# IS GREENLAND REALLY GREEN?

*Other Avon Books by*
**Laurence Moore**

LIGHTNING NEVER STRIKES TWICE AND OTHER FALSE FACTS

# IS GREENLAND REALLY GREEN?

## LAURENCE MOORE

AVON BOOKS ◆ NEW YORK

VISIT OUR WEBSITE AT
http://AvonBooks.com

IS GREENLAND REALLY GREEN? is an original publication of Avon Books. This work has never before appeared in book form.

AVON BOOKS
A division of
The Hearst Corporation
1350 Avenue of the Americas
New York, New York 10019

Copyright © 1996 by Laurence A. Moore
Published by arrangement with the author
Library of Congress Catalog Card Number: 96-13679
ISBN: 0-380-78587-0

Library of Congress Cataloging in Publication Data:

Moore, Laurence A.
  Is Greenland really green? / Laurence Moore.
    p.    cm.
1. Errors, Popular.  I. Title.
AZ999.M64   1996                    96-13679
001.9'6—dc20                        CIP

First Avon Books Trade Printing: October 1996

Printed in the U.S.A.

OPM   10  9  8  7  6  5  4  3  2  1

☞ ☜

*Wisdom comes by disillusionment.*

—GEORGE SANTAYANA

# Contents

# IS GREENLAND REALLY GREEN?

# 1
# Animals

**FALLACY:** Worms can grow to almost six feet in length.

**FACT:** There are worms, and then there are worms. The earthworms you see after a rainstorm can't grow to even a foot. Most of the world's other worms are equally footless, but many species are longer than a human is high. The longest known earthworm was discovered in South Africa. Don't know what you'd be fishing for if you used it as bait, though: it was twenty-two feet long. Not all worms live on or in land. The marine ribbon worm commonly grows as long as ninety feet. A report in 1864 cited a giant specimen of ribbon worm that washed ashore at St. Andrews, Scotland. It was more than 180 feet long. That one you'd use as bait for the Loch Ness Monster.

☞ 🐟

**FALLACY:** A basenji is a voiceless, hairless, Mexican dog.

**FACT:** A basenji is one of the spitz breeds—dogs whose tails usually curl up over their backs. Other spitz breeds are corgi, elkhound, Alaskan husky, malamute, Pomeranian, and Samoyed. (Mark Spitz is unrelated, but gets along swimmingly.) Neither hairless nor a longhair, a basenji has short, silky hair. This African native is best known as the barkless dog, but it does have a voice, making a sound somewhere between a whine and a yodel. The Mexican hairless, unrelated to the basenji, has tufts of hair on its head and tail but an otherwise hairless body. Interesting advertisement in the classified section: "For Sale. Puppies from a German Shepherd and an Alaskan Hussy."

☞ ☜

**FALLACY:**  A human can kill a bird, but a bird can't kill a human.

**FACT:**  A bird in the Southern Hemisphere stands six feet tall, cannot fly, and is native to northern Australia and New Guinea. No, not the ostrich. The male *Casuarius casuarius,* or Southern Cassowary, is noted for incubating the couple's eggs and raising their young. He is also noted for large, strong legs and toes with large, sharp claws that can kill a human. Al Bundy isn't the only one with killer feet.

☞ ☜

**FALLACY:**  Cuttlefish are fish.

**FACT:**  Despite the name, cuttlefish are not fish. Belonging to the genus *Sepia,* they look like ten-armed squid; like squid, they belong to the cephalopod group of marine mollusks. Cuttlefish are definitely not cuddle fish.

☞ ☜

**FALLACY:**  People are killed and eaten by alligators almost every year in Florida.

**FACT:**  A boy was killed by an alligator in the Loxahatchee River on 19 June 1993. He was the first person to be killed by an alligator in Florida in five years. Florida started keeping track of death-by-alligator cases in 1972, and that was only the sixth. As for being eaten, it's the alligators who should worry: many more people eat alligators than alligators eat people. If lemonade is made from lemons, what is Gatorade made from?

☞ ☜

**FALLACY:**  The last of the armor-plated animals, a type of dinosaur, became extinct 65 million years ago.

**FACT:**  Dinosaurs became extinct about 65 million years ago, but they didn't take the last armor-plated animal with them. Twenty species of armadillos are still roaming around, from South America to the southern United States. Members of the order Edentata, these nocturnal mammals range from the four-foot-long giant armadillo, *Priodontes giganteus,* to the six-inch fairy armadillo, *Chlamyphorus truncatus.* The only species in the United States is the thirty-inch nine-banded armadillo, *Dasypus novemcinctus.*

☞ ☜

**FALLACY:** Bald eagles are extinct in the United States.

**FACT:** The North American bald eagle, *Haliaeetus leucocephalus,* came close to extinction in the conterminous forty-eight states in the 1970s because of habitat loss, poaching, and the pesticide DDT; DDT was banned in the United States in 1972. Fortunately the bald eagle—also known as the American eagle—is alive and well in Alaska, saving the United States from exterminating its national bird. California, Indiana, Missouri, New York, North Carolina, and Tennessee have been importing bald eagles from Alaska in attempts to reestablish the species. And no, bald eagles aren't bald; it's only from a distance that their white head-feathers make them look that way.

☞ ☜

**FALLACY:** The largest colonies of bats number in the hundreds of thousands.

**FACT:** There are a lot more bats than most people realize, with more than 950 species in the order Chiroptera; bats account for about a fourth of all mammalian species. Colonies of thousands of bats are common. Colonies of a million bats are not uncommon. The world's largest known bat colony, located in Bracken Cave, Texas, reaches its peak after migration. At that time the number of Mexican free-tailed bats (*Tadarida brasiliensis*) calling Bracken Cave home reaches about 20 million—approximately the same as the human populations of Chicago, Dallas, Detroit, Houston, Los Angeles, New York City, Philadelphia, and San Diego combined.

☞ ☜

**FALLACY:** Millions of buffalo used to roam in North America.

**FACT:** A domesticated Indian water buffalo, *Bubalus bubalis,* is called a carabao; a Philippine buffalo is called a tamarua; a Celebese buffalo is called an anoa; an African buffalo is called the Cape buffalo. Even some humpbacked sucker fish of the genus Ictiobus are called buffalo. Bison are a different kettle of fish entirely. The European bison, *Bison bonasus,* is called a wisent. The North American bison, *Bison bison,* which is smaller than the European version, is often mistakenly called a buffalo. In 1850, roughly twenty million bison roamed freely on the

Great Plains; forty years later there were about five hundred. There are no North American buffalo, though, so heigh-ho Bison Bill!

☞ ☜

**FALLACY:** The blue whale, not the sulfur-bottom whale, is the world's largest.

**FACT:** The blue whale, *Sibbaldus musculus,* is a member of the rorqual group. One of the baleen whales, it was hunted almost to extinction. Except for its belly, it is bluish-gray. The sulfur-bottom whale, *Sibbaldus musculus,* is also a baleen member of the rorqual group—the same member. Depends on whether you're describing it by its blue-colored top or its sulfur-colored bottom. The blue, or sulfur-bottom, whale is not only the world's largest whale, it's the largest animal that has ever lived on Earth—and that's a whale of a lot of animal.

☞ ☜

**FALLACY:** The camel family became extinct in the Western Hemisphere millions of years ago.

**FACT:** The camel family, Camelidae, has six species. The two-humped Bactrian and the one-humped dromedary both live in the Eastern Hemisphere, from northern Africa to Mongolia. The other four species, all living in the South American Andes Mountains of the Western Hemisphere, are the alpaca, guanaco, llama, and vicuña.

☞ ☜

**FALLACY:** Birdlime is lime.

**FACT:** Birdlime is not limestone or the fruit of a lime tree or quicklime. Birdlime, usually made from the bark of the holly tree *Ilex aquifolium,* is a sticky substance smeared on twigs to snare small birds. That's why a twig so smeared is called a lime twig. Works a lot better than putting salt on a bird's tail.

☞ ☜

**FALLACY:** Dogs are the most common pet in the United States.

**FACT:** That was true until 1987. That year, for the first time in U.S. history, saw more feline than canine pets. An increasingly larger percentage of the human population lives in metropolitan areas, where it's easier to keep a cat than a dog. It's not merely a matter of size. Taking a dog out for an evening walk in most major cities might be worth your wallet, if not your life; cats don't have to be taken out. Remember the ancient maxim: "It's always darkest just before you step on the cat."

☞ ☜

**FALLACY:** Cats are clean because they're always washing themselves.
**FACT:** Think about it. Cats are covered with cat saliva when they finish licking themselves. Would you want to shake hands with people who washed their hands by licking them?

☞ ☜

**FALLACY:** A chameleon changes its skin color to look like what it's standing on.
**FACT:** A chameleon is an Old World lizard with a flattened body and eyes that move and see independently; some eighty-five species of Chamaeleontidae are native to the Middle East, Africa, southern Spain, Sri Lanka, and India. Although chameleons can rapidly change their skin color, they do so in response to emotion, light, and temperature, not because they've had a look at what they're standing on. If chameleons did change their skin color to match what they're standing on, what color would a chameleon be if it were standing on a mirror?

☞ ☜

**FALLACY:** Chickens are native to China and were domesticated almost 3,000 years ago.
**FACT:** Chickens are not native to China, but to a Southeast Asian arc around the Bay of Bengal from eastern India through Bangladesh, Burma, Thailand, Malaysia, and Sumatra. The Asian jungle fowl from which today's buckets of fried chicken are descended was domesticated more than 5,000 years ago.

☞ ☜

**FALLACY:** A camelopard is a cross between a camel and a leopard.
**FACT:** The camelopard is such a popular animal, there's even a Northern Hemisphere constellation named for it: Camelopardalis. This stately beast is not related to either a camel or a leopard, though. The name comes from confusion by ancient Greeks trying to describe the animal. It was called camelopard because they thought the head looked like a

camel's but the spots looked like a leopard's. Today it's more commonly called a giraffe.

☞ ☜

**FALLACY:** Seventeen-year locusts are locusts.

**FACT:** Locusts are grasshoppers of the family Acrididae, which often migrate in immense swarms. What are called seventeen-year locusts are actually cicadas, belonging to the family Cicadidae and the genus *Magicicada* and native to the eastern United States. Also called periodical cicada, they spend most of their lives underground as nymphs, emerging to become winged adults, eat, mate, lay eggs, and die. Male cicadas are noted for the high-frequency sound they make with a pair of resonating organs; when millions of them are doing it simultaneously and continuously, it has a decided effect not only on female cicadas but also on humans.

☞ ☜

**FALLACY:** A young horse is called a colt.

**FACT:** A young horse, especially one less than a year old, is called a foal. A young *male* horse is a colt. A young female horse is a filly. A cowgirl made a bet with a cowboy that she could ride into town on Tuesday and, staying only five days, ride out of town on Tuesday. He took the bet. He lost. Her filly's name was Tuesday.

☞ ☜

**FALLACY:** Most people in this country have seen a chicken.

**FACT:** Most people in this country have not seen a chicken. A picture of a chicken, yes, a plucked chicken carcass, yes, but not a chicken. Most people have seen parts of a chicken in a box or on their plate, but even if they had all the parts they wouldn't know how to reassemble a chicken.

☞ ☜

**FALLACY:** A *coydog* is a coy dog.

**FACT:** A coydog may be the child of a coy dog, but can't be a coy dog itself because it's not a dog. A coydog is the hybrid offspring of a coyote, *Canis latrans,* and a dog, *Canis familiaris.*

☞ ☜

**FALLACY:**   *Crocodile* is a regional name for an alligator.

**FACT:**   There are two species of alligator: the American alligator, *Alligator mississipiensis,* and the Chinese alligator, *Alligator sinensis.* Compared with crocodiles, alligators have wider, shorter snouts that don't taper toward the front. Compared with alligators, crocodiles are more aggressive and have a long fourth tooth in their lower jaw that sticks out when their mouth is closed. Alligators and crocodiles belong to different species and genera, but to the same family: Crocodilidae. And what of caimans? Going one step up the taxonomic ladder, the order Crocodylia includes alligators, caimans, crocodiles, and gavials.

☞ ☜

**FALLACY:**   Penguins and turkeys are the only birds that can't fly.

**FACT:**   Penguins can't fly at all, but wild turkeys definitely can. In addition to seventeen species of penguins, birds that can't fly include cassowaries, flightless cormorants, emus, kiwis, ostriches, rheas, and steamer ducks. Steamer ducks are named for the way they churn the surface of the water with their feet and wings like a paddle wheel steamboat, not for a cooking method.

☞ ☜

**FALLACY:**   Another name for an octopus is a cuttlefish.

**FACT:**   Octopuses and cuttlefish are both cephalopod marine mollusks, and both shoot out ink when in danger, but they're not the same animal. A cuttlefish looks more like a squid than an octopus, and if you're arm wrestling with one, keep in mind that a cuttlefish has ten tentacles.

☞ ☜

**FALLACY:**   The dormouse is a small species of indoor mouse, hence the original name "door mouse."

**FACT:**   The dormouse is not a mouse, and it doesn't live indoors. Rodents that look and behave like a cross between a mouse and a squirrel, they belong to the families Gliridae and Seleviniidae. Several species are found in Africa and Eurasia. The common dormouse of western Eurasia, when brought to a pleasant plumpness, was considered a tasty treat by ancient Romans. European species hibernate for up to six months; the *dor* in dormouse came not from "door," but from the Latin word for "dormant."

☞ ☜

**FALLACY:** Elephants have large ears to help them hear better.

**FACT:** Large ears help with hearing only if they focus sound. That's not why elephants have huge ears. The larger an animal's body is in relation to its skin surface, the more problem the animal has radiating excess heat. That's what the elephant's ears do.

☞ ☜

**FALLACY:** Primates have two eyelids.

**FACT:** Members of the order Primates—including apes, humans, lemurs, lorises, monkeys, and tarsiers—have two eyes, so they have four eyelids: two upper and two lower.

☞ ☜

**FALLACY:** Birds, unlike humans, can stare into the Sun without harming their eyes.

**FACT:** Many species of birds congregate in tall trees before sunset and face the Sun. Their eyes, like human eyes, would be damaged by staring into the Sun. Humans' eyes are on the front of the head while birds' eyes are on the sides. Although facing the setting Sun, birds are not staring into it.

☞ ☜

**FALLACY:** A fallow deer cannot have offspring.

**FACT:** In that sense, *fallow* refers to a field that has been plowed but not seeded. The Eurasian fallow deer, *Dama dama,* got its name long ago when *fallow* meant the color of its summer coat. It's much easier to say "fallow" than "somewhere between yellowish-brown and yellowish-red." Not only can fallow deer have offspring, without which there would be no more fallow deer, but they're known to fawn on them.

☞ ☜

**FALLACY:** *Sheepshead* is a culinary dish popular in the Middle East, made from the head of a sheep.

**FACT:** There are three types of sheepshead: *Archosargus probatocepha-*

*lus, Aplodinotus grunniens,* and *Semicossyphus pulcher.* The first lives along the Atlantic and Gulf coasts of the United States; the second is found from the Great Lakes to Texas; the third lives in the Gulf of California. All three are fish.

☞ 🕿

**FALLACY:** Houseflies come indoors before it's raining.

**FACT:** Houseflies come indoors before it starts raining—probably something to do with the lowering atmospheric pressure. As for "when it's raining," think about it: if you could fly would you do it when you had to dodge raindrops as big as your body?

☞ 🕿

**FALLACY:** A galliwasp is a wasp.

**FACT:** The long-bodied galliwasp is found from southern Mexico to northern Argentina and in the West Indies. A galliwasp is not a wasp, but it might eat a wasp because a galliwasp is a lizard of the genus *Diploglossus.* Galliwasps should not be confused with gallinippers; those little nippers are, indeed, insects.

☞ 🕿

**FALLACY:** Glass snakes are called that because they're transparent.

**FACT:** Glass snakes belong to a subfamily of the genus *Ophisaurus* of the family Anguidae. In that entire family there are no transparent animals—and no snakes. Found in both hemispheres, glass snakes are legless lizards, as indicated by the "saurus" in their genus name. At first glance they may look like snakes, but as soon as they blink you know that they're not: snakes don't have eyelids to blink with. Like many other lizards, glass snakes have the ability to break off their tail as a defense mechanism. Unlike other lizards, the glass snake has a tail that "shatters" into pieces when it breaks off. Each piece squirms independently, providing a confusing number of targets for a predator while the lizard itself make a fast getaway. Some glass snakes have a tail twice as long as the rest of their body, so the squirming pieces of tail are more than adequate to distract a predator. Yes, the tail does grow back. "We're off to see the Lizard, the wonderful Lizard of Oz!"

☞ ☜

**FALLACY:** The Great Dane species of dog was developed in Denmark.

**FACT:** Because the Great Dane is a breed, not a species, it can interbreed with other canines of the species *Canis familiaris.* Despite the name, the Great Dane was not developed in Denmark. This large breed of dog, which can be up to a yard high at the shoulder and weigh as much as 150 pounds, was developed from a mastifflike ancestor over 400 years ago in Germany as a boarhound.

☞ ☜

**FALLACY:** Aside from a colony of ants, a herd of cattle, and a school of fish, most groups of animals are just called "groups."

**FACT:** There may be more specific group names than you realize. Among many others: a charm of goldfinches, a cloud of gnats, a crash of rhinoceroses, an exaltation of larks, a knot of toads, a mob of kangaroos, a murder of crows, a skulk of foxes, a sleuth of bears, and a watch of nightingales.

☞ ☜

**FALLACY:** One of the nicknames for a hippopotamus is "water buffalo."

**FACT:** The water buffalo, *Bubalus bubalis,* is a large Asian animal whose nicknames include "carabao" and "water ox." The hippopotamus, *Hippopotamus amphibius,* is a large African animal. Its name comes from the Greek words for horse (*hippos*) and river (*potamos*), hence its nickname "water horse." You can lead a horse to water, but you can't make it float on its back.

☞ ☜

**FALLACY:** A horny toad is a toad who's horny.

**FACT:** A horny toad may or may not be horny, but it isn't a toad. Members of the genus *Phrynosoma,* found from southwestern Canada to Guatemala, have hornlike spikes on their head, back, and sides. Often called horny toads or horned toads, they're actually lizards. If you have a horny toad, you might want to head for Needles, California, in September; that's the site of an annual Horny Toad Race.

☞ ☜

**FALLACY:** The gazelle hound, not the greyhound, is the world's fastest dog.

**FACT:** The gazelle hound, also known as the Arabian hound but more formally called the saluki, was named after the ancient Arabian city of Saluq. Besides being the world's fastest dog, the saluki is the oldest breed of greyhound.

☞ ☜

**FALLACY:** All life on earth ultimately gets its energy from the Sun.

**FACT:** Photosynthetic plants capture energy directly from the Sun; some animals eat plants to get that solar energy, some animals eat other animals to get it. And that, we thought until recently, summed it up. It turns out that there are forms of life that don't depend upon solar energy. Whole colonies of organisms, including clams, crabs, mussels, and worms, live around undersea hydrothermal vents and couldn't care less about getting energy from the Sun. These colonies are based on chemosynthetic bacteria rather than on photosynthetic plants. The bacteria get energy by breaking down sulfur-based compounds coming up through the hydrothermal vents; other organisms eat the bacteria and are in turn eaten. At least one, a tube worm, neither eats nor excretes; it gets its energy directly from the bacteria, which live in its tissues.

☞ ☜

**FALLACY:** The ibex is an extinct animal.

**FACT:** The ibex is far from extinct. At least two species of the genus *Capra* still roam the mountains of Eurasia and northeast Africa. Ibex—which have heavy, ridged, back-sweeping horns, short tails, and beards—are wild goats.

☞ ☜

**FALLACY:** The leopard is the only cat of its size with spots.

**FACT:** Jaguars, about the same size as leopards, not only have spots, they have black spots and black-around-brown rings similar to the leopard's. Jaguars range from northern Mexico to Patagonia in Argentina, and the largest are found in Brazil's Mato Grosso; leopards live in Africa and Asia. The jaguar has a stockier body and thicker legs than a leopard. "Here, kitty" would be inappropriate with either.

☞ ☜

**FALLACY:**  The laughing jackass and the howling jackass are types of jackass.

**FACT:**  Humans not included, a true jackass is a male ass or donkey. The laughing jackass, found in Australia, is formally known as *Dacelo novaeguinae;* the howling jackass, found in Australia and New Guinea, is formally known as *Dacelo leachii.* Both species, also called kookaburras, are birds of the kingfisher family.

☞ ☜

**FALLACY:**  Wood lice are lice.

**FACT:**  Lice belong to the orders Mallophaga (bird lice) or Anoplura (sucking lice). Wood lice don't belong to either of those orders because they are not lice. What they are is isopod crustaceans, and what they're commonly called is sow bugs.

☞ ☜

**FALLACY:**  Crocodiles are the largest lizards.

**FACT:**  Although crocodiles are reptiles, they are (appropriately enough) crocodilians, not lizards. Although komodo dragons are not dragons, they are lizards. Also known as komodo monitor lizards and ora, and officially known as *Varanus komodoensis,* they live on several Indonesian islands. Carnivorous, they have on occasion attacked and killed humans. Komodo dragons can grow to more than ten feet in length and 300 pounds, making them the world's largest lizards. With modern technology, it's possible to monitor a monitor on a monitor.

☞ ☜

**FALLACY:**  A lobster's life span is about 20 years.

**FACT:**  Depends in part on how close it lives to Boston's restaurants. The largest species of lobster is the North Atlantic lobster, *Homarus americanus.* Also the heaviest of the crustaceans, the North Atlantic lobster may live as long as half a century.

☞ ☜

**FALLACY:**  Elephants live longer than any other mammal.

**FACT:**  There are African elephants (*Loxodonta africana*) and there are Asian elephants (*Elephas maximus*). African elephants do not live longer than any other mammal. Asian elephants, although taking the longest running start of any mammal with an average gestation period of 610 days, do not live longer than any other mammal. The longest-living mammal is that recent experiment of nature, *Homo sapiens sapiens*.

☞ ☜

**FALLACY:** Fish cannot breathe out of water.

**FACT:** Most fish cannot breathe out of water, but some can. The African clariid catfish, for example, can make an overland journey of several days from one body of water to another. About 400 million years ago, all vertebrates were fish. Those with sturdy, fleshy fins gradually developed the ability to stay out of water longer and longer; amphibians evolved from these air-breathing fish. Today's lungfish are found in central and western Africa (Protopteridae), South America (Lepidosirenidae), and Australia (Ceratodontidae). The African and South American families are elongated and look somewhat like eels; the Australian family has a wide body and large scales. Lungfish have both gills and lunglike organs and are able to breathe air.

☞ ☜

**FALLACY:** Mayflies are voracious eaters.

**FACT:** Mayflies are any of several insects of the order Ephemeroptera. "Ephemeral" suits them because after living as aquatic larvae for as long as four years, their adult lifespan as mayflies ranges from a few hours to a few days. Also called dayflies, mayflies do not eat.

☞ ☜

**FALLACY:** It takes the skins of hundreds of moles to make one pair of moleskin trousers.

**FACT:** The making of a pair of moleskin trousers requires not a single mole to give up its skin. The moleskin from which they're made is a heavy cotton twill with a thick velvetlike nap that supposedly feels as soft as the fur of a mole. Makes moles happy, that does.

☞ ☜

**FALLACY:** A mollusk has a hard outer shell and lives in the ocean.

**FACT:** Sounds like a submarine. Mollusks belong to the phylum Mollusca, the second-largest phylum of invertebrates after the arthropods.

Some have hard outer shells, some don't; some live in the ocean, some don't. Mollusks include abalones, chitons, clams, cockles, conches, cuttlefish, limpets, nautiluses, periwinkles, octopuses, oysters, scallops, shipworms, slugs, snails, squids, and whelks.

☞ ☜

**FALLACY:** Most North American mooses live in the northern United States.

**FACT:** The plural of moose is not mooses or meese or mice; it's moose. Rocky's friend Bullwinkle is, hooves down, the most widely known moose in the world; probably the next most famous is the curious creature seen during the opening credits of *Northern Exposure*. These long-legged, hump-shouldered characters with a nose almost big enough to be called a trunk belong to the genus *Alces* and are the largest members of the deer family. The males can weigh as much as 1,400 pounds, stand as high as eight feet at the shoulder, and have flat antlers as wide as seven feet. Only about 20 percent of North American moose live in the United States, Alaska included; the other 80 percent, more than 700,000, live in Canada.

☞ ☜

**FALLACY:** A musk rat is a rat.

**FACT:** A muskrat is a rodent, but not a rat (*Rattus*). A nocturnal North American water rodent with thick fur, *Ondatra* is related to the lemming and the vole and has partially-webbed feet and a wide tail. "Muskrat" comes not from musk rat, but from a Native American name for the animal, *musquash*.

☞ ☜

**FALLACY:** A numbat is a bat.

**FACT:** A numbat, *Myrmecobius fasciatus*, isn't numb and isn't even distantly related to a bat. A pouchless marsupial native to Australia and particularly fond of termites, a numbat also is called a banded anteater.

☞ ☜

**FALLACY:** A pack rat is a human, not a rodent, who collects things.

**FACT:** Human pack rats collect an amazing number of things, but they're not alone. Several species of rodents of the genus *Neotoma*, especially *Neotoma cinerea* of the Rocky Mountains, are known as pack rats. They collect all manner of things and store them in and around their nests, just as the human variety does. They're also known as wood rats, and as trade rats because they often leave something in place of what they take, such as a stone for a shiny object.

☞ ☜

**FALLACY:** Pandas are bears.

**FACT:** The two species of pandas, members of the family Ailuropodidae, are both native to bamboo forests in mountainous areas of Asia. The red panda, *Ailurus fulgens*, is found from southern China to northern Myanmar (formerly Burma) and is also called the lesser panda and the cat bear. The giant panda, *Ailuropoda melanoleuca,* is found in central China and is the one most people think of when they hear the word "panda." Although both species evolved from carnivores, they are vegetarians; although both have six digits on their hands, only the giant panda's extra digit has evolved to the point of being useful as a thumb. The red panda is anatomically similar to a racoon and resembles one. The giant panda looks like a bear, but is also anatomically similar to a racoon. Neither is a bear, or related to bears, which belong to the family Ursidae.

☞ ☜

**FALLACY:** Pit vipers are called that because they live in pits.

**FACT:** Pit vipers don't have a pit to hiss in. Not only do they not live in pits, no single species of snake is known as the pit viper. Copperheads are pit vipers, cottonmouth water moccasins are pit vipers, fer-de-lance are pit vipers, and rattlesnakes are pit vipers. Members of the family Crotalidae, pit vipers have heat-sensing organs in small depressions, called pits, below each eye. These infrared-sensing organs help them locate their warmblooded prey, especially at night.

☞ ☜

**FALLACY:** What the American colonists called robins were robins.

**FACT:** Early European immigrants paid little heed to the names used by Native Americans. Fond of the birds of their native land, the immigrants called almost every red-breasted bird they saw a "robin," short for Robin Redbreast. The North American birds were not related to robins, and all but one have been renamed. What they called the Canadian robin is the cedar waxwing, the golden robin is the northern oriole, the ground robin is the rufous-sided towhee, the robin snipe is the red knot, and the sea robin is the red-breasted merganzer. The real Eurasian and northern African robin is *Erithacus rubecula,* not a close relative of the species still called the American robin, *Turdus migratorius.*

☞ ☜

**FALLACY:**   A sea horse is a unique creature, unrelated to fish.

**FACT:**   There's no doubting the sea horse is a unique creature. Its upper part looks remarkably like the head and neck of a horse; it swims upright, adding to its horselike appearance; and at the bottom is a prehensile tail that it uses to anchor itself to sea plants. The male does not inject anything into the female during mating; on the contrary, the female injects her eggs into a pouch on the underside of the male, where they are fertilized and develop until born as live young. In spite of its unique appearance and unusual family practices, the sea horse is definitely a fish, belonging to the family Syngnathidae.

☞ ☜

**FALLACY:**   The easiest way to tell the sex of a walrus is by its tusks: males have them, females don't.

**FACT:**   Depending on what you had in mind for the walrus, *Odobenus rosmarus,* determining its sex by the presence or absence of tusks could be embarrassing. Both male and female walruses have tusks. Found only in the Arctic, the walrus is hunted for its skin, fat, and ivory, and is now an endangered species.

☞ ☜

**FALLACY:**   Dogs are only distantly related to wolves.

**FACT:**   Domesticated dogs, *Canis familiaris,* belong to the family Canidae. The two species of wild dogs or wolves, *Canis lupus* and *Canis rufus,* also belong to the family Canidae. Not only are wolves members of the dog family, but *Canis lupus,* also known as the gray wolf and the timber wolf, is the direct ancestor of today's domesticated dogs. There's probably no connection between that fact and this newspaper ad: "Dog for sale: eats anything, and is very fond of children."

☞ ☜

**FALLACY:**   Wolverines belong to the same family as wolves.

**FACT:**   The names are similar, but the critters aren't. Wolverines belong to the family Mustelidae, which has sixty-seven species including badgers, minks, otters, skunks, and weasels. Wolves belong to the family Canidae, which includes coyotes, dogs, foxes, and jackals. Nicknames for the wolverine include carcajou, skunk bear because of its scent gland, and glutton because it often kills more than it can eat.

☞ ☜

**FALLACY:**   Wood chucks are related to wood rats, not to ground hogs.

**FACT:**   "Wood rat" is two words, but "woodchuck" and "groundhog" are just one each. "Ground hog" is sausage. A wood rat is any of several Central and North American cricetid rodents, especially those of the genus *Neotoma;* very unratlike, they have furry tails. A woodchuck is a coarse-haired, chubby marmot, *Marmota monax,* found in Alaska, Canada, and the northeastern United States. "Woodchuck" comes from a Native American word; another common name for the critter is "groundhog." It would be just as correct to say that 2 February is Woodchuck Day. How much wood a woodchuck could chuck if a woodchuck could chuck wood would depend on whether or not the woodchuck's name was Chuck.

☞ ☜

**FALLACY:**   Wryneck is a muscular neck disorder.

**FACT:**   This isn't something you get from watching a long tennis match. The name does relate to the neck, but not the human neck. A wryneck is a small woodpecker of Africa, Asia, and Europe whose threat display involves hissing and moving its head and neck in a snakelike way. That's why one of its nicknames is snakebird. The two species in the genus are the African *Jynx ruficollis* and the Eurasian *Jynx torquilla.*

☞ ☜

**FALLACY:**   The young of most common animals are called young whatever, as in young antelope or young seal.

**FACT:**   For reasons probably best known to psychologists and philosophers, the young of most common nonhuman animals are given specific names. A young antelope is called a calf as is a young cow or elephant or hippo or rhino; whales also have calves. Some species even have sexual distinctions, such as colt versus filly and cockerel versus pullet. Bears and lions have cubs, and for some reason so do sharks, which are not mammals but fish. Swans have cygnets, deer have fawns, geese have goslings, goats have kids, and sheep have lambs. Dogs have pups, and so do seals and sea lions. And elver is not a baby elf; it's a baby eel.

☞ ☜

**FALLACY:** Mountain goats are goats.

**FACT:** Goats belong to the genus *Capra,* from which we get the name of the constellation Capricorn. Mountain goats belong to the genus *Oreamnos* and, because they live on the North American continent, were given the species name *americanus.* Although they have some of the characteristics of goats and are called mountain goats and Rocky Mountain goats, they are not goats but goat antelopes.

☞ ☜

**FALLACY:** Arctic sled dogs are among the world's fastest dogs.

**FACT:** Arctic sled dogs were bred for strength and endurance. Although they come nowhere close to the greyhounds' forty-plus-miles-per-hour record and are not among the world's fastest dogs, they do move along surprisingly rapidly, even with a heavy load. May have something to do with the distance between trees in the Arctic.

☞ ☜

**FALLACY:** *Cow chip, cow pie, meadow muffin,* and *road apple* are different names for the same thing.

**FACT:** Cow chip, cow pie, meadow muffin, and road apple are different names because there are differences among the things they name. Cow pies look like pies and are a constant danger in cow pastures; cow chips are the dry versions of cow pies and less of a danger because they won't stick to boots or squish between bare toes. Meadow muffins are about the size of a small muffin or apple and are most commonly found in horse pastures; when spotted on the road, they're called road apples.

☞ ☜

**FALLACY:** When killer bees crossed the border into Texas, they caused a local disaster.

**FACT:** The first swarm of Africanized "killer" bees found in the United States, numbering about 3,000, was discovered in October 1990 east of the border town of Hidalgo, Texas. Far from causing a disaster, the border-crossing bees provided Hidalgo with a tourist attraction: the first U.S. town to be visited by the bees. In 1992, Hidalgo spent nearly $20,000 to build a ten-foot-high statue of an Africanized bee.

☞ ☜

**FALLACY:** Tuna, like all fish, are cold-blooded.

**FACT:** Tuna, unlike most fish, can weigh up to a ton; also unlike most fish, tuna are warm-blooded. Marine biologists say that's one of the reasons tuna can move fast enough to swim virtually around the edge of the Pacific Ocean in a year, and to dive deeper than other fish. Another peculiarity of tuna among fish is that when they swim, they move only their tail.

☞ ☜

**FALLACY:** The ostrich is the largest bird in the Western Hemisphere.

**FACT:** The ostrich is the world's largest bird, standing as tall as nine feet and weighing as much as 350 pounds, as well as the fastest animal on two legs, reaching speeds of up to forty-five miles per hour. It is not a Western Hemisphere bird, however, but an Eastern Hemisphere bird, native to Africa. The largest bird in the Western Hemisphere is the rhea, a flightless bird native to the temperate plains of South America; they often graze along with cattle on the pampas and savannas. The rhea resembles the ostrich but is smaller, rarely exceeding five feet or weighing more than sixty pounds, and has larger wings. The male rhea digs a nest in the ground into which several females lay their eggs, then the male sits on the eggs, hatches them, and protects the young. One good tern deserves another.

☞ ☜

**FALLACY:** A giraffe has several times as many neck bones as a human.

**FACT:** A human has seven neck bones to support its head only a few inches above its shoulders. A giraffe stands about three times as tall as a human, most of that height legs and neck, and its head is many feet above its shoulders. The bones in a giraffe's neck are much longer than those in a human's, commonly about a foot long, but there are only seven of them, too.

☞ ☜

**FALLACY:**  The guppy was named for its place of discovery.

**FACT:**  That fish called the guppy, *Lebistes reticulata* or *Poecilia reticulata,* is a freshwater fish native to the West Indies and northern South America. It was named in Trinidad by a Trinidadian naturalist who sent the first specimens to the British Museum. His name was R. J. Lechmere Guppy.

☞ ☜

**FALLACY:**  The spaniel breed of dog was developed in the United States.

**FACT:**  Spaniels are small to medium breeds of dog with long, wavy hair and droopy ears. Spaniels were around before the United States was. Our modern English word came from Middle English, which came from an Old French word meaning "Spaniard." Before its name was shortened, a spaniel was called a "Spanish dog."

☞ ☜

**FALLACY:**  Mussels are called that because they cling so tightly to rocks with their muscles.

**FACT:**  If you go back far enough, there is a linguistic connection, but there's a big difference between mussels and muscles. Mussels are called mussels because whoever named them thought a mussel resembled a mouse. A mouse is so called because the name is derived from the Latin word for mouse, *mus.* The linguistic connection is that ancient Romans thought muscles moving around under the skin looked like little mice, and the Latin diminutive of *mus* is *musculus.* Mussels do not use their muscles to cling to rocks. They secrete a mass of strong, silky threads called byssus to hold them fast to rocks, pilings, or whatever.

☞ ☜

**FALLACY:**  An albatross is a sea bird of the Atlantic Ocean; a gooney is a sea bird of the Pacific Ocean.

**FACT:**  Fourteen species of albatross make up the family Diomedeidae. Most live in the southern Pacific Ocean, but some, including the black-footed albatross *Diomedea nigripes,* are found in the northern Pacific. The world's most famous albatross, featured in Samuel Taylor Coleridge's poem "The Rime of the Ancient Mariner," was a wandering albatross, *Diomedea exulans.* Generally speaking, a gooney is an albatross; specifically, a gooney is a black-footed albatross.

☞ ☜

**FALLACY:** The leghorn chicken is named for a spur (horn) on its leg.

**FACT:** The leg of a leghorn is no hornier than the leg of your average chicken. The leghorn, noted for its prolific egg production, got its name from a coastal town on the Ligurian Sea in northwestern Italy. In Italian, the name of the town is Livorno; in English, it's Leghorn.

☞ ☜

**FALLACY:** Shipworms are worms.

**FACT:** You'd think so from the name, but although shipworms will eat away at wooden ships or any other wood in the water, they are not worms. Belonging to the genera Teredo and Bankia, shipworms are marine mollusks, related not to worms, but to such folks as abalones, clams, oysters, scallops, snails, and squids.

☞ ☜

**FALLACY:** Fish reproduce by laying eggs.

**FACT:** Most fish reproduce by laying eggs, but not all. A notable exception to the general rule is the shark, which gives birth to live young. Their gestation period ranges from nine months to two years, and a litter of ten cubs is common.

☞ ☜

**FALLACY:** Yaks belong to the goat family.

**FACT:** Goats belong to the genus *Capra,* and the most common domesticated types belong to *Capra hircus.* Yaks, on the other hoof, belong to *Bos grunniens.* Much larger than goats, yaks are shaggy-haired oxen. Native to the mountains of central Asia, yaks got their English name from their Tibetan name, *gyagk.*

☞ ☜

**FALLACY:** A fish can live in fresh water, or a fish can live in salt water, but the same fish cannot live in both.

**FACT:** Most fish are born, live, and die in either fresh water or salt water. Some, however, not only can live in both fresh and salt water, but have to if the species is to continue. A fish born in fresh water that goes to live in salt water and then returns to fresh water to breed is called anadromous. Some better known anadromous fish are salmon, shad, striped bass, and sturgeon. A fish born in salt water that goes to live in fresh water and then returns to salt water to breed is called catadromous. Eels are the best known catadromous fish. More than 125 species of fish live in both fresh water and salt water during their life cycle.

☞ ☜

**FALLACY:** Penguins live only in very cold areas.

**FACT:** Most of these flightless sea birds do live in very cold areas of the far-southern Southern Hemisphere, but not all. Some live right on the Equator: significant numbers of Galapagos penguins are found on both Fernandina and Isabella Islands.

☞ ☜

**FALLACY:** Rice is being replaced at weddings by birdseed because if birds eat raw rice and then drink water, the rice grains expand and kill them.

**FACT:** Wedding rice causing birds to expand or otherwise expire is definitely a legend—and apparently an urban legend. People who live in the country are accustomed to seeing flocks of birds fly in at harvest season to eat all manner of grain, including rice. What humans swallow goes into their stomach; what birds swallow goes first into their crop and then into their gizzard. In a bird's gizzard, things are ground. Rice, for example, is ground into rice powder. Although the happy voices of well-fed birds may keep some people awake, there is no recorded case of anyone near a rice paddy being kept awake by the sound of exploding birds.

☞ ☜

**FALLACY:**   A gnu is a small, gazellelike animal; a wildebeest is a large, cowlike animal.

**FACT:**   A gnu is an African grazing antelope, as distinguished from all the other types of antelopes, and belongs to the genus *Connochaetes*. A wildebeest is an African grazing antelope, as distinguished from all the other types of antelopes, and belongs to the genus *Connochaetes*. A gnu by any other name is a wildebeest: they're the same animal. A gnu, but not a gnat, may be gnarled or even gnarly, and gnaws and gnashes grasses but never gnocchi; a gnome, but not a gnu or gnat, may give a gnathic gnar while gnawing gneiss or gnomons.

# 2

# Arts, Entertainment, Literature, Religion

**FALLACY:** Doc was the only one of the Seven Dwarfs who had a beard.

**FACT:** In Walt Disney's *Snow White and the Seven Dwarfs,* Doc did, indeed, have a beard. Bashful had a beard, too. So did Grumpy, Happy, Sleepy, and Sneezy (one beard each). Dopey was the only one of the Seven Dwarfs who did *not* have a beard. Snow White didn't have one, either.

☞ ☜

**FALLACY:** Another name for Lewis Carroll's *Alice in Wonderland* is *Through the Looking-Glass.*

**FACT:** The full title of the first is *Alice's Adventures in Wonderland,* written by Charles Lutwidge Dodgson under the pen name Lewis Carroll. Among the characters in addition to Alice are the Cheshire Cat, the Mad Hatter, the March Hare, the White Rabbit, and the Queen of Hearts: "The Queen was in a furious passion, and went stamping about, and shouting, 'Off with his head!' or 'Off with her head!' about once a minute." The book was such a success that he wrote a sequel called *Through the Looking-Glass,* which contains these classic lines of creative thought:

> 'Twas brillig, and the slithy toves
> Did gyre and gimble in the wabe;
> All mimsey were the borogoves,
> And the mome raths outgrabe.

24

☞ ☜

**FALLACY:** The expression "Time flies" is a direct translation of Virgil's words, *Tempus fugit.*

**FACT:** Those aren't Virgil's words. What he said in *Georgics* was: *"Sed fugit interea, fugit inreparabile tempus,"* which translates: "But meanwhile it is flying, irretrievable time is flying." Or, as Stephen Hawking might put it, "Time flies like an arrow, but fruit flies like an apple."

☞ ☜

**FALLACY:** *Amish, Mennonites,* and *Pennsylvania Dutch* are different names for the same people.

**FACT:** Although there is overlap, those are three different groups. The Mennonites, named after Menno Simons, branched off from the Anabaptists. The Amish, named after Jacob Amman, are a conservative branch of the Mennonites; the Amish don't accept such modern inventions as automobiles, electricity, or telephones. Although a minority of the original Pennsylvania Dutch settlers were Amish or Mennonite, the majority were Lutheran.

☞ ☜

**FALLACY:** The ancient island of Atlantis sank beneath the ocean.

**FACT:** The origin of the story of Atlantis is Plato's dialogue *Timaeus,* written about 350 B.C. The first sentence to mention the word is: "Now in this island of Atlantis there was a great and wonderful empire which had rule over the whole island and several others, and over parts of the continent, and, furthermore, the men of Atlantis had subjugated the parts of Libya within the Pillars of Hercules as far as Egypt, and of Europe as far as Italy." There is no mention of any such island in Egyptian records, in the writings of other early cultures, or in Greek literature before Plato. The story of Atlantis, as one of the first of the genre, deserves an honored place in the Science Fiction Hall of Fame. Aristotle, Plato's most famous student, made only one known comment about Atlantis: "He who invented it also destroyed it."

☞ ☜

**FALLACY:** George Orwell and Tom Wolfe are the real names of those authors.

**FACT:**  George Orwell and Tom Wolfe are the pen names of those authors. Their real names are, respectively, Eric Arthur Blair and Thomas Kennerly Jr.

☞ ☜

**FALLACY:**  *Yellow Submarine* was the Beatles' first movie.

**FACT:**  *Yellow Submarine,* in which the Beatles psychedelically save Pepperland from the Blue Meanies, came out in 1968. That made it their third movie, following *A Hard Day's Night* in 1964 and *Help* in 1965. Their fourth and last movie was *Let It Be* in 1970. In the words of a philosophical computer user: "We all live in a yellow subroutine."

☞ ☜

**FALLACY:**  The phrase "brave new world" was coined by Aldous Huxley.

**FACT:**  When Aldous Huxley wrote his acclaimed *Brave New World* and *Brave New World Revisited,* he took that title phrase from the writings of William Shakespeare, specifically from *The Tempest:*

> How many goodly creatures are there here!
> How beauteous mankind is! O brave new world,
> That has such people in't.

☞ ☜

**FALLACY:**  Humphrey Bogart is buried in Forest Lawn Cemetery.

**FACT:**  Humphrey DeForest Bogart was not buried; he was cremated in 1957. In the urn with his ashes is a silver whistle, put there by Lauren Bacall. The inscription on the whistle reads: "If you need anything, just whistle." That was the classic line Bacall said to Bogart in their first picture together, *To Have and Have Not.*

☞ ☜

**FALLACY:**  "If only we could see ourselves as others see us!" is a famous old quote.

**FACT:**  "If only we could see ourselves as others see us!" is a famous new misquote from a famous old quote. The original, from *To a Louse* by Robert Burns, is:

> *O wad some Pow'r the giftie gie us*
> *To see oursels as others see us!*
> *It wad frae mony a blunder free us,*
> *And foolish notion.*

Burns is also the source of several other very familiar thoughts for which he is seldom credited, and which are often misquoted.

> *Should auld acquaintance be forgot,*
> *And never brought to mind?*

is from his *Auld Lang Syne.*

> *Gin a body meet a body*
> *Coming through the rye;*
> *Gin a body kiss a body,*
> *Need a body cry?*

is from *Coming Through the Rye.*

> *The best laid schemes o' mice an' men*
> *Gang aft a-gley.*

is from *To a Mouse.*

From Louse to Mouse, there's no denying that Robert Burns is definitely quotable. And misquotable.

☞ ☜

**FALLACY:** "Don't count your chickens before they're hatched" is a nineteenth-century expression.

**FACT:** Actually it's a sixth-century expression—sixth century B.C. It comes from Aesop's fable "The Milkmaid and Her Pail." The milkmaid says: "The milk in this pail will provide me with cream, which I will make into butter, which I will sell in the market, and buy a dozen eggs, which will hatch into chickens, which will lay more eggs, and soon I shall have a large poultry yard." She then accidentally drops the pail, spilling the milk. Her mother says: "Do not count your chickens before they are hatched." This Aesop's fable is completely unrelated to the Robin Hood tale about that other famous fowl, Fryer Duck.

☞ ☜

**FALLACY:** Dooley Wilson played the piano music in the movie *Casablanca.*

**FACT:** Dooley Wilson played the piano-playing Sam in the movie *Casablanca,* but he did not play the piano music; he was a better singer than a pianist. The piano was actually played by Elliott Carpenter. That was, though, Dooley Wilson singing the songs he seemed to be singing: "As Time Goes By," "It Had To Be You," and "Knock on Wood." The last film Dooley Wilson appeared in was *Passage West,* in 1951; he died in 1953.

☞ ☜

**FALLACY:** *Catcher in the Rye* was written by Holden Caulfield.

**FACT:** His only novel, *Catcher in the Rye* was written by J(erome) D(avid) Salinger, who spent the rest of his time writing short stories. The *hero* of J. D. Salinger's 1951 novel was Holden Caulfield. *Catcher in the Rye* frequently catches the wry eye of censors. A mind, like a parachute, works best when it's open. The worst thing about censorship is XXXXXXXXXX.

☞ ☜

**FALLACY:** Diane Chambers was in more than twice as many episodes of *Cheers* as Rebecca Howe.

**FACT:** Shelley Long's character, Diane Chambers, appeared in fewer episodes of *Cheers* than Kirstie Alley's character, Rebecca Howe. According to Paramount Television, Diane Chambers appeared in 124 episodes, ending in 1987; Rebecca Howe appeared in 154.

☞ ☜

**FALLACY:** *Cheers* was brought to an end over the objections of Ted Danson.

**FACT:** Ted Danson, who played Sam Malone on *Cheers,* had a good reason to object to the end of the series: he was making $450,000 per week. The series wasn't brought to an end over his objections, though. His decision to leave the series brought about its demise after eleven seasons. Among the other major characters on the show: Kirstie Alley's Rebecca Howe, Kelsey Grammer's Dr. Frasier Crane, Woody Harrelson's Woody Boyd, Shelley Long's Diane Chambers, Bebe Neuwirth's Lilith, Rhea Perlman's Carla Tortelli LeBec, John Ratzenberger's Cliff Clavin, and George Wendt's Norm Peterson.

☞ ☜

**FALLACY:**  The actor who played Clarabell the Clown on the *Howdy Doody Show* disappeared along with that TV series.

**FACT:**  Buffalo Bob Smith opened each show with, "Say, kids, what time is it?" and the Peanut Gallery shouted back, "It's Howdy Doody time!" Almost all the actors could be identified by sight or, if heavily made up, by voice. The actor who played Clarabell was heavily made up but couldn't be identified by voice either because Clarabell didn't talk; taking a page from Harpo Marx, he honked a horn. Clarabell was one of actor Bob Keeshan's most famous characters; at least as famous was another of his characters: Captain Kangaroo. Speaking of Harpo, you'll come up with the name of another famous entertainer if you spell his name backward.

☞ ☜

**FALLACY:**  Perry Mason, Mickey Spillane, Sam Spade, and Rex Stout were fictional detectives.

**FACT:**  Perry Mason was the fictional detective created by author Erle (not Earle) Stanley Gardner and played to perfection by Canadian-born actor Raymond Burr. Mickey Spillane was an author, not a fictional detective; one of his best known characters was Mike Hammer. Sam Spade was a fictional detective created by author Dashiell Hammett; Hammett also created Nick Charles, better known as the urbane sleuth in *The Thin Man,* and wrote *The Maltese Falcon.* Rex Stout was the very real author who created the fictional detective Nero Wolfe.

☞ ☜

**FALLACY:**  George Eliot's *Middlemarch* is his masterpiece and the best known of his works.

**FACT:**  *Middlemarch* is considered the best of Eliot's works by critics, but both *The Mill on the Floss* and *Silas Marner* are better known. In person, the author might have taken umbrage at being referred to as a male, since George Eliot was the pen name of Mary Ann Evans. One of her classic lines from *Felix Holt:* "An election is coming. Universal peace is declared, and the foxes have a sincere interest in prolonging the lives of the poultry."

☞ ☜

**FALLACY:** T. S. Eliot was one of the most famous English-born poets.

**FACT:** T(homas) S(tearns) Eliot, author of many famous works including *The Waste Land, Four Quartets,* and the play *Murder in the Cathedral,* received the 1948 Nobel Prize for Literature. He was not, however, born in England, although he spent most of his life there. He was born in 1888 in St. Louis, Missouri.

☞ ☜

**FALLACY:** The singer Engelbert Humperdinck made that name up.

**FACT:** The singer Engelbert Humperdinck did not make that name up. It wasn't what his folks called him, though; they called him Gerry Dorsey. He borrowed the name from a famous German composer. The original Engelbert Humperdinck wrote the opera *Hänsel und Gretel.*

☞ ☜

**FALLACY:** The hands of animated characters have only four fingers so that children will know they're not real.

**FACT:** Children have less trouble telling reality from make-believe than many adults do. Some characters animated today have only four fingers (three fingers and a thumb) because of tradition. In the beginning of the art, animation was drawn one frame at a time. Hands were among the most difficult features to draw; eliminating one finger made it much easier. Most animated characters today are drawn by computer (set your laser printers to "Stun"), but the tradition lives on. Some animated characters, even those drawn long ago, have the full complement of five fingers; Mickey Mouse doesn't, but Snow White does. Bart Simpson, on the other hand, doesn't. As Homer said when he first saw Bart at the hospital, "So long as he's got eight fingers and eight toes, he's okay with me."

☞ ☜

**FALLACY:** Mary Wollstonecraft wrote *Frankenstein.*

**FACT:** Mary Wollstonecraft wrote *Vindication of the Rights of Women,* a classic published in 1792. She died in 1797, ten days after the birth of her second daughter, Mary Godwin, whose father was William Godwin. Mary Godwin married the English poet Percy Bysshe Shelley in 1816. Her famous novel, *Frankenstein, or the Modern Prometheus,* was published in 1818, under the name Mary Wollstonecraft Shelley.

☞ ☜

**FALLACY:** Boris Karloff played the title role in the classic movie *Frankenstein.*

**FACT:** Boris Karloff did not play the title role in the classic movie *Frankenstein.* Colin Clive portrayed Frankenstein. Boris Karloff played the role of the monster created by Frankenstein.

☞ ☜

**FALLACY:** Frankenstein's monster didn't have a name, because Doctor Frankenstein didn't name him.

**FACT:** Many people believe that because Universal cut the scene from the movie in which Frankenstein gave the monster a name; most other people believe the monster's name was Frankenstein. There was no Doctor Frankenstein in the story; Frankenstein was a student of physiology. The name of the monster was Adam.

☞ ☜

**FALLACY:** George and Ira Gershwin were one of America's most famous husband-wife musical teams.

**FACT:** George Gershwin was a composer who wrote such famous concert pieces as *Rhapsody in Blue* and *An American in Paris.* Ira Gershwin was a lyricist who wrote the words for many of the Gershwins' works, including the folk opera *Porgy and Bess.* Ira was George's older brother.

☞ ☜

**FALLACY:** "Margaret Mitchell" was the pen name under which Peggy Marsh wrote *Gone With the Wind.*

**FACT:** In 1900, Eugene Mitchell, one of the founders of the Atlanta Historical Society, became the happy father of a daughter named Margaret Munnerlyn Mitchell. Margaret married John Marsh, becoming Margaret Marsh. The young woman whose nickname was Peggy wrote her classic Civil War novel under her original name, Margaret Mitchell. The title she chose, and which Macmillan used when it published the Pulitzer Prize-winning book in 1936, was *Gone with the Wind*—the word *with* was not capitalized. She found her title in Ernest Dowson's poem "Non Sum Qualis Eram":

> *I have forgot much, Cynara! gone with the wind,*
> *Flung roses, roses, riotously, with the throng,*
> *Dancing, to put thy pale, lost lilies out of mind.*

☞ ☜

**FALLACY:** The name "Hawkeye" was invented for a character in M*A*S*H.

**FACT:** The name Hawkeye goes back a lot further than the folks of the 4077th, or even the Korean War. In 1841, James Fenimore Cooper published *The Deerslayer,* which completed his series of books called the *Leatherstocking Tales.* The title character, Leatherstocking, was also known as Deerslayer, Natty Bumppo, Pathfinder, and Hawkeye. Alan Alda knew that.

☞ ☜

**FALLACY:** "Here Comes the Bride" was written for church weddings.

**FACT:** The name of the piece is "The Bridal Chorus." It was written by Richard Wagner for his opera *Lohengrin.* The scene does not take place in a church, but in a bedroom. A chorus sings "The Bridal Chorus" as the newly married couple, Elsa and Lohengrin, enter the bedroom and are undressed by servants. Although there are a lot of people and things on stage, the central feature is a large bed. The scene ends while still G-rated.

☞ ☜

**FALLACY:** "Home is the sailor, home from the sea, and the hunter home from the hill," is part of a happy poem about coming home.

**FACT:** When that sailor returned home it wasn't from "the sea," it was from "sea"; the poem was not about coming home, but about dying and being buried. In Robert Louis Stevenson's "Requiem," from his book *Underwood:*

*Under the wide and starry sky*
*Dig the grave and let me lie.*
*Glad I did live and gladly die,*
  *And I laid me down with a will.*
*This be the verse you grave for me:*
*"Here he lies where he longed to be;*
*Home is the sailor, home from sea,*
  *And the hunter home from the hill."*

☞ ☜

**FALLACY:**  The theme music for *The Howdy Doody Show* was written for that show.

**FACT:**  The theme music for *The Howdy Doody Show* didn't originate with that show. In 1891, Henry J. Sayers wrote a song that became famous in both the United States and Europe: "Ta-ra-ra-bom-der-é." With new words, that was the theme music for *The Howdy Doody Show.* The tune didn't originate with Sayers, either, though; he said he had heard it in a brothel in St. Louis.

☞ ☜

**FALLACY:**  The first James Bond movie was *007.*

**FACT:**  There has been no James Bond movie named *007.* The first movie in the series was *Dr. No,* released in 1962.

☞ ☜

**FALLACY:**  *I Love Lucy* was in the Nielsen top ten from 1952 to 1971.

**FACT:**  The A. C. Nielsen ratings during that period ran from October to April. *I Love Lucy* first appeared in the top ten in the October 1951 to April 1952 list, coming in at number three; it held the number one spot for the next three years, came in at number two the year after that, then returned to number one in the 1956–1957 ratings—the last time the show appeared. In the 1962–1963 Nielsens, a new program, *The Lucy Show,* came in at number five; it stayed in the top ten until the 1967–1968 ratings—the last time it appeared. The following year a new show, *Here's Lucy,* turned up on the list and stayed there until 1970–1971—the last time it appeared in the Nielsen top ten. Evidently, for those who believe the reruns have more commercial and less program: you're right. Although many viewers aren't aware of it, up to four minutes of each of the original *I Love Lucy* episodes have been removed to make more room for commercials.

☞ ☜

**FALLACY:** On the *Kukla, Fran, and Ollie* TV show, Ollie was also known as Cecil the Seasick Sea Serpent.

**FACT:** On the *Kukla, Fran, and Ollie* show, Ollie was known as Ollie. Ollie was a hand puppet; Kukla was a hand puppet; Fran was a human, Fran Allison; and the puppeteer was Burr Tillstrom. There was a Dumb Cecil Bill character, but that wasn't Ollie. Among the other hand-puppet characters were Beulah the Witch, Dolores Dragon, Fletcher Rabbit, Madame Oglepuss, Mercedes, and Windbag Colonel Crackie. The characters of another TV puppet show, *Time for Beany,* included Beany, Caboose Goose, and Cecil the Seasick Sea Serpent.

☞ ☜

**FALLACY:** James Dean became famous even though he made only two movies.

**FACT:** During his short acting career Jams Dean was in three major movies: *East of Eden,* which made him a star; *Rebel Without A Cause,* which made him a hero to alienated youth; and *Giant,* which was released after his death. Dean was born in 1931 in Indiana, and died in 1955 in a car crash in California.

☞ ☜

**FALLACY:** There is only one Lama of Tibet.

**FACT:** Lamaism is a Mongolian and Tibetan form (Mahayana) of Buddhism, with shamanistic and tantric rituals. According to this theocratic system, both church and state are headed by the Dalai Lama. There is only one Dalai Lama, but all of the priests are lamas. No, there's no connection with the four-footed folks in South America; although they belong to the genus Lama, those are llamas.

☞ ☜

**FALLACY:** The oldest paintings still in existence are about 500 years old.

**FACT:** The oldest paintings still in existence are many times that old.

In northern Spain, for example, is the Altamira cave, on its ceiling are Paleolithic paintings 15,500 years old. Near Montignac in southwestern France, in the Lascaux cave, there are 17,000-year-old paintings. In late December 1994, more than 300 paintings were discovered in the Chauvet cave near the town of Vallon-Pont-d'Arc, in the Ardèche region of southwestern France; they were painted more than 30,000 years ago.

☞ ☜

**FALLACY:** Elizabeth Taylor was born in the United States.

**FACT:** Elizabeth Rosemond Taylor was born in London, England, but she has been in the United States for quite a while. She was not yet a teenager when she starred in the first of the Lassie films, Metro-Goldwyn-Mayer's 1943 classic *Lassie Come Home*.

☞ ☜

**FALLACY:** None of the main actors in the movie *M\*A\*S\*H*, which was based on the novel *M\*A\*S\*H*, was also in the TV series.

**FACT:** The 1970 movie was called *M\*A\*S\*H*, but the novel wasn't. Twentieth Century-Fox bought the rights to the novel, which was called *MASH*, and added the asterisks for the movie title. Almost none of the main actors in the movie was also in the TV series, but one was: Gary Burghoff, better known as Radar O'Reilly.

☞ ☜

**FALLACY:** Herman Melville's *Moby Dick* made him rich and famous.

**FACT:** Herman Melville's 1846 *Typee* and 1847 *Omoo* were successes, but his 1851 *Moby Dick; or The Whale* was a flop. The public didn't like it, the critics didn't like it, nobody seemed to like it until a Melville renaissance in the 1920s. It is now considered not only his best work, but a masterpiece. Unfortunately, Melville died in 1891, an impoverished customs inspector in New York City.

☞ ☜

**FALLACY:** The little-known author of *Winnie the Pooh* wrote only that one book.

**FACT:** The author—Alan Alexander Milne, who wrote as A. A. Milne—became internationally known in 1924 with the publication of *When We Were Very Young*, a book of children's verse he had written for his son. *Winnie-the-Pooh* followed in 1926, featuring Christopher Robin and his toy bear, Pooh; Milne's son's name was Christopher Robin. *Now We Are Six* was published in 1927, and *The House at Pooh Corner* in 1928.

☞ ☜

**FALLACY:** Michael Jackson has more compact disks on the market than anyone else.

**FACT:** It isn't Michael Jackson who has more compact disks on the market than anyone else, and it isn't Beethoven, or Madonna, or the Beatles. In commemoration of the bicentennial of the death of Wolfgang Amadeus Mozart in 1791, Philips Classics released 180 compact disks containing his complete official works. That gives Mozart the record for most compact disks.

☞ ☜

**FALLACY:** "Never Never Land" is purely fictional and exists only in the novel *Peter Pan.*

**FACT:** In Northern Territory, Australia, southeast of Darwin, there is an area called Never Never Land. Mrs. Aeneas Gunn wrote about it in her 1908 book, *We of the Never Never.* Considering that James Matthew Barrie's *Peter Pan*—a play, not a novel—opened in London on 27 December 1904, there may be a connection. Barrie's story came out in book form first as *Peter and Wendy* and in 1911 as *Peter Pan and Wendy.* Although many people now refer to the magic island of the mind as Never Never Land, that's not exactly what Barrie named it: "Of all delectable islands the Neverland is the snuggest and most compact; not large and sprawly, you know, with tedious distance between one adventure and another, but nicely crammed." As to how to get there, here are the directions from Peter Pan himself: "Second star to the right and straight on 'til morning."

☞ ☜

**FALLACY:** Picasso signed his works with his full name, Pablo Picasso.

**FACT:** Picasso was born in Malaga, Spain, in 1881. Together, he and Georges Braque founded the school of Cubism. His first major Cubistic painting was *Les Demoiselles d'Avignon,* 1906–1907. Of all the works he created before his death in 1973, none has approached the fame of

*Guernica*, named for a Spanish town bombed by the Nazis in 1937. He never signed his works with his full name, for a very good reason: there wouldn't have been room left for the artwork. His full name was Pablo Diego Jose Francisco de Paula Juan Nepomuceno Maria de los Remedios Cipriano de la Santisima Trinidad Ruiz y Picasso.

☞ ☜

**FALLACY:** Once you have a street address, you can't change it.

**FACT:** Depends on how good your reason is—and who you are. If your reason is that you're superstitious about the number you have, you'd need an awful lot of political influence to pull it off. Ronald and Nancy Reagan, for example. Friends bought them a $2.5 million house in August 1988, back when that was a lot of money. The address was 666 St. Cloud Road, in the wealthy Bel Air district in the hills of western Los Angeles. The Reagans said they wanted to change the street address because 666 was the mark of the devil. In February 1989, the address was officially changed to 668 St. Cloud Road.

☞ ☜

**FALLACY:** If the address you put on an envelope is nearly correct, the U.S. Postal Service will deliver it.

**FACT:** The U.S. Postal Service moves in mysterious ways. For about a decade, mail reached me in a small coastal town if the envelope had no more than my P.O. box number and the town's ZIP code—nothing else, just those two numbers. To confirm an item in this book, I sent a letter to the Canadian Embassy in Washington, D.C. The Canadian Embassy had moved to a different street that year, and its ZIP code had changed by one number in the last digit. A full month after I mailed the letter it arrived back with these notices stamped on the envelope: AT-TEMPTED—NOT KNOWN and UNKNOWN. The U.S. Postal Service, in Washington, couldn't find the Canadian Embassy, in Washington.

☞ ☜

**FALLACY:** The Br'er Rabbit stories were written by an author who used the pen name Uncle Remus.

**FACT:** The Br'er Rabbit stories, including *The Tar Baby,* published in 1904, and *Uncle Remus and Br'er Rabbit,* published in 1906, were narrated by a character called Uncle Remus. The writer of those tales had already published *Uncle Remus: His Songs and His Sayings* in 1881. The Br'er Rabbit stories were written by an author who used his own name: Joel Chandler Harris.

☞ ☜

**FALLACY:** George Sand created a scandal when he became Frédéric Chopin's lover.

**FACT:** French novelist George Sand went so far as to write an autobiographical work, *A Winter on Majorca,* about life with Chopin. Among Sand's approximately 100 books were the acclaimed *Fanchon the Cricket* and *The Haunted Pool.* Sand believed strongly in equality of the sexes, was an ardent nature lover, and had two children from *her* one marriage. "George Sand" was the pen name of Amandine Aurore Lucie Dupin.

☞ ☜

**FALLACY:** The real name of the author who wrote *The Wizard of Oz* under the pen name L. Frank Baum was Frank Oz.

**FACT:** Frank Oz is involved with one of the best known children's shows of all time, but it isn't the one with Dorothy and Toto. It's the one with Bert and Ernie and the Cookie Monster and Big Bird: *Sesame Street.* Frank Oz is the voice of Bert. *The Wizard of Oz* was one of a series of Oz books written by L(yman) Frank Baum.

☞ ☜

**FALLACY:** *The Canterbury Tales* were written in Old English.

**FACT:** Geoffrey Chaucer's late-fourteenth-century work, *The Canterbury Tales,* was written in Middle English. Old English was an Anglo-Saxon language so different from modern English that someone who knows only modern English would find it incomprehensible. Middle English, on the other hand, is recognizable as English:

HERE BYGYNNETH THE BOOK OF THE
TALES OF CAUNTERBURY

*Whan that Aprille with his shoures sote*
*The droghte of Marche hath perced to the rote,*
*And bathed every veyne in swich licour,*
*Of which vertu engendred is the flour; . . .*

And in modern English:

> *When April with his showers sweet*
> *The drought of March has pierced to the root,*
> *And bathed every vein in such moisture,*
> *Of which virtue engendered is the flower;* ...

☞ ☜

**FALLACY:**  *The Autobiography of Alice B. Toklas* was written by Alice B. Toklas.

**FACT:**  *The Autobiography of Alice B. Toklas,* published in 1933, was written by Gertrude Stein. Alice B. Toklas's best known piece of writing was her cookbook, which listed marijuana among the ingredients for several recipes, including her famous brownies.

☞ ☜

**FALLACY:**  The character Huckleberry Finn first appeared in Mark Twain's novel *The Adventures of Huckleberry Finn.*

**FACT:**  The character Huckleberry Finn first appeared in Mark Twain's novel *The Adventures of Tom Sawyer* in 1876. That's also where Huck's best friend, Tom Sawyer, first appeared. Mark Twain, a.k.a. Samuel Langhorne Clemens, published *The Adventures of Huckleberry Finn* in 1884 as a sequel to *The Adventures of Tom Sawyer.* The last lines of the first book suggest he was thinking of writing a second:

> Most of the characters that perform in this book still live, and are prosperous and happy. Some day it may seem worth while to take up the story of the younger ones again and see what sort of men and women they turned out to be; therefore it will be wisest not to reveal any of that part of their lives at present.

Among his best known works are "The Celebrated Jumping Frog of Calaveras County," *Life on the Mississippi,* and *A Connecticut Yankee in King Arthur's Court;* among his most controversial are *Letters from Earth* and *The Mysterious Stranger.*

☞ ☜

**FALLACY:**  Mark Twain was born in Hannibal, Missouri.

**FACT:**  Mark Twain was born in 1835 in Florida. Florida, Missouri, that is. It wasn't until 1839 that his family moved to Hannibal.

☞ ☜

**FALLACY:**  There was only one Roy Rogers, but there were a series of horses named Trigger.

**FACT:**  Roy Rogers and Trigger made more than eighty-five motion pictures together—the same Roy Rogers and the same Trigger. When Trigger died in 1965, he was taken to a taxidermist; he is now in the Roy Rogers and Dale Evans Museum in Victorville, California. Dale's horse, Buttermilk, is also there, as is their dog, Bullet. Dale Evans's real name was Frances Octavia Smith; Roy Rogers's was Leonard Sly Jr. After taking occasional flack over the years for having Trigger "stuffed," Roy responded: "Would you rather I put him in the ground and let the worms eat him? I don't like to say 'stuffed' because they don't stuff them anymore. They make a sculpture out of fiberglass and stretch the hide over that." In the case of this one and only Trigger, beauty *is* only skin deep.

☞ ☜

**FALLACY:**  The United States, because of separation of church and state, does not have diplomatic relations with churches.

**FACT:**  Despite separation of church and state, the United States has full diplomatic relations with the Roman Catholic Church. Technically, the representative is the United States Ambassador to the Vatican, a "country" of 108.7 acres with a population of about 800. The independent state of Vatican City was established by the 1929 Treaty of Conciliation signed by the church and Italian Premier Benito Mussolini. Following Congress's repeal of the 1867 ban on diplomatic relations with the Vatican, President Ronald Reagan appointed his close friend William A. Wilson as ambassador on 9 April 1984.

☞ ☜

**FALLACY:**  The Irving Berlin song "White Christmas," from the movie *White Christmas,* was Bing Crosby's first big hit.

**FACT:**  Russian-American Irving Berlin, who changed his name from Israel Baline, won the 1942 Academy Award for Best Song for his

"White Christmas." He composed the song for a movie, but not *White Christmas*. Bing Crosby recorded the song in 1942 for the Paramount production *Holiday Inn*. Crosby was chosen for the picture because he was already a famous crooner. His first big hit, which sold more than a million copies, was "Sweet Leilani," recorded in 1937. The Crosby–"White Christmas" combination was so popular that it was used in a second movie in 1954, and the movie was named after the song: *White Christmas*.

☞ ☜

**FALLACY:**  In *The Wild Ones*, Marlon Brando rode a Harley.

**FACT:**  The title of that classic 1954 movie was *The Wild One*, singular. It was a fictionalized version of the very real takeover of Hollister, California, by bikers on 4 July 1947. Hollister had about 4,000 residents on that Independence Day; about 4,000 bikers turned up for the annual motorcycle races. In the movie, Johnny (Marlon Brando) was the leader of the Black Rebel Motorcycle Club. The motorcycle that Johnny was so proud of was a British bike, a Triumph, not a Harley-Davidson.

☞ ☜

**FALLACY:**  Among Yogi Bear's most memorable lines are: "I'm smarter than the average bear!" and "Exit, stage left!"

**FACT:**  Yogi Bear is definitely smarter than the average bear, but it isn't Yogi who exits stage left. That's Snagglepuss the lion, who also says, "Heavens to Mergatroyd!" The characters are often confused in memory because their voices sound a lot alike. May have something to do with the fact that the voices of both Yogi and Snagglepuss are done by Daws Butler.

☞ ☜

**FALLACY:**  "Alas, poor Yorick. I knew him well." is from Shakespeare.

**FACT:**  Alas, poor Shakespeare. Many people remember his classic quote that way, but that's not the way he wrote it. The original, from *Hamlet*, goes:

*Alas, poor Yorick. I knew him, Horatio; a fellow of infinite jest, of most excellent fancy; he hath borne me on his back a thousand times; and*

*now, how abhorred in my imagination it is! my gorge rises at it. Here*
*hung those lips that I have kissed I know not how oft.*

☞ ☜

**FALLACY:** Paleolithic cave paintings have been found throughout Europe and the Middle East.

**FACT:** Paleolithic (Old Stone Age) cave paintings have been found only in southern France and northern Spain. Among the most famous of the caves are Altamira, on Spain's northern coast, and Lascaux, in the Dordogne River Valley of southwestern France.

☞ ☜

**FALLACY:** More Jews were killed in World War II than members of any other religion.

**FACT:** There was so much chaos and destruction in World War II that no exact fatality figures exist. It is estimated that 55 million people were killed. The populations of the European and Western Hemisphere countries involved, and of Australia, New Zealand, and the Philippines, were predominantly members of the Christian religion, so more Christians were killed in World War II than members of any other religion. There are two important points to keep in mind, however: this refers to numbers, not to percentages; Jews, along with communists, homosexuals, and Gypsies, were targeted by the Nazis for extermination. More than 45 percent of all the people killed in World War II, about 25 million, were citizens of the Soviet Union. Approximately 8 million Chinese civilians were killed, few of whom were members of either the Christian or the Jewish religions.

☞ ☜

**FALLACY:** "Every day, in every way, I am getting better and better" was coined by Dale Carnegie.

**FACT:** Dale Carnegie's main claim to fame was his 1936 book, *How to Win Friends and Influence People.* "Every day, in every way, I am getting better and better" was not a Dale Carnegieism; it was coined by the leader of a self-improvement movement popular in the 1920s, Émile Coué.

☞ ☜

**FALLACY:** Henry Brandon was the one and only movie actor who played Dr. Fu Manchu.

**FACT:** The evil Dr. Fu Manchu was indeed played by actor Henry Brandon, but only as one among many. Dr. Fu Manchu was created by Arthur Sarsfield Ward, who wrote more than a dozen Dr. Fu Manchu novels under the pseudonym Sax Rohmer. In addition to Brandon, the character was played in movies by Warner Oland and other actors who went on to greater fame, including Boris Karloff and Christopher Lee.

☞ ☜

**FALLACY:** Ripley came up with the thought that "Truth is stranger than fiction."

**FACT:** Robert Le Roy "Believe It or Not" Ripley did not come up with the thought that "Truth is stranger than fiction." Which is fine because he never claimed credit for it. The credit for that thought goes to George Gordon Byron, also known as Lord Byron, who wrote in his poem "Don Juan":

> 'Tis strange—but true; for truth is always strange;
> Stranger than fiction.

☞ ☜

**FALLACY:** *Gadsby* is one of F. Scott Fitzgerald's most famous novels.

**FACT:** *Gadsby*, published in 1939, couldn't be one of F. Scott Fitzgerald's most famous novels because it was written by Ernest Vincent Wright. Although a perfectly respectable novel in its own right, *Gadsby*'s main claim to fame is that in the entire book of more than 50,000 words, Wright never once used the letter *e*. One of F(rancis) Scott (Key) Fitzgerald's most famous novels is *The Great Gatsby,* published in 1925.

☞ ☜

**FALLACY:** "Music hath charms to sooth the savage beast" is a well-known quote.

**FACT:** "Music hath charms to sooth the savage beast" may be well known, but that's not the quote. The original—by William Congreve, in Act I, Scene 1, of his 1697 work *The Mourning Bride*—has no *hath*, no *the*, and no *beast*: "Music has charms to sooth a savage breast." The common misquote of "beast" for "breast" may have originated because it had charms to sooth a savage censor.

☞ ☜

**FALLACY:** A book has only half as many pages as the numbers indicate because pages are printed on both sides.

**FACT:** Leaving aside the unnumbered ones, a book has just as many pages as the numbers indicate. Those things you turn are leaves, not pages. Each side of a leaf is a page.

☞ ☜

**FALLACY:** Three of the most famous Arabian novels are *Aladdin, Ali Baba,* and *Sinbad.*

**FACT:** Open sesame! Those are not novels. The stories about Aladdin and the magic lamp, Ali Baba and the forty thieves, and Sinbad the sailor are many-centuries-old tales in *Arabian Nights* or *The Thousand and One Nights,* a collection of anonymously authored Arabian, Indian, and Persian stories written in Arabic and translated into English by Richard Francis Burton. Although each tale is complete unto itself, they are connected by a framework story. Scheherazade is newly married to Schariar, who kills his wives the day after he marries them. She tells him one fascinating story each night but leaves the ending for the next night; because Schariar wants to hear the ending, he spares her one day at a time. After 1,001 nights he has fallen in love with her.

☞ ☜

**FALLACY:** Dr. Jekyll was a monster.

**FACT:** Only Mrs. Jekyll would know for sure, but that's not the way Robert Louis Stevenson described the doctor in his 1886 novel, *The Strange Case of Dr. Jekyll and Mr. Hyde.* It was the good doctor who prepared the potion that turned him into the evil Mr. Hyde.

☞ ☜

**FALLACY:** "I must go down to the sea again" is from a poem by Tennyson.

**FACT:** That classic line is almost always misquoted. There is no *go* in it, and the word is *seas.* It's not from a poem by Tennyson; it's from *Sea Fever,* by John Masefield:

> *I must down to the seas again,*
> > *to the lonely sea and the sky,*

> *And all I ask is a tall ship and a star*
>   *to steer her by,*
> *And the wheel's kick and the wind's song*
>   *and the white sail's shaking,*
> *And a grey mist on the sea's face*
>   *and a grey dawn breaking.*

What Tennyson wrote, in *Crossing the Bar*, was:

> *Sunset and evening star,*
> *And one clear call for me!*
> *And may there be no moaning of the bar*
> *When I put out to sea.*

☞ ☜

**FALLACY:**  Gulliver, of *Gulliver's Travels* fame, traveled to two places: the land of the little people and the land of the big people.

**FACT:**  Lemuel Gulliver, the title character of Jonathan Swift's 1726 satire, *Gulliver's Travels,* traveled to many places. Two of the places were Lilliput, where the people were six inches tall, and Brobdingnag, where the people were seventy feet tall. A third place Gulliver visited was the land of the Houyhnhnms, where horses were the intelligent species and a human-shaped species, called Yahoos, were work animals. Referring to a citizen of yet another land he'd traveled to, Laputa, Gulliver said: "He had been eight years upon a project for extracting sunbeams out of cucumbers, which were to be put into vials hermetically sealed, and let out to warm the air in raw inclement summers."

☞ ☜

**FALLACY:**  The first canine movie star was Rin Tin Tin, not Lassie.

**FACT:**  The first canine movie star was neither Rin Tin Tin nor Lassie. Lassie's first film, in which he was ably assisted by Elizabeth Taylor, was *Lassie Come Home,* in 1943. Rin Tin Tin's first film was *Where the North Begins,* in 1925. The first canine movie star was Rover, hero and title character of *Rescue by Rover,* in 1903.

☞ ☜

**FALLACY:**  Saying "Abracadabra" was supposed to bring about magic.

**FACT:**  *Abracadabra* wasn't supposed to be spoken, it was supposed to be written; the word, which comes from Late Latin, wasn't used at all as it is by today's magicians. The word was written on an amulet in the form of an upside-down pyramid, then worn around the neck to ward off sickness or other evil. To be effective, it had to be written like this:

A B R A C A D A B R A
A B R A C A D A B R
A B R A C A D A B
A B R A C A D A
A B R A C A D
A B R A C A
A B R A C
A B R A
A B R
A B
A

☞ ☜

**FALLACY:**  When the rest of the Texas Rangers with him were killed, Ranger John Smith became the Lone Ranger.

**FACT:**  "Return with us now to those thrilling days of yesteryear!" When the rest of the Texas Rangers with him were killed, Ranger John Reid became the Lone Ranger. Ranger John Smith is in charge of Yogi Bear's Jellystone Park.

☞ ☜

**FALLACY:**  In their day, Camille Saint-Saëns, Evelyn Waugh, and Flo Ziegfeld were among the most famous women in the arts.

**FACT:**  Camille Saint-Saëns' full name was Charles Camille Saint-Saëns; he was a French composer. Evelyn Waugh's full name was Evelyn Arthur St. John Waugh; he was an English novelist. Flo Ziegfeld's full name was Florenz Ziegfeld; he was an American theatrical producer.

☞ ☜

**FALLACY:** Norman Rockwell painted almost a hundred covers for the *Saturday Evening Post.*

**FACT:** Norman Rockwell painted almost a hundred covers for the *Saturday Evening Post*—for starters. Then his paintings appeared on another hundred covers. Then his paintings appeared on another hundred covers. Norman Rockwell paintings appeared on a total of 322 *Saturday Evening Post* covers.

☞ ☜

**FALLACY:** The theme music of the TV series *M\*A\*S\*H* had no words and was called simply "The Theme from M\*A\*S\*H."

**FACT:** The theme of the TV series *M\*A\*S\*H* was a theme *song*. The music was by Johnny Mandel, the words were by Mike Altman, and the title was "Suicide is Painless." There are differences among the movie version of the song, the TV version, and the sheet music, but these words remained in the refrain:

> *Suicide is painless*
> *It brings on many changes*
> *And I can take or leave it if I please.*

☞ ☜

**FALLACY:** *The Satanic Verses* was Salman Rushdie's only major book.

**FACT:** Bombay-born British writer Salman Rushdie was a noted author long before his 1988 novel, *The Satanic Verses*. He came out with *Grimus* in 1975, and his 1980 *Midnight's Children* won the Booker Prize. Other works include *Shame* in 1983 and *The Jaguar Smile: A Nicaraguan Journey* in 1987. Following the death sentence passed on him by Ayatollah Khomeini and reaffirmed by other Muslim clerics since Khomeini's death, Rushdie published *Haroun and the Sea of Stories* in 1990, *Imaginary Homelands* in 1991, and *East, West* in 1995.

☞ ☜

**FALLACY:** In the famous poem "The Night Before Christmas," Rudolph is the best known of Santa's reindeer.

**FACT:** Clement Clarke Moore's poem, published in a newspaper in 1823, is "A Visit from St. Nicholas." Many people call it by that other name because the opening words are " 'Twas the night before Christmas . . ." Rudolph is not one of Santa's reindeer in the poem; he was created more than a century later in a Christmas jingle, "Rudolph the Red-Nosed Reindeer." Because of popularizations showing Rudolph in front with pairs of reindeer behind him, it is sometimes thought that Santa had an odd number of reindeer. In Clement Moore's "A Visit from St. Nicholas" there are eight:

> More rapid than eagles his coursers they came,
> And he whistled, and shouted, and called them by name:
> "Now, Dasher! now, Dancer! now, Prancer and Vixen!
> On, Comet! on, Cupid! on, Donder and Blitzen!
> To the top of the porch! to the top of the wall!
> Now dash away! dash away! dash away, all!''

☞ ☜

**FALLACY:** Finnan Haddie is a folk hero from Celtic literature.

**FACT:** Finnan Haddie is not a folk hero, Celtic or otherwise. *Finnan* is an alteration of the name of a village in northeast Scotland, Findon; *haddie* is an alteration of haddock. Finnan haddie is smoked haddock. It's perfectly legal to smoke haddock so long as you don't inhale.

# 3
# Earth

**FALLACY:** Hurricanes were given only female names until the beginning of the 1990s.

**FACT:** Historically, hurricanes were given only female names because most meteorologists were of the male persuasion. It was on 12 May 1978 that the U.S. Department of Commerce decreed that henceforth hurricanes would be bisexual.

☞ ☜

**FALLACY:** The source of the Amazon River is in the jungles of Brazil.

**FACT:** The source of the Amazon (Amazonas) River is neither in a jungle nor in Brazil. The most distant reported source of water flowing through the Amazon is Laguna McIntyre, at the junction of the Ucayali and Marañón Rivers in the snow-shrouded Andes Mountains in northern Peru, at an altitude of more than three miles. It's definitely not a jungle out there.

☞ ☜

**FALLACY:** Victoria Falls in Africa is the world's highest waterfall.

**FACT:** Victoria Falls on the Zambezi River is well known because David Livingstone, of "Dr. Livingstone, I presume?" fame, was the first European to see it, but at 350 feet it's not particularly high; six other African waterfalls are higher. Victoria Falls was the name given to it by Europeans, but the people who have lived in the area since long before the first European arrived call the falls *Mosi oa Tunya* (The Smoke That Thunders). Yosemite Falls in North America, 2,425 feet in more than one drop, is higher than any in Africa. With a single drop of 2,648 feet and a total drop of 3,212 feet, the world's highest waterfall is Angel Falls in South America. No, it is not named for an angel. It's named for a pilot who flew over it: Jimmy Angel.

☞ ☜

**FALLACY:** Antarctica is about a third as large as the continent of Australia.

**FACT:** Australia has an area of 2,966,200 square miles. Highest point is 7,310-foot Mt. Kosciusko, New South Wales; lowest point is Lake Eyre, South Australia, 52 feet below sea level. Highest recorded temperature was 128° Fahrenheit at Cloncurry, Queensland; lowest recorded temperature was −8° at Charlotte Pass, New South Wales. Antarctica's lowest recorded temperature was −129° at Vostok; highest recorded temperature was 59° at Esperanza on the Antarctic Peninsula. Lowest point is unknown, but highest point is 16,864-foot Vinson Massif. Only about 2 percent of Antarctica is not covered by ice, but underneath all that ice Antarctica makes up about 9 percent of Earth's continental crust. Antarctica has an area of 5,400,000 square miles, making it 1.8 times as large as Australia. Unlike Australia, Antarctica never has a shortage of ice cubes.

☞ ☜

**FALLACY:** The farthest that one human can get from another is a point on the opposite side of Earth.

**FACT:** Points on diametrically opposite sides of Earth are antipodes; the distance between them is the diameter of Earth, about 8,000 miles. That's much farther than the roughly 200-mile distance to an orbiting space shuttle, but the astronauts who went to the Moon got a lot farther away than that. The farthest one human has ever been from another was in 1971, when Alfred M. Worden of the Apollo 15 mission, in orbit around the Moon, was over its far side. The closest human was on the other side of the Moon, more than 2,233 miles away; the farthest was on the far side of Earth.

☞ ☜

**FALLACY:** The highest layer of Earth's atmosphere is the stratosphere.

**FACT:** The layer of Earth's atmosphere that rests on the planet, and in which we live and weather occurs, is the troposphere. The troposphere ranges up to about 10 kilometers; less at the poles, more at the equator. Above that is the stratosphere, of ozone-layer fame, which goes up to 50 kilometers. Above the stratosphere is the ionosphere, which extends from 50 kilometers to 400 kilometers. Beyond 400 kilometers is the outermost layer of earth's atmosphere, the exosphere.

☞ ☜

**FALLACY:** There are Northern Lights, but no Southern Lights.

**FACT:** The northern lights, or aurora borealis, are often just colorful glows but sometimes look like curtains or rays or even tunnels of light in the far northern skies. The far southern skies weren't left out, though, and do have their counterpart: the southern lights, or aurora australis. *Aurora* is Latin for "dawn"; *borealis* and *australis* are Latin for "northern" and "southern." High-energy particles from the Sun spiral down Earth's magnetic field lines toward the poles. When they interact with atoms in the atmosphere, they cause the auroras. Green, for example, the most common auroral color, is caused by atomic oxygen. It's usually possible to see auroras only in the higher northern or southern latitudes, but when conditions are right they can be seen more than halfway to the equator. After an especially good party, of course, they might be seen just about anywhere.

☞ ☜

**FALLACY:** Barrow, Alaska, is the northernmost point of North America.

**FACT:** Barrow, Alaska, an Inupiat Eskimo community, is the northernmost town of the United States; when the Sun sets there for the winter, it doesn't rise again for sixty-five days. Point Barrow, not the town of Barrow, is the northernmost point of the United States. The northernmost point of North America, however, is not on the mainland. It's Cape Columbia, at the northern tip of Ellesmere Island, a barren, mountainous island of about 76,000 square miles in Canada's Northwest Territories, in the Arctic Ocean. Forget the suntan lotion and the bikini; bring lots of dogs for the much-colder-than-three-dog nights.

☞ ☜

**FALLACY:** Hudson Bay in Canada is the largest bay on Earth.

**FACT:** Hudson Bay, connected to the Atlantic Ocean, covers an area of 475,000 square miles. The Bay of Bengal, connected to the Indian Ocean, covers an area of 839,000 square miles, making it the largest bay on Earth. Hudson Bay does hold the world record for the bay with the longest shoreline: more than 7,600 miles—or, for you traditional folks, more than 60,800 furlongs.

☞ ☜

**FALLACY:**  About half a dozen U.S. states, including Alaska and Maine, extend north of Canada's southernmost point.

**FACT:**  Canada's southernmost point is in Lake Erie, south of Pelée Island. U.S. states completely north of Canada's southernmost point are: Alaska, Idaho, Maine, Michigan, Minnesota, Montana, New Hampshire, North Dakota, Oregon, South Dakota, Vermont, Washington, and Wisconsin. States that extend north of Canada's southernmost point are: California, Connecticut, Illinois, Indiana, Iowa, Massachusetts, Nebraska, Nevada, New York, Ohio, Pennsylvania, Rhode Island, Utah, and Wyoming. Twenty-seven of the fifty United States extend north of Canada's southernmost point.

☞ ☜

**FALLACY:**  The correct name now is Cape Kennedy; its old name was Cape Canaveral.

**FACT:**  Well, no and yes. No, the correct name now is not Cape Kennedy; yes, its old name was Cape Canaveral. That cape on Florida's east coast was known as Cape Canaveral until 1963, when the name was changed to Cape Kennedy. In 1973, the name was changed back to Cape Canaveral. That's the cape itself. On Cape Canaveral are NASA's Kennedy Space Center and, near the space center, the Cape Canaveral Air Force Station. The final score of that great space game, by the way, was Deep Space 9, Babylon 5.

☞ ☜

**FALLACY:**  Continents are easy to identify because they're far apart.

**FACT:**  Antarctica is a long way from Africa, Australia, or South America, but not all continents are so far apart. Eurasia and North America are separated by only the fifty-six-mile width of the Bering Strait; Africa and Eurasia are separated by only the nine-mile width of the Strait of Gibraltar.

☞ ☜

**FALLACY:**  Coral reefs range in length from a few hundred feet to nearly a hundred miles.

**FACT:**  Coral reefs are calcium carbonate formations consisting mainly of the skeletons of corals, animals belonging to the class Anthrozoa. Coral reefs form only in warm, shallow, tropical waters. The world's largest coral reef system is the Great Barrier Reef, located, appropriately enough, in the Coral Sea; it ranges from thirty to ninety miles offshore from the northeastern coast of Australia. Thicker than 400 feet in some places, the Great Barrier Reef is more than 1,200 miles long.

☞ ☜

**FALLACY:**  The Dominican Republic is on the island of Dominica.

**FACT:**  The Commonwealth of Dominica is on the island of Dominica; it has a population of about 90,000 and a land surface of 290 square miles. The island of Dominica, located in the West Indies between Guadeloupe and Martinique, is the northernmost of the Windward Islands. The Dominican Republic, though, is on the island of Hispaniola, which is east of Cuba and Jamaica and also in the West Indies. The Dominican Republic has a population of about 8 million and a land surface of nearly 19,000 square miles. The Dominican Republic comprises the eastern two thirds of the island of Hispaniola; the western third is the nation of Haiti.

☞ ☜

**FALLACY:**  Fiji is a large island in the South Pacific.

**FACT:**  There is no large island in the South Pacific named Fiji. The Sovereign Democratic Republic of Fiji, in the southwestern Pacific Ocean southwest of Western Samoa, is comprised of hundreds of islands. The 180th parallel runs through the group, but the International Date Line jogs east to place all of Fiji in the Eastern Hemisphere. About 90 percent of the population lives on the two main islands, Viti Levu and Vanua Levu; both the capital, Suva, and the nation's tallest mountain, 4,345-foot Tomaniivi, are on Viti Levu.

☞ ☜

**FALLACY:**  Florida is closer to Cuba than to any other country.

**FACT:**  Florida is ninety miles from Cuba. Florida is forty miles closer to the Commonwealth of the Bahamas than it is to Cuba.

☞ ☜

**FALLACY:** France is slightly smaller than the United States.

**FACT:** France shares borders with four more countries than does the United States: Belgium, Germany, Italy, Luxembourg, Spain, and Switzerland. The United States covers 3,787,318 square miles; France covers 210,026 square miles. France is four-fifths the size of Texas, which some Texans claim is slightly larger than the United States.

☞ ☜

**FALLACY:** The official name of England is Great Britain.

**FACT:** The Scots and the Welsh hate to hear that. Great Britain is an island. England, Scotland, and Wales (Cymru) are located on the island of Great Britain. The official name of England is England. The official name of the United Kingdom is the United Kingdom. Unless you're looking for a Brobdingnagian brouhaha, don't say a word about those people with a brogue on the island west of Great Britain.

☞ ☜

**FALLACY:** The Gobi desert is a small, low-altitude, dangerously hot sea of sand in Mongolia containing nothing of value.

**FACT:** The Gobi desert is certainly inhospitable to humans, although some Mongol herders do live along its fringes. It is not small, covering 500,000 square miles. Because it is on the Mongolian Plateau, it is not low altitude, ranging from 3,000 to 5,000 feet. It is seldom hot except during its very short summer; far more dangerous are its extreme cold and its violent sand- and windstorms. Only the western part of the Gobi is sandy, most of the rest being shallow alkaline basins. It extends approximately 1,000 miles east-west across not only southeastern Mongolia but also northern China. There are significant deposits of coal at Tawan-Tolgoi, Mongolia, and of oil at Saynshand, Mongolia, and Yumen, China. Probably of greatest importance, the Gobi desert is one of the richest sources on the planet for dinosaur fossils.

☞ ☜

**FALLACY:** Most gold nuggets weigh only a few ounces; the very biggest weigh only a few pounds.

**FACT:** First off, a clarification: gold is measured in troy weight, and in the troy system there are twelve ounces, not sixteen ounces, to a pound. The largest pure nugget ever found, discovered in Australia in 1869, contained 2,248 troy ounces, or 187 troy pounds, of gold. One troy pound equals 0.8232 customary pounds, so in the world of the sixteen-ounce pound, that comes out to 154 pounds of gold.

☞ ☜

**FALLACY:** The Cape of Good Hope is the southern tip of Africa.

**FACT:** The Cape of Good Hope is the best known cape *near* the southern tip of Africa, but it isn't the tip. The southern tip of Africa is about 100 miles southeast of the Cape of Good Hope: Cape Agulhas.

☞ ☜

**FALLACY:** Because the Great Lakes are on the border, part of each is in Canada and part is in the United States.

**FACT:** Lakes Erie, Huron, Ontario, and Superior are partly in Canada and partly in the United States. Lake Michigan, though, is south of the border and entirely in the United States.

☞ ☜

**FALLACY:** The Great Plains are a low, flat area in the United States Midwest.

**FACT:** Many citizens of the United States are surprised to learn that the Great Plains are not contained within their country's borders. The Great Plains are indeed great, extending about 400 miles east from the Rocky Mountains and more than 1,500 miles from the Saskatchewan River in northwestern Canada south into New Mexico and Texas, for an area of roughly 600,000 square miles. Far from being low-altitude, the Great Plains range from 1,500 feet in the east to 6,000 feet in the west. The native vegetation was buffalo grass, which supported the bison, which supported the Native Americans. By the time buffalo grass was replaced by overfarming in the southern part of the Great Plains, the bison and the Native Americans and the topsoil were gone with the wind, and a new expression was added to the language: Dust Bowl. Many farms have since been replaced with housing tracts and highways, shopping malls and parking lots.

☞ ☜

**FALLACY:**  Continents are the largest of the tectonic plates.

**FACT:**  Not only are continents not the largest of the tectonic plates, they aren't tectonic plates at all. The North American continent, for example, neither begins nor ends at the edge of a plate. The eastern edge of the North American tectonic plate lies along the Mid-Atlantic Ridge, appropriately named because it's in the middle of the Atlantic Ocean. Part of the western edge of the North American tectonic plate lies along the San Andreas fault. Although San Francisco is on the eastern side of the fault, and therefore on the North American plate, Los Angeles is on the western side, placing it on the Pacific Plate. San Franciscans and Los Angelenos have long considered themselves residents of two different worlds; this confirms it.

☞ ☜

**FALLACY:**  The Persian Gulf is the world's largest gulf.

**FACT:**  The Persian Gulf, also called the Arabian Gulf, is an arm of the Arabian Sea, which in turn is part of the Indian Ocean. The Persian Gulf covers an area of 89,000 square miles. That makes it considerably larger than the Gulf of Oman, but it's just a drop in the bucket compared to the world's largest gulf: the Gulf of Mexico, with an area of 582,000 square miles. For those interested in farming the sea, that's a surface area of 372,480,000 acres.

☞ ☜

**FALLACY:**  Icebergs, which are frozen ocean water, are huge beneath the ocean's surface but cover only a few square miles above it.

**FACT:**  Melt an iceberg and you get fresh water, not salt water; they are not frozen ocean water. Icebergs break off from ice sheets or glaciers, made of the snow of millennia compressed into ice by its own weight. The world's largest icebergs come from Antarctica. The largest measured so far was 200 feet thick, and 208 miles long by 60 miles wide—nearly 12,500 square miles. The state of Maryland has a land area of 9,775 square miles.

☞ ☜

**FALLACY:**  Illinois is east of the Mississippi River.

**FACT:**  Most of Illinois is east of the Mississippi, but not all of it. On a map, look at its southwest border with Missouri, south of St. Louis, where the Mississippi is running northwest to southeast. Find Randolph County. Look on the other side of the Mississippi. There sits the town of Kaskaskia on a piece of Illinois that used to be east of the river until the Mississippi changed its course during a flood in 1881. Nature doesn't pay much attention to such foolish notions as property lines.

☞ ☜

**FALLACY:** Manhattan is North America's largest island.

**FACT:** Manhattan Island is 22 square miles. Manitoulin Island, Canada, in Lake Huron, is 1,070 square miles. Long Island, New York, is 1,320 square miles. Vancouver Island, Canada, is 12,080 square miles. Newfoundland Island, Canada, at 42,030 square miles, is North America's largest island.

☞ ☜

**FALLACY:** Israel is only about the size of Kansas.

**FACT:** Israel is only about one-tenth the size of Kansas, which covers 82,282 square miles. To give a better comparison, New Jersey covers 8,722 square miles; Israel covers 7,992 square miles. New Jersey's population is about 8 million; Israel's population is about 5 million.

☞ ☜

**FALLACY:** Key West is the westernmost of southern Florida's islands.

**FACT:** The Marquesas Keys are west of Key West. The Dry Tortugas (Turtles), home of the Fort Jefferson National Monument, are west of the Marquesas Keys.

☞ ☜

**FALLACY:** Africa has no mountains more than a mile or two in height.

**FACT:** Africa doesn't have any mountains as tall as Asia's 29,022-foot Everest, South America's 22,834-foot Aconcagua, or North America's 20,320-foot McKinley (Denali), but it does have three that are more than three miles high. Margherita, between Uganda and Zaire, rises to 16,763 feet, or 3.18 miles. Kenya, appropriately in Kenya, reaches 17,058 feet, or 3.23 miles. Kilimanjaro, on the border between Kenya and Tanzania, tops out at 19,340 feet, or 3.66 miles, making it the highest mountain on the African continent.

☞ ☜

**FALLACY:**  The ocean is salt water; lakes are fresh water.

**FACT:**  The ocean is definitely salt water, but lakes are large inland bodies of either fresh water or salt water. Great Salt Lake in Utah, for example.

☞ ☜

**FALLACY:**  For obvious reasons, it's not possible to have a lake inside a lake.

**FACT:**  In Lake Huron there's an island called Manitoulin. On Manitoulin Island is Manitou Lake, a lake inside a lake. Within Manitou Lake there are islands.

☞ ☜

**FALLACY:**  Long Island is in the Atlantic Ocean east of New York City.

**FACT:**  Long Island is in the Atlantic Ocean east of Manhattan, but not east of New York City. The largest island in the conterminous United States at 1,320 square miles, it contains both Nassau County and Suffolk County, which take up most of the island. Its western end, however, contains two of New York City's boroughs: Brooklyn and Queens. New York City wouldn't be New York City without Queens, and Brooklyn is the only place in the United States where Oil can discover earl.

☞ ☜

**FALLACY:**  The country with the lowest average altitude is the Netherlands.

**FACT:**  The land of the Netherlands, hidden behind its dikes, has an average altitude of only thirty-seven feet above sea level. But if you think the people of the Netherlands are worried by big waves, consider the people of the Maldives in the Indian Ocean: the highest point in their atolls-and-islands nation is only eight feet above sea level.

☞ ☜

**FALLACY:**  Cyprus is the largest island in the Mediterranean Sea.

**FACT:**  As Mediterranean islands go, Cyprus, which had human inhabitants at least as long ago as 4000 B.C., is a big one at 3,570 square miles. Sardinia, a source of raw materials for the Roman Empire, is larger at 9,300 squares miles. The largest island in the Mediterranean Sea is Sicily, originally settled by the ancient Greeks in the eighth century B.C. and now part of Italy; there are 9,920 square miles of Sicily.

☞ ☜

**FALLACY:**  Miami is only ninety miles north of Cuba.

**FACT:**  Miami is 150 miles northeast of Key West. Key West is ninety miles north of Cuba, across the Straits of Florida.

☞ ☜

**FALLACY:**  The Canadian province of Newfoundland is an island.

**FACT:**  The Canadian province of Newfoundland is a strange arrangement. The island of Newfoundland, at the mouth of the Gulf of St. Lawrence, is home to the provincial capital, St. John's, and to most of the population. St. John's is out on the eastern edge of the island, not only as far from the rest of Canada as possible, but farther east than most of Greenland's west coat. Newfoundland Island, however, is not all of the province of Newfoundland. Labrador, the northeastern part of the Canadian mainland from the Strait of Belle Isle north to Cape Chidley and inland as far as Schefferville and Labrador City, is also part of the province. Labrador is more than twice as large as Newfound Island.

☞ ☜

**FALLACY:**  Zealand, after which New Zealand was named, is now called the Netherlands.

**FACT:**  Zealand, after which New Zealand was named, is now called Zealand. Largest of the Danish islands at more than 2,700 square miles, Zealand is home to Denmark's capital, Copenhagen. The child is far larger than the parent, though. New Zealand, an independent nation, consists of two large islands and a scattering of small ones, with an overall area of nearly 104,000 square miles. That makes New Zealand more than 38.5 times as large as Zealand. New Zealand's capital, Wellington, is on the southern coast of North Island, close to the northern coast of South Island.

☞ ☜

**FALLACY:**  There's about as much oxygen in the atmosphere today as there always has been.

**FACT:**  About 21 percent of Earth's atmosphere today is oxygen. When life first appeared on the planet at least 3.5 billion years ago, there was virtually none; by 2 billion years ago there was a significant amount. According to current theory, archaic cyanobacteria seeking hydrogen evolved the ability to split water molecules to find it. For each two atoms of hydrogen the bacteria got from a molecule of water, they discarded one atom of a toxic waste product: oxygen.

☞ ☜

**FALLACY:** The continent of Pangaea, like the continent of Atlantis, is strictly science fiction.

**FACT:** Unlike the island of Atlantis, the continent of Pangaea is strictly science. Earth's crust is broken into tectonic plates that drift like rafts; many carry continents on them. The most recent time when all the continents came together into one supercontinent was about 250 million years ago. That supercontinent is called Pangaea (all earth). About 180 million years ago Pangaea began breaking up, first into two huge continents called Gondwana and Laurasia, and eventually into the six continents we have today. The tectonic plates, and therefore the continents riding on them, are still moving.

☞ ☜

**FALLACY:** The Sargasso Sea is fiction, not fact.

**FACT:** The first tales of the Sargasso Sea came from superstitious sailors and were far more fiction than fact. Although surrounded by water rather than by land, the Sargasso Sea really does exist. It is a region of the Atlantic Ocean from the West Indies on the west to the Azores on the east, at about 30° north latitude, which puts it within the horse latitudes—bands of high pressure with only light and variable winds. In the days when ships depended on sails, to be in the Sargasso Sea was to be becalmed, with no prevailing winds to take you anywhere. The huge masses of floating gulfweed, or sargassum, added to the sailors' feeling of being trapped, and its shifting shapes gave rise to many a tale of sea monsters.

☞ ☜

**FALLACY:** The Caspian Sea is a sea.

**FACT:** The word *sea* refers to the ocean generally or to some connected part of it such as the Mediterranean Sea, the Sargasso Sea, or the South

China Sea. The Caspian Sea is a large inland body of water. That makes it a lake, not a sea.

☞ 🕮

**FALLACY:** There is such a thing as a *sea breeze*, but no such thing as a *land breeze*.

**FACT:** Even people who don't live near the coast are familiar with the term *sea breeze*, which means a cool, moist breeze blowing onshore from the ocean. People who do live near the coast are also familiar with the term *land breeze*, a warm, dry breeze blowing offshore from the land. Although high- and low-pressure areas can cause these breezes, the most common cause is that the land heats and cools more rapidly than the water. As the land heats after sunrise, the warm air over it rises, drawing in cooler air from the ocean. After sunset, as the land cools below the temperature of the water surface, warm air rises over the ocean, drawing in cooler air from the land.

☞ 🕮

**FALLACY:** The names *Black Sea, Red Sea, White Sea,* and *Yellow Sea* have nothing to do with the colors of the seas.

**FACT:** The Black Sea, called *Pontius Euxinus* by the ancient Romans, has dark-looking water because of a layer with a high concentration of hydrogen sulfide. The Red Sea, long ago called *Sinus Arabicus,* got its name from a reddish seaweed that flourishes in it. The White Sea, *Beloye More,* is white because it is frozen over much of the year. The Yellow Sea, *Hwang Hai,* is yellow because of mud washed into it by rivers.

☞ 🕮

**FALLACY:** The longest river in Europe is the Rhine.

**FACT:** The Rhine is definitely impressive. It rises in southeastern Switzerland, forms part of the border between France and Germany, then divides into two parts in the Netherlands before reaching the North Sea— 820 miles from its source. The Danube is even more impressive. It rises in southwestern Germany's Black Forest and flows east and south to Austria (Vienna), Slovakia, Hungary (Budapest), Yugoslavia (Belgrade), Romania, Bulgaria, and Ukraine before reaching the Black Sea—1,770 miles from where it began. Most impressive of all European rivers is the Volga, which rises in the Valdai Hills northwest of Moscow. It flows past Gorky, Kazan, Saratov, and Volgograd to empty into the Caspian Sea near Astrakhan—2,200 miles from its source, making the Volga the longest river in Europe.

☞ ☜

**FALLACY:** Waves move across the ocean.

**FACT:** As wind blows over the surface of the ocean, it imparts energy to the water in the form of waves. Those waves of energy move through the ocean, but the water itself does not move horizontally; the water is merely raised and lowered as the wave passes through it.

☞ ☜

**FALLACY:** Wichita Falls is near Wichita, Kansas.

**FACT:** Wichita is in southern Kansas, southwest of Kansas City, on the Arkansas River. Although Topeka is the capital, Wichita has the largest population of any city in Kansas. Wichita Falls is in northern Texas, northwest of Fort Worth, on the Wichita River. Wichita Falls isn't among the ten most populated cities in Texas. Between Wichita and Witchita Falls, in addition to parts of Kansas and Texas, is all of Oklahoma.

☞ ☜

**FALLACY:** West Virginia is west of Virginia.

**FACT:** Parts of West Virginia are west of Virginia, but parts of Virginia are west of West Virginia. Big Stone Gap, Virginia, is west of all of West Virginia, and so too are Bonny Blue and Blackwater and Rose Hill and Ewing Hill.

☞ ☜

**FALLACY:** The Yellow River is the longest river in China.

**FACT:** The Yellow River (Huang He) reaches the Yellow Sea after traveling 3,000 miles from its source. That makes it longer than Africa's Congo River or North America's Mississippi River. China's Chang Jiang River, also called the Yangtze River, travels 4,000 miles before reaching the East China Sea, making it the longest river not only in China, but in all of Asia. The Chang Jiang is the world's third longest river, after the Nile and the Amazon.

☞ ☜

**FALLACY:** No country is larger than an entire continent.

**FACT:** Australia covers an entire continent. Because the country of Australia also includes Tasmania and other islands, it is larger than the continent of Australia. The only other countries larger than the continent of Australia are Brazil, Canada, China, Russia, and the United States.

☞ ☜

**FALLACY:** An iceberg weighs a lot less than a steel ship of the same size.

**FACT:** Ice is definitely less dense than steel, and weighs a lot less, but that's not the point. The point is that an iceberg is ice all the way through, whereas a steel ship is mostly air. An iceberg weighs a lot more than a steel ship of the same size, and rides a lot lower in the water. When they're floating, of course, neither weighs anything.

☞ ☜

**FALLACY:** Russia's Siberia is larger than Texas but smaller than Alaska.

**FACT:** There are 266,807 square miles of Texas. Siberia is larger than that. There are 591,000 square miles of Alaska. Siberia is larger than that. Together, there are 857,807 square miles of Alaska and Texas. Siberia is larger than that. There are 2,900,000 square miles of Siberia.

☞ ☜

**FALLACY:** Most of New York City is on mainland North America.

**FACT:** Most of New York City is on islands off mainland North America. Four out of five of New York City's boroughs are on islands: Brooklyn, Queens, Manhattan, and Staten Island. Only the Bronx, north of Manhattan, is on the mainland.

☞ ☜

**FALLACY:** Mount Vesuvius is Europe's largest active volcano.

**FACT:** Mount Vesuvius—Vesuvio in its native Italian—is ten miles southeast of Naples, overlooking the Bay of Naples. It has had at least six major eruptions, including 1906 and 1994, since the cataclysm in August of the year 79 that destroyed Herculaneum, Pompeii, and Stabiae. Although the height of Mount Vesuvius is different after each eruption, it is usually about 4,000 feet. Stromboli, northeast of Sicily, has erupted more than half a dozen times since the twentieth century but is only

3,000 feet high. Europe's largest active volcano, on Sicily's east coast, is Mount Etna, which at 11,000 feet is snowcapped much of the year. In this century Etna has had significant eruptions in 1928, 1964, 1971, 1986, and 1994. Mount Vesuvius does hold the records, though, for both largest and smallest active volcano on the European mainland: it is the *only* active volcano on the European mainland.

☞ ☜

**FALLACY:** Abyssinia is in Africa, Batavia is in the Dutch East Indies, and East Pakistan is east of Pakistan.

**FACT:** Abyssinia isn't anywhere anymore; it's now Ethiopia. Batavia is now Jakarta, the capital of Indonesia, which used to be the Dutch East Indies. What used to be East Pakistan is east of Pakistan and also east of a huge swath of India, but now it's Bangladesh.

☞ ☜

**FALLACY:** New York is the largest state east of the Mississippi River.

**FACT:** The twenty largest states are all west of the Mississippi River; New York's 49,108 square miles makes it the thirtieth largest state, so it's not the largest state east of the Mississippi. The three largest states on that side of the river are, in increasing size, Michigan, Florida, and Georgia. At 58,910 square miles, Georgia is the largest state east of the Mississippi River.

☞ ☜

**FALLACY:** To go by boat from New York City to New Orleans, you have to go around Florida.

**FACT:** You can go by boat from New York City to New Orleans without going around Florida, and you don't have to go around the continent or around the planet to do it. From New York City you go up the Hudson River to Albany, take the New York State Barge Canal to Buffalo on Lake Erie, sail from Lake Erie to Lake Michigan, take the Illinois Waterway from Chicago to the Mississippi River, and from there on it's downhill all the way to New Orleans.

☞ ☜

**FALLACY:** The Dead Sea is a sea.

**FACT:** The Dead Sea, about fifty miles long and ten miles wide, is not a sea. It is an extremely salty lake in the Jordan Trough of the Great Rift Valley, fed by the Jordan River but having no outlet; evaporation concentrates its salts. At nearly 1,300 feet below sea level, it is the lowest point on Earth not under the ocean. It got its name from the fact that, because of its high salinity, it is devoid of life.

☞ ☜

**FALLACY:**   The Alps are in two countries, Italy and Switzerland.

**FACT:**   The Alps were pushed up as the African tectonic plate collided with the European plate 140 million years ago. Covering 100,000 square miles, the Alps are in seven countries: Austria, France, Germany, Italy, Liechtenstein, Slovenia, and Switzerland. Of those seven countries, only Liechtenstein is entirely in the Alps. Three of Europe's best known rivers—the Rhine, the Rhône, and the Po—have their source in the Alps.

☞ ☜

**FALLACY:**   The Matterhorn is Europe's highest mountain.

**FACT:**   The 14,691-foot Matterhorn is one of the most famous peaks in the Alps, but it is not the highest peak in the Alps. Mont Blanc, at 15,771 feet, holds the record as the highest peak not only in the Alps, but in all of Europe. Mont Blanc is also higher than the highest Rocky Mountain high.

☞ ☜

**FALLACY:**   Jackson Hole and Woods Hole are two of the deepest holes in the United States.

**FACT:**   Jackson Hole, partially in Grand Teton National Park, is a lush, fertile valley on the Snake River in the Rocky Mountains of northwestern Wyoming. Woods Hole, a town between Vineyard Sound and Buzzards Bay at the southwestern tip of Cape Cod in Massachusetts, is the home of the world renowned Woods Hole Oceanographic Institution.

☞ ☜

**FALLACY:**   The deepest lake in the United States is Lake Superior.

**FACT:**   Lake Superior has a depth of 1,330 feet. Only part of Lake Superior is in the United States, but that isn't the point. The point is that Crater Lake in Oregon is 1,932 feet deep, making it the deepest lake in the United States.

☞ ☜

**FALLACY:**   The Atlantic coastline of the United States is much longer than the Pacific coastline.

**FACT:**   Maine extends well north of northernmost Washington state, and even the northernmost point in Florida is south of the southernmost point in California, so at first glance it would appear that the Atlantic coastline is much longer than the Pacific coastline. First glances can be deceiving. The only state bordering the Arctic Ocean is Alaska. The states with borders along the Gulf of Mexico are Alabama, Florida, Louisiana, Mississippi, and Texas. The states comprising the Atlantic coastline are Connecticut, Delaware, Florida, Georgia, Maine, Maryland, Massachusetts, New Hampshire, New Jersey, New York, North Carolina, Pennsylvania, Rhode Island, South Carolina, and Virginia. The states with Pacific coastlines are Alaska, California, Hawaii, Oregon, and Washington. Of the total 12,383-mile U.S. coastline, the coast along the Arctic Ocean is 1,060 miles long, the Gulf of Mexico coast accounts for 1,631 miles, 2,069 miles border the Atlantic Ocean, and the Pacific Ocean coastline is 7,623 miles long. That makes the Pacific coastline more than three and a half times as long as the Atlantic.

☞ ☜

**FALLACY:**   Thanks to modern science, we know the exact height of worldwide sea level.

**FACT:**   Thanks to modern science, specifically including satellites, we can now measure sea level at any particular point very accurately. As for a worldwide sea level, there is no such thing; although there is only one ocean on Earth, the surface of that ocean is not level. There are temporary high places and low places: those caused by the high and low tides, for example, and those caused by high- and low-pressure areas. There are also permanent high places and low places, caused by the different gravitational pulls of lower-than-average or higher-than-average concentrations of mass beneath the seafloor. When scientists refer to sea level, what they are referring to is the average level of the surface of the ocean.

☞ ☜

**FALLACY:**   The two most famous bridges at Niagara Falls are Honeymoon Bridge and Rainbow Bridge.

**FACT:**   If you've seen Niagara Falls from Honeymoon Bridge you've been around for a while. Honeymoon Bridge was destroyed by an ice jam in the winter of 1938, and was replaced by Rainbow Bridge. There's another famous Rainbow Bridge, but you'd have to have *very* good eyesight to see Niagara Falls from there. It's in Rainbow Bridge National Monument in Utah, just north of the Arizona border.

☞ ☜

**FALLACY:**  All of the world's mountain ranges are growing shorter because of erosion.

**FACT:**  All of the world's *inactive* mountain ranges are growing shorter because of erosion, but active mountain ranges are growing taller despite erosion. The Himalayas, for example, are rising as India continues to crash into southern Asia. The Andes are rising, too, as the Nazca Plate carrying Pacific Ocean crust dives under the South American Plate.

☞ ☜

**FALLACY:**  Chile is a hot and dry country.

**FACT:**  Chile is indeed a hot and dry country; it is also a cold and wet country, and a temperate country. Nearly 3,000 miles long north-south but only about 250 miles east-west at its widest point, Chile stretches through 37 degrees of latitude and therefore several climate zones. The north is hot and dry; the Atacama Desert is one of the driest places on Earth. The central section, where most of the population lives, has a Mediterranean climate. The south is cold and humid, with dense forests, snow-topped mountains, and glaciers.

☞ ☜

**FALLACY:**  The Spice Islands are in the Indian Ocean.

**FACT:**  The Spice Islands, where cloves and nutmeg were first found, aren't anywhere anymore. They were renamed the Moluccas (Maluku). The Moluccas are in eastern Indonesia, between Celebes (Sulawesi) and New Guinea.

☞ ☜

**FALLACY:**  Iceland is an ice-covered island whose harbors are frozen most of the year.

**FACT:**  Since Iceland has that name and is just south of the Arctic Circle, you'd suspect it's an ice-covered island with frozen harbors, but it's not. Iceland is in a volcanic zone and has several active volcanoes. Geysers and hot springs are plentiful, providing cheap heating. The tundralike north and east live up to Iceland's name, and about three-fourths of the island is uninhabitable because of such things as glaciers, lakes, and a lava desert. The south and west, however, influenced by the warm waters of the Gulf Stream, are mild and humid, and the harbors don't freeze.

☞ ☜

**FALLACY:**   Greenland is green.

**FACT:**   Greenland's 840,000 square miles make it the world's largest island. Far from being green, 84 percent of Greenland is covered by an ice sheet with an average thickness of 1,000 feet and a maximum thickness of more than 10,000 feet. Although it used to be correct to say that Greenland is white, that's no longer true. When this Danish territory came under home rule on 1 May 1979, its Greenlandic name became its official name: *Kalaallit Nunaat.* In order to avoid a worldwide shortage of the letter *a,* many people still call it Greenland.

☞ ☜

**FALLACY:**   Mount McKinley is the highest peak in the Rocky Mountains, followed by Mount Whitney.

**FACT:**   Mount McKinley (Denali), the highest peak on the North American continent, rises to 20,320 feet. Mount Whitney, the highest peak in the conterminous United Sates, tops out at 14,494 feet. Mount Elbert, at 14,433 feet, is the highest peak in the Rocky Mountains. How can that be? Mount McKinley (Denali) is in the Alaska Range, not the Rockies; Mount Whitney is in the Sierra Nevada, not the Rockies.

☞ ☜

**FALLACY:**   All of North America is north of all of Africa.

**FACT:**   Three African countries—Algiers, Morocco, and Tunisia—extend north of latitude 35° North. Although all of Canada is north of that latitude, all of Mexico is south of that latitude. Parts of California, North Carolina, and Oklahoma are south of 35° N. Most of Arizona, Arkansas, and New Mexico, and almost all of South Carolina and Texas, are south of that latitude. All of Louisiana, Mississippi, Alabama, Georgia, and Florida are south of 35° North.

☞ ☜

**FALLACY:** Kansas City, Missouri, and Kansas City, Kansas, are directly across the Mississippi River from each other.

**FACT:** Kansas City is in northeastern Kansas; Kansas City is in northwestern Missouri. Both are, appropriately, at the junction of the Kansas River and the Missouri River and have grown into one large metropolitan area. They originally gained importance because the Missouri River flows from there to the Mississippi River, making the area a transportation hub. Not coincidentally, this area was also the eastern end of the Santa Fe Trail. Kansas City, Missouri, and Kansas City, Kansas, are not on the Mississippi river at all. They're not on opposite sides of the Missouri River, either; they're both on the west side. They are, however, directly across the Kansas River from each other: Kansas City, Missouri on the east bank; Kansas City, Kansas on the west. North of the two Kansas Citys, the Missouri River is Missouri's western border. On the other side of the state, the Mississippi River is all but a tiny portion of Missouri's eastern border.

☞ ☜

**FALLACY:** The only country north of Finland is Lapland.

**FACT:** The only country north of Finland is Norway, which arcs over the top of both Sweden and Finland; because of this, neither Sweden nor Finland reaches the Arctic Ocean. Most of Lapland is above the Arctic Circle; most of Lapland's soil is tundra. There are some significant mineral deposits, but the mainstay of Lapland's economy can be summed up in one word: reindeer. Although Lapland is large, there are fewer than 50,000 Laplanders or Lapps. Lapland is not a country, but a geographic region that includes large parts of Norway, Finland, Sweden, and Russia's Kola Peninsula. More than half of all Lapps live in a Norwegian province covering about 30 percent of Norway and is named, appropriately enough, the province of Lapland.

☞ ☜

**FALLACY:** The correct name is Pike's Peak, with an apostrophe.

**FACT:** Named for Zebulon Montgomery Pike, the correct name for that 14,110-foot mountain in Central Colorado is Pikes Peak. Although rich in history, it doesn't have an apostrophe to its name.

## ④
# Food, Drugs, Plants

**FALLACY:**  Belladonna comes from the belladonna lily.

**FACT:**  The belladonna lily, *Amaryllis bella-donna,* is native to southern Africa. Belladonna is a liquid extract from a totally unrelated plant, *Atropa belladonna,* also called deadly nightshade because of the atropine it contains. It's interesting that belladonna, which can be fatal if not handled properly, means "beautiful woman" in Italian. Brings to mind the fateful sentence that Adam said to Eve just before she invented separate bedrooms: "I wear the plants in this family!"

**FALLACY:**  A sea anemone is an ocean plant.

**FACT:**  An anemone is a land plant of the genus Anemone, sometimes called a wildflower. A sea anemone is a marine animal of the order Actiniaria; there are about 800 known species. Its body is a flexible cylinder, with the bottom attached to a submerged object and the top encircled by stinging tentacles. When the top is open, spreading the tentacles, a brightly colored sea anemone may look like a flowering plant, but it's an animal.

**FALLACY:**  Apples, like bananas, will spoil faster if you put them in a refrigerator.

**FACT:**  The belief that bananas will spoil faster if you put them in a refrigerator comes from an old jingle. The intent of the jingle was to tell people to keep bananas out of the refrigerator—until they had ripened.

Once ripened, bananas, like apples, will last longer in the refrigerator. Apples left at room temperature will spoil about ten times faster than refrigerated apples.

☞ ☜

**FALLACY:** Barleycorn is a type of corn.

**FACT:** Sprouted barleycorn is called malt, and is used for brewing beer and distilling whiskey; John Barleycorn is an old nickname for liquor. Barleycorn is not a type of corn, which is the grain of the corn plant, a grass of the genus *Zea*. Barleycorn is the grain of the barley plant, a grass of the genus *Hordeum*, the major grain for making bread in Europe into the sixteenth century. A barleycorn is also a unit of measure equal to the width of a standard grain of barley, about one-third of an inch.

☞ ☜

**FALLACY:** They get whole fruit inside a bottle the same way they get a ship inside a bottle.

**FACT:** Aside from the occasional cheater who cuts the bottom off a bottle, slips the object in, then puts the bottom back on, people do not get whole fruit inside a bottle the same way they get a ship inside a bottle. The ship is folded into a package that will slip through the bottle opening, then unfolded inside by pulling on strings that are later cut off; long-handled instruments are used to manipulate the ship inside the bottle and to cut the strings. Folding whole fruit to get it into a bottle presents rather large problems. It's much easier to follow the traditional method of slipping a bottle over the twig of a fruit tree that has a tiny apple or pear or whatever, then letting the fruit grow inside the bottle.

☞ ☜

**FALLACY:** The correct name for those small cabbages is "Brussel sprouts."

**FACT:** The correct name is Brussels sprouts, not Brussel sprouts, because the capital of Belgium is Brussels, not Brussel. Botanically, they're the *gemmifera* variety of *Brassica oleracea*. The average Brussels sprout has about one gram of fiber, and the spunky little sprouts have more vitamin C by weight than oranges. According to several recent studies, cruciferous vegetables such as broccoli, Brussels sprouts, cabbage, and cauliflower seem to have a link to a lower risk of some forms of cancer.

If they tasted like ice cream or pizza instead of like broccoli, Brussels sprouts, cabbage, and cauliflower, we'd all be a lot healthier.

☞ ☜

**FALLACY:** The best place to keep butter is in the butter-keeper compartment in the refrigerator door.

**FACT:** One of the worst places to keep butter is in the butter-keeper compartment in the refrigerator door. Not only is that compartment closer to the outside and therefore subject to warming, it is often also enclosed, providing a barrier to the refrigerated air of the inside. An unopened package of butter will stay good for up to four months in the freezer and up to 30 days in the coldest part of the refrigerator; how long it will last in the butter keeper depends on how much warmer it is in there.

☞ ☜

**FALLACY:** Butter-and-eggs belong on the breakfast table.

**FACT:** Butter and eggs may belong on the table of those who don't count cholesterol, but butter-and-eggs is *Linaria vulgaris,* a perennial plant native to Eurasia. You could grace your breakfast table with this plant, but would you really want to share your morning meal with what is popularly known as toadflax?

☞ ☜

**FALLACY:** The drug used most often by America's youth is aspirin.

**FACT:** The drug used most often by America's youth is not aspirin, and no, it's not one of the illegal drugs. In a virtual flood of colas and the occasional cup of coffee or tea or cocoa, and in a mountain of chocolate candy, the drug used most often by America's youth is the alkaloid $C_6H_{10}N_4O_2$—caffeine. This is your brain, sunny-side up.

☞ ☜

**FALLACY:** You gain a lot of weight from a quart of cream, less weight from a quart of milk, and no weight from a quart of water.

**FACT:** Doesn't matter how many calories there are in those quarts, only how much they weigh. If they each weigh one pound, for example, you will gain one pound no matter which one you ingest. Where the calories come in is how much you'll weigh later on. You'll be rid of the pound of water in a few hours. You'll be rid of the water from the milk and cream in a few hours, too, but it will take a lot longer to burn off the other ingredients, especially the fat. Until you've burned off the other ingredients, you'll weigh as much more than your starting weight as they weigh.

☞ ☜

**FALLACY:** Fat has the most calories, carbohydrates have far less, and alcohol has none.

**FACT:** Of those three, fat does have the most calories: nine per gram. Carbohydrate has four calories per gram, but it doesn't come in second, because alcohol has seven calories per gram. If a regular twelve-ounce can of beer has sixteen grams of alcohol (4.6 percent), a six-pack adds up to 672 calories from the alcohol; add in the carbohydrate calories, and you're up to 840 calories. If you drink a six-pack of stout (5.2 percent alcohol) rather than beer, you'll discover that stout is well named for several reasons: 757 calories from alcohol and 1,056 total calories.

☞ ☜

**FALLACY:** Cantaloupes smell great; muskmelons smell terrible.

**FACT:** Beauty is in the nose of the beholder. A cantaloupe is the *reticulatus* variety of *Cucumis melo*. A muskmelon is any of several varieties of *Cucumis melo*—but most commonly the one called a cantaloupe. The muskmelon is not to be confused with the musk ox, which smells terrible to everybody except another musk ox.

☞ ☜

**FALLACY:** Tapioca root is better cooked, but is often eaten raw.

**FACT:** There is no such thing as a tapioca root because there is no such thing as a tapioca plant. Tapioca is a starch extracted from the root of the cassava plant, *Manihot esculenta,* of the Euphorbiaceae family, also called the manioc plant. Cassava root is rarely eaten raw more than once because it is poisonous until processed.

☞ ☜

**FALLACY:** Cutting down on fat and cholesterol, Americans are eating much less cheese than they were a quarter century ago.

**FACT:** Americans definitely have been cutting down on the percentage of fat and cholesterol in their diet. According to a recent report, though, Americans are now eating more than twice as much cheese as they did a quarter century ago. A clue to the disparity is that although cheddar is still the most popular cheese, mozzarella has soared up the list to the number two spot. The huge increase in cheese consumption has been caused by the huge increase in pizza consumption. Four teenage turtles have a lot to answer for.

☞ ☜

**FALLACY:** *Ambrosia* and *nectar* are different names for the same substance.

**FACT:** Ancient ambrosia, the food of the gods, made them immortal. Modern ambrosia is a dessert made of oranges and flaked coconut. Nectar, the drink of the gods, is a sweet liquid secreted by flowers to attract pollinators; it is gathered as nourishment by hummingbirds, and by bees as the raw material for honey. Ambrosia is food; nectar is drink. Then there's this from the menu of a modern restaurant: "Lunch Special: Chicken or Turkey, $4.95; Beef, $5.95; Children, $3.95."

☞ ☜

**FALLACY:** To be chili, it has to have chili beans.

**FACT:** To be chili it has to have chili peppers; it can have almost anything else, and often does, but it doesn't have to have a single bean. Besides, there is no such thing as a chili bean—the beans usually added are pinto beans or kidney beans. Alphabetically, a typical basic chili may contain cereal (usually corn meal), chili pepper, cumin, garlic, onion, oregano, paprika, salt, tomato, and water. Chili made by a corporation may also include corn syrup, hydrogenated oil, modified food starch, monosodium glutamate, sugar, and the corporate chemists only know what else. Beans are commonly added to chili, but they are not part of the chili; the combination is called chili with beans. Meat is also not a necessary ingredient of chili. If meat is added, the basic chili becomes chili con carne. If more chili peppers are added than you can comfortably deal with, the antidote to that fire-in-the-mouth feeling is found in milk and milk products such as cheese, sour cream, and yogurt; cold beer is a boon, too.

☞ ☜

**FALLACY:** Chewing coca leaves has the same effect as snorting cocaine.

**FACT:** There is a vast difference between chewing coca leaves and snorting cocaine, just as there is a vast difference between smoking tobacco as a ritual drug on rare occasions and carrying a twenty-cigarette pack to be smoked routinely all day. Native Americans knew how to use American herbal drugs; European Americans still don't. People have chewed coca leaf for at least 5,000 years, the Incas among them. It was a European, Friedrich Gaedka, who isolated cocaine crystals from the coca leaf in 1885. Imagine isolating nicotine from the tobacco plant, and snorting that. It would kill you.

☞ ☜

**FALLACY:**  Butter, cheese, cream, eggs, and milk are dairy products.

**FACT:**  Butter, cheese, cream, and milk are dairy products; eggs are not. To be a dairy product, it must be or come from milk. Doesn't have to be milk from a cow, though. Goat milk qualifies, as does mare's milk. It should be noted that among cows, hamburger is grounds for divorce.

☞ ☜

**FALLACY:**  The cork tree is unique, unrelated to any common tree.

**FACT:**  That cork in your bottle came from the bark of the cork tree, *Quercus suber,* an evergreen native to the Mediterranean region. The genus name *Quercus* translates from Latin as "oak." The cork tree is one species of the very common oak.

☞ ☜

**FALLACY:**  Corkwood comes from the cork tree.

**FACT:**  Two different species, both having lightweight, soft wood, are called corkwood. One is a small, deciduous tree native to the southeastern United States, *Leitneria floridana.* The other is a tropical Western Hemisphere tree, *Ochroma pyramidale,* commonly known as balsa and famous as the main structural material in model airplanes. Neither species is even in the same genus as the cork tree, *Quercus suber.*

☞ ☜

**FALLACY:**  DDT was a spinoff of weapons research in the United States during World War II.

**FACT:**  DDT, formally known as *d*ichloro*d*iphenyl*t*richloroethane or $C_{14}H_9Cl_5$, is a colorless, odorless insecticide that will not dissolve in water. It was synthesized by Paul H. Müller of Switzerland in 1939. He was awarded the Nobel Prize in Physiology or Medicine in 1948 for "discovery of the high efficiency of DDT as a contact poison against several arthropods." DDT was banned in the United States in 1972.

☞ ☜

**FALLACY:** A truly fresh egg floats.

**FACT:** Eggs, not noted for their swimming ability, go through a spectrum of aquatic antics as they age. A truly fresh egg will lie peacefully on the bottom of a water-filled pot. One that came out of a hen a few days ago will also stay on the bottom, but it will be leaning upward. About the time it becomes a ten-day-old, it will stand straight up on the bottom. By the time it's old enough to float, it's too old to be eaten.

☞ ☜

**FALLACY:** Eggs Benedict was named after Benedict Arnold.

**FACT:** Eggs Benedict was named quite a while after Benedict Arnold, who was born in 1741 and died in 1801. Socialite Samuel Benedict and his hangover made it into New York City's Waldorf-Astoria Hotel one morning in 1894, and asked the maître d'hôtel for bacon and poached eggs on toast with Hollandaise sauce. The maître d' substituted ham for the bacon and an English muffin for the toast, and Eggs Benedict was born. Sam's hangover didn't kill him, and neither did the heartburn he probably got from all that fat, but his cholesterol count as he staggered back out of the restaurant must have been impressive.

☞ ☜

**FALLACY:** Fresh fish in a store should have white eyes and a slightly fishy smell.

**FACT:** If that fresh fish in a store has white eyes, it's not fresh. It takes quite a while for a fish's eyes to cloud over after it dies. Another clue is the gills. If the gills are red, the fish is fresh; if they've turned gray or brown, it's not. As for smell, a freshly caught fish smells wet and clean like the ocean, not fishy. A fishy smell means the fish is far from fresh, and bacteria have begun their work; the stronger the smell, the more you should toss that one back.

☞ ☜

**FALLACY:** Except in exotic gourmet restaurants, people rarely eat flowers.

**FACT:** That holiday eggnog just wouldn't be the same without cloves, the dried flower buds of a tropical evergreen tree. Since at least ancient Roman times, people have eaten the flowers of two types of cabbage variety *Brassica oleracea botrytis*: broccoli and cauliflower. Not at all nasty, nasturtium flowers are used in salads and gelatin desserts.

☞ ☜

**FALLACY:** If you're talking with someone who has garlic breath, there's absolutely no defense against it.

**FACT:** The absolute defense against someone else's garlic breath is to eat garlic, after which you won't notice that they've eaten garlic. And garlic, as is well known, is an absolute defense against vampires: there is not a single scientifically documented case of someone eating garlic and then being bitten by a vampire.

☞ ☜

**FALLACY:** Most garlic eaten in the United States is imported from Europe.

**FACT:** Garlic (*Allium sativum*) was originally imported to the United States from Mediterranean Europe. Most garlic eaten in the United States today, however, is imported from California. Garlic is grown in many states, but California is the main supplier to the country, growing more than 300,000,000 pounds of the gustatory delight each year.

☞ ☜

**FALLACY:** Hash, which must contain meat to be real hash, was invented in the United States.

**FACT:** Hash, to be real hash, must be chopped food. That's all. No one knows where or when it was first made, but it definitely wasn't in the United States. The English noun comes from the French verb *hacher,* "to chop"; the French noun *la hache* translates as "axe" and the diminutive *la hachette* as, reasonably enough, "hatchet." The first hash was made many thousands of years before there was a United States or a France, or even a corned beef.

☞ ☜

**FALLACY:** A tablespoon of pure fat has a lot more fat, and calories, than a hot dog.

**FACT:** Fat and oil are different words for the same thing; generally speaking, if it's solid at room temperature it's called fat, if it's liquid at room temperature it's called oil. A tablespoon of pure fat, such as canola oil, corn oil, olive oil, or peanut oil, contains fourteen grams of fat. There are nine calories per gram of fat regardless of its source, so a tablespoon of fat has 126 calories. A regular hot dog has 150 calories, of which 126 are from fat. That means that a tablespoon of pure fat has exactly as much fat as, and forty-nine fewer calories than, a hot dog.

☞ ☜

**FALLACY:** Eating ice cream when the weather is cold is illogical, because it makes you colder.

**FACT:** Eating ice cream when the weather is cold is very logical. It's eating ice cream when the weather is hot that's illogical. The small temperature drop your body will experience from eating a cup of ice cream is inconsequential when compared with the large number of calories the ice cream makes available for your body to turn into heat. An eight-ounce cup of one major house brand of plain vanilla ice cream has 320 calories; a cup of a premium brand has 540 calories. A cup of light beer, by comparison, has 95 calories. Beer float, anyone?

☞ ☜

**FALLACY:** Indian bread is a type of bread.

**FACT:** Indian bread has no flour, is not baked, and is not a type of bread. The name "Indian bread" refers to any of various plants that Native Americans used as food. The Indian bread most directly related to the name is breadroot, *Psoralea esculenta,* a member of the pea family that has a large, starchy root. Another common name for breadroot is prairie potato. A prairie oyster is definitely something else.

☞ ☜

**FALLACY:** Because most lawns are small, they don't use much fertilizer and mowing them doesn't create much air pollution.

**FACT:** The average lawn in the United States may be smaller than a football field, but there are a lot of them. More synthetic fertilizer is used on U.S. lawns each year than is used on all the food crops of the 900 million people of India, the world's second-most-populous nation. Then there are the host of herbicides, fungicides, pesticides, and other

-icides, some of which evaporate into the air, some of which sink into the groundwater, and some of which run off into streams and rivers. As for gas lawn mowers, running one for an hour creates more air pollution than driving a car 300 miles.

☞ ☜

**FALLACY:** The lima bean originated in Italy.

**FACT:** *Phaseolus limensis,* also called the butter bean, did not originate in Italy or anywhere else on the Eurasian continent. Named for a capital city in the geographical area where it originated, the tropical American lima bean got its name from Lima, Peru.

☞ ☜

**FALLACY:** Linseed oil is made from the linseed plant.

**FACT:** Couldn't be, because there is no linseed plant. Linseed oil is extracted from the seed of the same plant that gives us linen, the flax plant. Not coincidentally, linen got its name from *linum,* the Latin word for flax.

☞ ☜

**FALLACY:** When it comes to food, Low Fat, Lean, and Light/Lite all mean the same thing.

**FACT:** When it comes to food, Low Fat, Lean, and Light/Lite mean three different things, each defined by government regulations. To be Low Fat, a food must have three grams or less of fat per serving. To be Lean, a food must have less than ten grams of fat, less than four grams of saturated fat, and less than ninety-five milligrams of cholesterol per serving. To be Light/Lite, a food must have a third fewer calories or no more than half the fat of the regular version, or no more than half the sodium of the regular version. And Fat Free doesn't mean exactly that; it means less than half a gram of fat per serving.

☞ ☜

**FALLACY:** Hot dogs and hamburgers are the most economical meats.

**FACT:** Hot dogs are about 30 percent fat. That means that the real price of the meat is 30 percent higher than the label price—not even considering what else is in hot dogs besides fat and meat. Regular ground beef is also about 30 percent fat. Ham is one of the most expensive meats:

besides a high natural fat content, up to 25 percent of a ham's weight is injected chemical-laden water; considering the price of ham, that's mighty expensive water.

☞ ☜

**FALLACY:**  In the nineteenth century, whiskey was about the only drink watered down to increase profit.

**FACT:**  In the nineteenth century, before enforceable laws against adding water to beverages to increase profit, unscrupulous vendors added water to virtually every beverage they thought they could get away with. In addition to whiskey and beer, milk was commonly watered. Commenting on circumstantial evidence in the 11 November 1850 entry in his *Journal,* Henry David Thoreau used milk as an example: ''Some circumstantial evidence is very strong, as when you find a trout in the milk.''

☞ ☜

**FALLACY:**  Mushrooms are edible: toadstools are poisonous.

**FACT:**  A mushroom is an aboveground fleshy fungus of the class Basidiomycetes; most of them have a stem topped by an umbrellalike fruiting structure (pileus). A toadstool is an aboveground fleshy fungus of the class Basidiomycetes; most of them have a stem topped by an umbrellalike fruiting structure (pileus), which a toad is using as a stool. In truth, there is no such thing as a toadstool. Some people call poisonous mushrooms toadstools, but that is folklore, not botany. Go ask Alice.

☞ ☜

**FALLACY:**  Plants of the nightshade family are poisonous.

**FACT:**  Nightshade plants belong to the family *Solanaceae.* One of them, *Atropa belladonna,* is popularly called deadly nightshade. Another poisonous member of the family, *Solanum dulcamara,* is called bittersweet nightshade. Jimson weed, mandrake, and tobacco are also members of the family. Among the alkaloids derived from nightshade plants are atropine, nicotine, scopolamine, and solanine. Only members of the Addams Family would put members of the nightshade family on the dining table, right? Wrong. Eggplant belongs to the same family, but whether or not you'd serve that to someone you liked is debatable. Nearly all of us, though, regularly enjoy parts of two other nightshade plants: potatoes and tomatoes.

☞ ☜

**FALLACY:** The oak apple is an apple.

**FACT:** This is not an apple you'd want to sink your teeth into. An oak apple is a large swelling on oak twigs and leaves caused by the larvae of gall wasps.

☞ ☜

**FALLACY:** Onions and potatoes are root crops.

**FACT:** Neither onions nor potatoes are root crops. Root crops have large, edible roots. A turnip is a large, edible root, so the turnip is a root crop. The onions we eat are bulbs, not roots. The potatoes we eat are stem tubers, not roots. Cogito ergo spud: I think, therefore I yam.

☞ ☜

**FALLACY:** Orchids are rare plants growing only in the tropics.

**FACT:** The Orchidaceae family is one of the world's largest families of flowering plants with over 17,000 different species. Orchids grow wild not only in the tropics, but over a wide range of latitudes and on every continent except Antarctica. "Orchid" comes from the Greek word *orkhis*, "testicle"; the plants were given that name not because they're so good at breeding, but because of the shape of their root. Hardy plant that it is, the orchid might be a good plant to plant for the person who complains that every plant they plant commits herbicide.

☞ ☜

**FALLACY:** The meat in oxtail soup comes from the tail of an ox.

**FACT:** Depends on which oxtail soup you sup. The meat in some oxtail soups comes from the tail of an ox, some started off hanging behind heifers, some comes from cows, some from the back end of bulls.

☞ ☜

**FALLACY:** Temperature-hot food can make you sweat, but cold food that is chili-pepper-hot can't.

**FACT:** Temperature-hot food can make you sweat, and because we're mostly liquid, hot liquid works even better. Chili-pepper-hot food or liquid can also make you sweat, even if it's cold. The ingredient in peppers (black pepper is not a pepper) that makes your mouth burn is capsaicin, known in some circles as $C_{18}H_{27}NO_3$. It affects the same nerve endings in the mouth that are affected by a rise in temperature; that's why chili-pepper-hot foods and liquids cause you to sweat, just as high-temperature foods and liquids do. Because the nerve endings being stimulated are those in the front of the head, you'll also notice it's your face that does most of the sweating.

☞ ☜

**FALLACY:** If it doesn't have petals, it isn't a flower.

**FACT:** The vast majority of flowers have petals, but by no means all. Birch, oak, and willow flowers, called catkins, do not have petals. Members of the genus *Rafflesia* also have flowers without petals. The plant with the largest flowers—more than a yard in diameter and weighing up to 15 pounds—is Rafflesia arnoldii, unpopularly known as the stinking corpse lily; its flowers have no petals.

☞ ☜

**FALLACY:** The male organ of a plant is called the pistil.

**FACT:** Between pistil and stamen, many people pick pistil as a plant's male organ both because of the first letter and because of association with *pistol*. It isn't, though. A pistil is a plant's female organ, comprised of an ovary, stigma, and style. Which leaves the stamen, comprised of an anther and an upright stalklike filament, as the male organ. The stamen makes a dusty pollen, which contains the sperm. Remember this to remember what's what: pistil-packing mama and staMEN.

☞ ☜

**FALLACY:** The Christmas plant called pointsetta got its name from its pointed petals.

**FACT:** Although many people call that plant a pointsetta, that's not its name—and it has no petals. The poinsettia plant, *Euphorbia pulcherrima,* is a spurge native of Mexico. What look like red petals are actually modified leaves called bracts. The plant got its name from the man who was U.S. minister to Mexico between 1825 and 1829 and U.S. secretary of war between 1837 and 1841: Joel Robert Poinsett.

☞ ☜

**FALLACY:** Popcorn has to be completely dry or it won't pop.

**FACT:** Completely dry popcorn will burn, but it won't pop. What makes popcorn pop is the pressure built up inside the kernel when the moisture turns to steam. If there's no moisture, there won't be any steam, therefore there won't be any pressure, therefore there won't be any pop. An entirely different process is involved in "pop goes the weasel."

☞ ☜

**FALLACY:** Saffron is a spice from the safflower plant.

**FACT:** The safflower plant, *Carthamus tinctorius,* of the family Compositae, is not the source of saffron. That mistake is made so often, though, either intentionally or unintentionally, that another name for the safflower plant is false saffron. The saffron plant is a species of crocus, *Crocus sativus,* of the iris family Iridaceae. One reason why saffron is so expensive is that it takes the stigmas of 64,000 flowers to provide one pound of the spice.

☞ ☜

**FALLACY:** Seaweed grows close to shore because its roots need to reach the bottom.

**FACT:** Seaweeds are marine algae. The simplest of the green seaweeds, which grow in shallow waters, is blue-green alga (Chlorophyceae). The most common seaweed, brown alga (Phaeophyceae), can grow at depths of fifty to seventy-five feet; kelp is a brown seaweed. Red-alga seaweed (Rhodophycaea) is found as deep as 200 feet. Most seaweeds have holdfasts with which they cling to underwater objects. These holdfasts may look like roots, but they aren't; seaweeds simply hold fast with them, they don't feed through them. As for seaweeds growing close to shore, some do, some don't. The Sargasso Sea, in the horse latitudes between the West Indies and the Azores in the Atlantic Ocean, got its name from the huge masses of sargassum seaweed growing there. Also called gulfweed, sargassum floats along happily on top of the Atlantic Ocean, with never a thought of putting down roots.

☞ ☜

**FALLACY:** Tulips are native to the Netherlands.

**FACT:** The tulip, belonging to the genus *Tulipa* and a member of the lily family, is native to a wide area from the eastern Mediterranean through Asia. The first tulip bulb in the Netherlands was carried there by humans, brought from Turkey in the mid-1500s, and spread from there throughout Europe. The name comes from the Ottoman Turkish word *tülbend,* ''gauze, muslin.'' Turbans were often made of muslin, and a tulip apparently looked like a turban to the namer of the flower.

☞ ☜

**FALLACY:**  Hostess Twinkies last almost forever.

**FACT:**  Around some people Hostess Twinkies last less than a few seconds, but if left unmolested, they remain fresh for about as long as other bakery products. Continental Baking Company, the corporation that makes them, says the shelf life of Twinkies is one week, after which they're tasty for another week, after which they taste like cardboard (that may not be exactly how Continental put it). Modern marshmallows, on the other hand, may indeed last almost forever.

☞ ☜

**FALLACY:**  A small cucumber used for pickling is a jerkin.

**FACT:**  You could pickle a jerkin if you wanted to, but you'd end up with a pretty chewy pickle. A jerkin is a short, collarless, sleeveless, tight-fitting leather jacket. A small cucumber used for pickling is a gherkin.

☞ ☜

**FALLACY:**  Oranges have more vitamin C than any other common fruit or vegetable.

**FACT:**  Ounce for ounce, broccoli has more vitamin C than oranges. So do Brussels sprouts. So do green bell peppers. So does red cabbage. So do strawberries. Let that green bell pepper ripen on the vine until it's a red bell pepper, and it'll have more than three times as much vitamin C as the same amount of orange.

☞ ☜

**FALLACY:**  More shrimp is eaten in this country than any other seafood.

**FACT:**  In spite of the popularity of shrimp—including the oxymoronic ''jumbo shrimp''—it comes in second; more tuna is eaten in this country than any other seafood. According to the U.S. Department of Commerce, Americans eat about 4 billion pounds of seafood each year. After tuna and shrimp come cod and pollock, not because people buy a lot of them at the fish counter, but because there's a lot of them in prepared seafood products such as imitation crab, fish sticks, and—posing an anatomical mystery—fish fingers.

☞ ☜

**FALLACY:** Watermelon, native to North America, has about half a dozen varieties.

**FACT:** The watermelon vine, *Citrullus lanatus,* is native to Africa. According to the National Watermelon Association, Americans eat 3 billion pounds a year of the more than 50 varieties of watermelon grown in this country.

☞ ☜

**FALLACY:** *Wheat bread* and *whole-wheat bread* are different names for the same thing.

**FACT:** Regardless of the name on the package, if the first item in the list of ingredients is "wheat flour," you don't have whole-wheat bread. Some cunning companies add brown coloring to their white bread and put WHEAT BREAD in large letters on the wrapper. That's legal because "wheat bread" includes all breads made from wheat, but they're trying to con the customer into thinking it's whole wheat. Whole-wheat bread is made from the entire wheat grain, including the bran and the germ; white or "wheat" bread is made from what's left of the grain after the bran and germ have been removed.

☞ ☜

**FALLACY:** Since wine should be opened and allowed to "breathe" before it is drunk, the same is true of beer.

**FACT:** It's just as true for beer as it is for wine: they should be opened and allowed to "breathe" for at least a second before they are drunk. There is virtually no gaseous exchange between the contents of an open bottle of wine and the atmosphere in any reasonable period of time. Consider the volume of liquid; consider the tiny opening at the top.

☞ ☜

**FALLACY:** When a vintner labels a wine as a "varietal," only grapes of that variety can be used in making it.

**FACT:** When a vintner labels a wine as a "varietal," grapes of other than that variety can be used in making it. According to federal law, up to 25 percent of the grape juice used can be from other varieties of grapes. The most common grape variety used in winemaking is the Thompson seedless.

☞ ☜

**FALLACY:** According to federal law, anything labeled "frozen yogurt" must be exactly that.

**FACT:** There is no federal standard for "frozen yogurt," and most of the ones on the market are a long way from being, literally, frozen yogurt. Closer in nutritive value to ice milk than to ice cream, most frozen yogurts are only slightly fermented. If you want real frozen yogurt, either make or buy yogurt and freeze it yourself. Not only will you save a lot of money, you can make it the way you like it.

☞ ☜

**FALLACY:** *Caviar* is a Russian word meaning "sturgeon eggs."

**FACT:** Caviar isn't a Russian word, and it doesn't mean sturgeon eggs. The Russian word for caviar is *ikra.* The English word caviar came from an Italian word, which came from a French word, which came from a Turkish word, which came from the Persian word *khayah,* "egg." Caviar is the salted and processed roe of any large fish, including but not limited to sturgeon. When it comes to buying these expensive fish eggs, keep in mind the ancient adage: *Caviar emptor!*

☞ ☜

**FALLACY:** Roquefort cheese can be made anywhere, from any cow's milk.

**FACT:** Roquefort cheese cannot be made just anywhere, and nowhere can it be made from cow's milk. "Roquefort" is a trademark for a pungent blue cheese made near the town of Roquefort, south of Bordeaux in southwestern France. It is made from sheep's milk, which has a higher fat content than cow's milk, resulting in a rich, creamy cheese. Another unusual thing about Roquefort cheese is that it is ripened in caves.

☞ ☜

**FALLACY:** Membership in the rose family is limited to roses.

**FACT:** The rose family is Rosaceae. In addition to roses, the family includes almonds, apples, apricots, blackberries, cherries, loganberries, nectarines, peaches, pears, plums, quinces, raspberries, and strawberries.

☞ ☜

**FALLACY:** The official name of licorice is anise.

**FACT:** The official name of licorice is *Glycyrrhiza glabra,* and that's a mouthful. It's a Mediterranean plant with blue flowers, but it's not from the flowers that we get the flavor; that come from its sweet root. Anise, *Pimpinella anisum,* is an aromatic herb, also from the Mediterranean. Its seedlike fruit, and the oil from it, have a licoricelike taste. The liqueur anisette is flavored with anise.

☞ ☜

**FALLACY:** Sweetbread is a sweet bread.

**FACT:** Sweet bread is a sweet bread; sweetbread is definitely something else. Specifically, sweetbread is the pancreas or thymus of a young animal, most often a calf or a lamb. "Mary had a little lamb—the doctor was surprised."

☞ ☜

**FALLACY:** Bourbon whiskey got its name from the place in France where it was first made.

**FACT:** Bourbon whiskey is distilled from a mash containing at least 51 percent corn, in addition to malt and rye. That's a clue, because corn was originally an American plant, not European. Bourbon whiskey got its name from Bourbon County, Kentucky.

☞ ☜

**FALLACY:** The tangerine arrived in Europe from China.

**FACT:** The tangerine arrived in Europe from Africa. Morocco, specifically. The city of Tangier, most specifically—from where the tangerine got its name.

☞ ☜

**FALLACY:** Buckwheat, a type of wheat, is a cereal grain.

**FACT:** Wheat is any of several species of the genus *Triticum,* most commonly *Triticum aestivum.* Buckwheat is a Central Asian plant, *Fagopyrum esculentum,* that produces clusters of small, triangular fruits resembling seeds or grains. Buckwheat is not a type of wheat. Cereal grains come from grasses, such as barley, corn, maize, millet, oats, rice, rye, sorghum, and wheat. Buckwheat is not a cereal grain.

☞ ☜

**FALLACY:**  Yorkshire pudding is pudding.

**FACT:**  Yorkshire pudding isn't even close to being pudding. First, roast some beef. Then make a batter of eggs, flour, and milk, and bake that in the pan drippings from the roast beef. What you end up with is a *bread* called Yorkshire pudding.

☞ ☜

**FALLACY:**  The only ingredients in peanut butter are peanuts and salt.

**FACT:**  The purest of peanut butters contain only peanuts. Next step from there is the addition of salt, because so many people prefer salted peanuts. From there on down, you'd be amazed by what corporations manage to slip into the jar and still call it peanut butter. Among the added ingredients in major brands are: fully hydrogenated cottonseed oil, dextrose (a sugar), diglyceride (an ester of glycerol and two fatty acids), molasses, monoglyceride, fully hydrogenated rapeseed oil, partially hydrogenated soybean oil, and sugar (sucrose).

☞ ☜

**FALLACY:**  Shoofly pie is made from the fruit of the shoofly plant.

**FACT:**  The shoo-fly plant, also known as apple of Peru or *Nicandra physalodes,* is grown as an ornamental and is not used in pies. A shoofly, with no hyphen, is a child's rocker with a seat between two side panels made in the outline of an animal, often with the animal painted on them. The main ingredient in a shoofly is wood. The main ingredients in a shoofly pie are brown sugar and molasses, with a crumblike topping of butter, flour, and sugar. It got its name from the fact that the most commonly heard expression when this pie was set out to cool was, "Shoo, fly!"

☞ ☜

**FALLACY:**  Kiwi fruit is native to Australia.

**FACT:**  Kiwi birds—three flightless species of the genus *Apteryx* related to the emu and the ostrich—are native not to Australia, but to New

Zealand. Kiwi fruit, *Actinidia chinensis,* is native to neither Australia nor New Zealand, but to China, which is why the fuzzy fruit is also known as Chinese gooseberry. Next time you get a chance, take a gander at a gooseberry.

☞ ☜

**FALLACY:** If the hamburger at the store is red on the outside but darker inside, it's beginning to go bad.

**FACT:** If the hamburger at the store is red on the outside but darker inside, it's the way it should be. The darker interior is the normal color. When iron in the outer layer combines with oxygen from the air it forms hemoglobin, turning that layer of the meat red. Hamburger that has begun to go bad has an odor, and feels slightly slimy.

☞ ☜

**FALLACY:** Because most of a chicken's fat is in its skin, you should always skin a chicken before roasting it.

**FACT:** Because most of a chicken's fat is in its skin, you should always skin a chicken before *eating* it. Removing the skin before roasting will give you a drier chicken, but not a leaner one. No significant amount of fat goes from the skin into the meat during cooking. If you remove the skin before roasting, not only does moisture escape from the meat, but the outer layer will be dry and tough because it hasn't been basted by the skin. The best of both worlds is to cook with the skin on, then remove it.

☞ ☜

**FALLACY:** Pumpernickel bread takes its name from the German baking family who became famous for making it.

**FACT:** Pumpernickel is a dark rye sourdough bread baked from coarsely ground whole grain. People unused to such heavy, high-fiber bread commonly notice rumblings as the bacteria in their intestines gear up to handle it. Pumpernickel would be an unfortunate family name in Germany because it is a combination of the words *pumpern,* "to break wind," and *Nickel,* "goblin."

☞ ☜

**FALLACY:** The Venus flytrap is one of only a handful of carnivorous plants.

**FACT:** Depends on the size of the hand. Venus's-flytrap, *Dionaea mus-cipula,* native to the coastal plains of the Carolinas, is one of more than 350 species of carnivorous plants. Pitcher plants—belonging to the genera *Darlingtonia, Nepenthes,* and *Sarracenia*—are carnivorous, as are water plants of the genus *Utricularia* called bladderworts. No carnivorous plant is large enough to eat a human, but some are large enough to eat a frog.

☞ ☜

**FALLACY:** Regular ground beef is the single largest source of calories, protein, and fat in the U.S. diet.

**FACT:** According to the U.S. Department of Agriculture, the single largest source of calories in the U.S. diet is whole milk, followed by cola-flavored soft drinks, then margarine. Whole milk is also the largest source of protein. Cola-flavored soft drinks are the largest source of sugar. Margarine is the largest source of fat, contributing 7.13 percent of the total, followed by whole milk at 5.42 percent, and shortening at 4.14 percent; regular ground beef is the sixth largest source of fat, contributing 2.67 percent.

☞ ☜

**FALLACY:** The smuggling of morphine or heroine is a federal offense.

**FACT:** The smuggling of morphine or heroin is definitely a federal offense. Smuggle as many heroines as you want to, though. It's a common practice in those works of fiction known long ago as penny dreadfuls and known today as romance novels or bodice rippers.

☞ ☜

**FALLACY:** Manila hemp is hemp.

**FACT:** Manila hemp, *Musa textilis,* is native to the Philippines. Fibers from the stalks are used to make cord, fabric, paper, rope, and twine. "Manila help," however, is just a nickname for this species of banana plant whose actual name is abaca. The real hemp plant, *Cannabis sativa* of the mulberry family, is native to central Asia and is the source of both hemp and marijuana.

☞ ☜

**FALLACY:** There are millions of farms in the United States.

**FACT:** The largest number of farms the country has ever had was 6.8

million, in 1935. Although the acreage of farms has been increasing, the number of farms has been decreasing: in 1980 there were 2,437,000; in 1992, 2,094,000. According to a 1994 Census Bureau report, the total number of farms was down to 1,925,300—no longer "millions." The last time there were so few farms in the United States was 1850; Millard Fillmore became president that year, there would be two more presidents before Abraham Lincoln, and the Civil War was still more than a decade in the future.

☞ ☜

**FALLACY:** There's a lot more fat in chili than there is in regular ground beef.

**FACT:** Beans are often added to chili; the following deals with just the chili itself, sold in stores as chili-without-beans. Most people expect that a can of chili contains sixteen ounces. Many chili makers, though, routinely shave an ounce off this, and sell fifteen-ounce cans. The amount of fat in fifteen ounces of chili varies widely by company. One major brand has 22 grams of fat; another, 38 grams; another, 44 grams; yet another, 60 grams. Ground beef also comes in a variety of types. Fifteen ounces of 10 percent–fat ground beef has 42.5 grams of fat; 15 percent has 63.8 grams; 20 percent has 85.0 grams; and 30 percent—regular ground beef—has 127.58 grams of fat. The good thing about eating chili and beans on a cold day is that it warms you up; the bad thing about eating chili and beans on a cold day is that you can't open the windows.

# History

**FALLACY:** Julius Caesar was the first Roman emperor.

**FACT:** Julius Caesar was never a Roman emperor, and there were none before him. The title hadn't been invented by the time of his death on 15 March 44 B.C., because Rome was not officially an empire. Octavian, Julius Caesar's grandnephew, won a series of political and military battles for control of Rome, culminating in the 31 B.C. Battle of Actium in which he defeated Antony and Cleopatra. The Roman senate made him emperor (*Imperator*) in 29 B.C. and gave him the honorary title Augustus in 27 B.C. Octavian, therefore, was the first Roman emperor. It is not true, however that Octavian was the originator of the famous phrase *Veni, Vidi, Velcro*—"I came, I saw, I stuck around."

**FALLACY:** Alexander Graham Bell was born in New Jersey.

**FACT:** Alexander Graham Bell was not born in New Jersey. Alexander Graham Bell was not born in the United States. Alexander Graham Bell was born in 1847. In Scotland. Your library reference desk will verify that, by telephone.

**FALLACY:** Because the Wright brothers made the first flying machine, they were the first people to fly in one.

**FACT:** Orville and Wilbur Wright made the first engine-powered, sustainable-manned-aircraft flights on 17 December 1903. That was way too late for them to have made the first flying machine, or to be the first people to fly in one. The first flying machine was an unmanned glider designed and flown by George Cayley in 1808; the first manned flying machine was also a glider designed by Cayley, flown in 1853. That was several years before the Jefferson Airplane's first flight.

☞ ☜

**FALLACY:** The Allies of World War I were the Allies of World War II.

**FACT:** There was no such thing as "World War I" until World War II because nobody knew it was going to be a double-header. People at the time called the first one the "Great War," but it wasn't all that great. World War I was between the Allies and the Central Powers: Austria-Hungary, Germany, and the Ottoman Empire. Russia was one of the Allies in World War I, but the Russian Revolution occurred between the wars, so the Soviet Union replaced Russia as one of the Allies in World II. France was one of the Allies in World War I and also at the outbreak of World War II, but was overrun by Germany and surrendered on 22 May 1940. Britain and the United States were Allies in both wars. Italy was one of the Allies during World War I, but one of the Axis Powers in World War II, along with Japan and Germany. You can't tell the players without a scorecard.

☞ ☜

**FALLACY:** Audubon was born in New England.

**FACT:** John James Audubon—naturalist, ornithologist, and artist—was born in 1785 at Les Cayes, which was then in Santo Domingo but is now in Haiti. He arrived in the United States in 1803. His most famous works were *The Birds of America,* which contained his drawings and paintings, and, in collaboration with William MacGillivray, the accompanying five-volume text, *Ornithological Biography.* Audubon never met a bird he didn't like.

☞ ☜

**FALLACY:** The Boar War was a European war between Britain and the Netherlands.

**FACT:** Those wars (there were two) involved no boars or other pigs. The Boer Wars were African wars between Dutch Europeans who wanted to control land inhabited by Native Africans, and British Europeans who wanted to control it. The Boers, also called Afrikaners, were the Dutch contenders. The European invaders finally resolved their differences in 1902, and in 1910 came up with a country called South Africa.

☞ ☜

**FALLACY:**   Boot Hill is an Old West town.

**FACT:**   Boot Hill is not a town, and never was. One of the best known Old West towns, Tombstone, is in southeastern Arizona. Tombstone was the site of the famous 1881 shootout at the O. K. Corral and has a cemetery named Boot Hill. Tombstone, including Boot Hill and the O. K. Corral, was designated a national historic landmark in 1962.

☞ ☜

**FALLACY:**   Beer was first brewed in Germany.

**FACT:**   When beer was first brewed, there was no Germany. No one knows exactly when or where beer was first brewed, but we do know it was being brewed more than 5,000 years ago. Pottery jars, which held beer then and retain its residue, have been discovered at Godin Tepe in the Zagros Mountains. That area is now in western Iran, but 5,000 years ago Godin Tepe was a Sumerian trading post. The Sumerian culture of Mesopotamia was centered in the lower Tigris–Euphrates Valley in what is now Iraq. Among its other advances in civilization were growing barley, and writing in cuneiform on clay tablets. The symbol for beer was linear markings inside a jar.

☞ ☜

**FALLACY:**   The Chippewa tribe originally lived near the Great Lakes.

**FACT:**   No Chippewa lived near the Great Lakes, or anywhere else. Native Americans who lived north of Lakes Huron and Superior were called "Chippewa" by undocumented alien immigrants from Europe. The Native Americans knew, but the Europeans didn't, that they were the Ojibwa group of the Algonquin people.

☞ ☜

**FALLACY:**   Columbus made his trip to the Western Hemisphere in 1492.

**FACT:**   Columbus's trip to the Western Hemisphere in 1492 was his first, but not his only. He headed west again in 1493, this time with seventeen ships. His third trip was in 1498, and his fourth in 1502. Although he had been to the Western Hemisphere four times, to the day he died he believed that he had reached Asia.

☞ ☜

**FALLACY:** The ancient capital of the Inca empire was abandoned after it was plundered by Spanish invaders.

**FACT:** The ancient capital of the Inca empire, in the Andes in southern Peru, was Cuzco. Spanish invaders arrived in the City of the Sun in 1533, murdered the rulers, enslaved the population, stole everything of value, and largely destroyed the city. They then built a colonial city among the ruins, from which to control the surrounding area. Although not one of the major cities of Peru, Cuzco is today the capital of the department of Cuzco.

☞ ☜

**FALLACY:** Dolly Varden was a Revolutionary War heroine.

**FACT:** No more than Dolly Parton. Dolly Varden, also known as *Salvelinus malma,* is a large, colorful trout found in the streams of western North America and eastern Asia. It was named for a colorfully costumed coquette in Charles Dickens's 1841 novel *Barnaby Rudge.* Partons, on the other hand, are hypothetical elementary particles; very small, and they don't necessarily come in pairs. Speaking of things hypothetical, what if there were no hypothetical questions?

☞ ☜

**FALLACY:** The Dow Jones Industrial Average has been above 1,000 since 1970.

**FACT:** On 12 January 1906, the Dow closed above 100 for the first time, at 100.25. On 12 March 1956 it closed above 500 for the first time, at 500.24. On 14 November 1972 it closed above 1,000 for the first time, at 1,003.16. Just two years later, though, on 6 December 1974, it closed at 577.60. On 27 April 1981 it reached an eight-year high of 1,024.05. On 12 August 1982 it was again below 1,000, closing at 776.92; by 3 November it was up to 1,065.49. It closed at 1,121.81, its first time above 1,100, on 24 February 1983; on 26 April it broke 1,200 to close at 1,209.46; on 20 May 1985 it broke 1,300. During 1987 it broke 2,000, 2,100, 2,200, 2,300, 2,400, 2,500, 2,600, and 2,700 before the October Crash. At the bottom of the crash it dropped well below 2,000 but never closed below 1,000. The Dow Jones Industrial Average has been above 1,000 since November 1982.

☞ ☜

**FALLACY:** Amelia Earhart disappeared on a solo attempt to cross the Pacific Ocean.

**FACT:** Amelia Earhart was the first woman to fly across the Atlantic Ocean, as a passenger in 1928 and solo in 1932. She was also the first person to fly solo from Hawaii to California, in 1935. In July 1937 she set off on her last flight—not just to cross the Pacific but also to make the first flight around the world at the equator. She disappeared somewhere between New Guinea and Howland Island. Amelia Earhart wasn't flying solo, though; Frederick J. Noonan was also on that final flight.

☞ ☜

**FALLACY:** Albert Einstein was born before Thomas Edison.

**FACT:** Thomas Edison and Albert Einstein were both alive between 1879 and 1931. Einstein, though, was born a generation after Edison. Thomas Edison was born in 1847, is credited with over 1,000 inventions including the phonograph in 1877, and died in 1931. Albert Einstein was born in 1879, two years after Edison's phonograph, revolutionized physics with his relativity theories, and died in 1955.

☞ ☜

**FALLACY:** France hasn't had any territory in North America since the Louisiana Purchase.

**FACT:** The loss of New France (Canada) to the British in the mid-1700s, followed by the Louisiana Purchase in 1803, effectively ended France's role as a colonial power in North America. When such large areas of land trade hands, however, bits and pieces are often left over, and that was true of France's North American holdings. Saint Pierre and Miquelon is a group of nine islands very close to Newfoundland's southern Burin Peninsula. Claimed by France in 1604, they changed hands between the British and the French three times, and were a French Overseas Territory from the early 1800s until 1976. In 1976 the islands were upgraded to an Overseas Department, and in 1985 they became a Territorial Collective. St. Pierre and Miquelon sends a deputy and a senator to the French Parliament. The largest of the islands is Miquelon; the capital, Saint Pierre, is on Saint Pierre Island. Total population is about 6,500. A long-standing dispute between Canada and France over fishing rights and territorial waters was finally resolved by an international court of arbitration in 1992.

☞ ✌

**FALLACY:** Jimmy Hoffa is not legally dead because his body was never found.

**FACT:** Theories abound as to what really happened to James Riddle Hoffa. Except for people who believe he's hanging out with Judge Crater and Elvis Presley, most agree he was murdered by the mob. Some say his body was fed to alligators in a Florida swamp, some say it's part of a freeway on-ramp, others say it was sent to a sausage factory. Whether or not Jimmy Hoffa is really dead, he is definitely legally dead. Acting on a petition by his son, the courts declared Jimmy Hoffa "presumed dead" in 1982; he became legally dead three years later. As for Elvis, he was last seen making crop circles in Europe.

☞ ✌

**FALLACY:** It was impossible to go around the world in eighty days when Jules Verne was alive.

**FACT:** That's what Jules Verne thought when he wrote his 1873 *Around the World in Eighty Days* as a science fiction novel, and that's what he told Elizabeth Cochrane in 1889 as she started her attempt to go around the world in less than eighty days. The most famous female reporter in the United States, she was better known by her pen name: Nellie Bly. She not only matched Phileas Fogg's fictional feat, she beat it. Nellie Bly made it around the world, from New York City to New York City, in 72 days, 6 hours, 11 minutes, and 14 seconds. Yes, Jules Verne's character's name was Phileas, not Phineas.

☞ ✌

**FALLACY:** The time when dinosaurs lived is called the Jurassic.

**FACT:** The time when dinosaurs lived is called the Mesozoic. There are three parts of the Mesozoic era: the Triassic period, from 248 to 213 million years ago; the Jurassic period, from 213 to 144 million years ago; and the Cretaceous period, from 144 to 65 million years ago. Dinosaurs, a subgroup of reptiles, evolved during the Triassic and became extinct at the end of the Cretaceous. Hence the name of that blockbuster 1990s movie, *Mesozoic Park*.

☞ ✌

**FALLACY:** Magellan was the first person to sail around the world.

**FACT:** Portuguese explorer Ferdinand Magalhães (Magellan) started out from Spain in 1519 with a five-ship fleet, but he didn't make it around the world. During a battle with inhabitants of the Philippines, he was killed. The crew members of the ships that made it back to Spain in 1522 were the first people to sail around the world.

☞ ☜

**FALLACY:** "King Tut," the pharaoh Tutankhamen, amassed so much treasure because he lived so long.

**FACT:** Tutankhamen amassed so much treasure because he was the pharaoh. His treasure-filled tomb at Thebes was discovered by Howard Carter in 1922. Tutankhamen became pharaoh of the XVIIIth dynasty at the ripe old age of twelve and died at the age of eighteen.

☞ ☜

**FALLACY:** Marco Polo was the first European to visit China.

**FACT:** Marco Polo, born into a wealthy Venetian merchant family, began his first trip to China in 1271 when he was seventeen and arrived at the court of Kublai Khan, at the site of present-day Beijing, in 1275. He was accompanying his father and an uncle, both of whom had been to China in 1266. Many Europeans had visited China before Marco Polo. We remember him because of the book he wrote, which we call *The Travels of Marco Polo* but which he called *Il milione (The Million)*.

☞ ☜

**FALLACY:** Mata Hari was a German woman who worked as a spy for the Nazis in World War II.

**FACT:** Mata Hari wasn't German, and when she was born in Leeuwarden, Netherlands, she was named Margaretha Geertruida Zelle. Her first husband was a captain in the Royal Dutch East Indies Army, which led to her stage name as a belly dancer: Mata Hari, Malay for "Eye of the Day." She did most of her dancing in Paris, where she was a member of the German secret service. It has often been suggested, but never proven, that she was a spy not only for the Germans but also for the French, passing information both ways. It's easily proven, however, that she didn't work for the Nazis: she was born in 1876 and seduced secrets from high-ranking officers during World War I. If she did pass German secrets to the French, the French were remarkably ungrateful: they shot her as a spy in 1917.

☞ ☜

**FALLACY:**  The Pantheon was built by the ancient Greeks in Athens.

**FACT:**  The Pantheon, a circular temple completed in 27 B.C., was built by the ancient Romans in Rome. The Latin word *Pantheon* comes from the Greek word *Pantheion,* "shrine of all the gods." The Pantheon is unrelated to the Parthenon, built by the ancient Greeks in Athens.

☞ ☜

**FALLACY:**  Wyatt Earp is buried in Tombstone, Arizona.

**FACT:**  Wyatt Berry Stapp Earp is best known for being part of the 1881 shootout at the O.K. Corral in Tombstone, Arizona. His ashes are buried at The Hills of Eternity cemetery in Colma, California, south of San Francisco. (To make room in San Francisco, which is bordered on three sides by water, the city moved its cemeteries to Colma in 1914.) His wife, Josephine, lived until near the end of World War II. Their tombstone reads:

WYATT EARP
1848–1929

JOSEPHINE EARP
1861–1944

☞ ☜

**FALLACY:**  Paper was first made by the ancient Egyptians.

**FACT:**  The ancient Egyptians wrote on papyrus, a predecessor of paper. The Chinese are credited with being the first humans to make paper, from pulped rags and plant fiber, near the beginning of the second century. Most paper today is made from wood pulp. The Chinese, however, did not make the first paper. Long before there were any Chinese, or any other humans for that matter, social wasps were building paper nests out of wood pulp and saliva.

☞ ☜

**FALLACY:**  Martin Luther King's "I Have A Dream" speech should be called "I Still Have A Dream" because those are the words it starts with.

**FACT:** Although the pertinent part of Martin Luther King Jr.'s speech at the Lincoln Memorial in Washington on 28 August 1963 does begin with "I still have a dream," calling it "I Have A Dream" better reflects its content.

> I still have a dream. It is a dream deeply rooted in the American dream. I have a dream that one day this nation will rise up and live out the true meaning of its creed: "We hold these truths to be self-evident: that all men are created equal." I have a dream that one day on the red hills of Georgia the sons of former slaves and the sons of former slaveowners will be able to sit down together at the table of brotherhood. I have a dream that my four little children will one day live in a nation where they will not be judged by the color of their skin but by the content of their character.

☞ ☜

**FALLACY:** The Parthenon in Athens was a temple of the god Parthenos.

**FACT:** The name does come from the Greek word *parthenos,* but it doesn't refer to a god of that name. *Parthenos* translates as "virgin." The Parthenon, built on Athens's acropolis between 447 and 432 B.C., was the main temple of the city's patron goddess, Athena. Just as the state of Virginia was named for Elizabeth the Virgin Queen, the Parthenon was named for Athena Parthenos.

☞ ☜

**FALLACY:** Plymouth Rock marks the spot where the Pilgrims stepped off the Mayflower.

**FACT:** Plymouth Rock was not mentioned in the diaries of the Pilgrims who landed in 1620. The first historical mention wasn't until the eighteenth century, when the town was planning to cover the rock with a wharf; the elderly son of one of the pilgrims recalled that his father had told him it had been used as a stepping stone. An attempt to move the rock into town during the Revolutionary War succeeded in breaking it in two. Over the years it has been moved, glued back together, and carried off in small pieces for souvenirs. A tourist shrine was built for the 300th anniversary of the 1620 Mayflower landing, and the granite rock was moved there. There is no evidence that Plymouth Rock had any connection at all to the Pilgrims.

☞ ☜

**FALLACY:** Prussia used to be a nation; now it is one of the states of Germany.

**FACT:** At one time Prussia was not only one of the German nations, it was the largest and most powerful kingdom among them, with its capital at Berlin. In 1871 the Prussian king was proclaimed Emperor William I of the German Empire. Prussia is not now one of the states of Germany because it no longer exists. It was abolished in 1947 following World War II, its territory divided among Germany, Poland, and the USSR.

☞ ☜

**FALLACY:** One of the most significant battles of the Korean War was fought at Poznan.

**FACT:** Between the start of the Korean War on 25 June 1950 and the armistice that ended it on 27 July 1953, not a single battle was fought at Poznan. Pusan, South Korea's second-largest city and one of its most important seaports, is on the country's southeastern coast. Although it was South Korea's capital during the war and the main entry point for troops and supplies, no battle was fought at Pusan, either. Poznan is the fourth-largest city in Poland.

☞ ☜

**FALLACY:** The Rosetta Stone, named for the scholar who deciphered it, has the same text in two different languages.

**FACT:** Building on the work of Thomas Young, Jean François Champollion deciphered the Egyptian hieroglyphs on the Rosetta Stone in the early 1800s. The broken black basalt slab, discovered in 1799, got its name from the fact it was found near the town of Rosetta in the Nile River delta. The importance of the Rosetta Stone is that it has the same text, a decree issued by Ptolemy V, in three different languages: demotic, Egyptian hieroglyphs, and Greek. Until the discovery of the Rosetta Stone, Egyptian hieroglyphics were indecipherable.

☞ ☜

**FALLACY:** The first successful underwater cable was under the Atlantic Ocean between Europe and the United States.

**FACT:** The first successful underwater cable, completed in 1850, was

on the bottom of the English Channel between England and France. The
success of this telegraph led to underwater cables on the bottom of the
Irish Sea, the Mediterranean Sea, and the North Sea. The first successful
trans-Atlantic cable was completed in 1866.

☞ ☜

**FALLACY:** People everywhere know the War of 1812 as a war between
the United States and Britain.

**FACT:** When people in the United States think of the War of 1812,
they think of the British capturing and burning Washington. When people
in most of the rest of the world, including Britain, think of the War of
1812, they think of Napoleon capturing and burning Moscow and of
Tchaikovsky's *1812, Ceremonial Overture* commemorating that war.

☞ ☜

**FALLACY:** Crazy Horse was a member of the Dakota, not the Sioux.

**FACT:** In his own language, his name was Ta-Sunko-Witko. He was a
chief of the Oglala, and the organizer of the Sioux Uprising when Native
American land was being stolen in the Black Hills and the northern
Great Plains. He defeated General George Crook at Rosebud Creek, and
Lieutenant Colonel George Custer at the Little Big Horn. At the time,
the Oglala were one of seven groups making up the Teton, also called
the Lakota. The Teton were the westernmost of the larger group called
both Dakota and Sioux, who lived from Minnesota to Montana and Saskatchewan to Nebraska. It's correct to say, therefore, that Ta-Sunko-
Witko, or Crazy Horse, was a member of the Dakota, Lakota, Oglala,
Teton, and Sioux. In the same way, John Lennon was a member of the
groups called European, British, English, Liverpudlian, and Beatles.

☞ ☜

**FALLACY:** George Washington was born on 22 February.

**FACT:** According to the calendar on the wall when he was born, George
Washington arrived on 11 February 1731; according to the calendar on
the wall today, George Washington was born on 22 February 1732: a
difference of one year and eleven days. British colonies were still using
the Julian calendar when Washington was born. In 1752, Britain and her
colonies shifted over to the Gregorian calendar; the day following 2
September 1752 became 14 September 1752. That accounts for the

eleven-day difference. Another change was that New Year's Day was shifted from 25 March to 1 January. Although 24 March 1751 was followed by 25 March 1752, under the new Gregorian calendar 31 December 1752 was followed by 1 January 1753. Since Washington was born in February, that accounts for the one-year difference.

☞ ☜

**FALLACY:** William Tell was an Englishman who shot an apple off his son's head.

**FACT:** Many Americans believe that, but not many Britons. First off, the story of William Tell is tradition, not history. According to the legend, a Swiss—not English—patriot named William Tell was forced by Gessler, the local Austrian bailiff, to shoot an apple off his son's head with a crossbow from a distance of eighty paces. He succeeded in doing so and later killed the tyrannical Gessler, which led to a general uprising against the Austrian bailiffs. This traditional tale is really an allegory about the forming of a defensive league against the Hapsburgs of Austria by three cantons in 1291, the beginning of the struggle for Swiss independence.

☞ ☜

**FALLACY:** The first flight at Kitty Hawk, with Orville and Wilbur Wright at the controls, lasted only a few minutes.

**FACT:** The Wright brothers' plane, the *Flyer,* had room for only one person. The person on the maiden flight near Kill Devil Hill, Kitty Hawk, North Carolina, on 17 December 1903, was Orville. He flew 120 feet at an average altitude of 10 feet. The entire flight lasted 12 seconds. Four flights took place that day, during the last of which Wilbur broke Orville's records for both time and distance: 852 feet on a flight lasting 59 seconds.

☞ ☜

**FALLACY:** Everybody knows about Socrates, but nobody knows if there was a Mrs. Socrates.

**FACT:** Yes, they do, and yes, there was. Her name wasn't Mrs. Socrates, of course. It was Xanthippe—sharp-tongued, scolding, shrewish Xanthippe. As tradition has it, she was the reason Socrates spent so much time out and about and so little time at home.

☞ ☜

**FALLACY:** The Bayeux tapestry, although famous, is small.

**FACT:** The Bayeux tapestry—actually an embroidery, not a tapestry because it isn't woven—is made of colored wool on a linen backing. It tells of events leading up to the invasion of Anglo-Saxon England by William of Normandy and the Battle of Hastings in 1066. Supposedly made under the direction of Williams' wife, Queen Matilda, and now in the Bayeux Museum in France, *Telle du Conquest, dite tapisserie de la reine Mathilde* is far from small: roughly 20 inches by 225 feet, or 375 square feet.

☞ ☜

**FALLACY:** Sigmund Freud is buried in Germany.

**FACT:** Sigmund Freud's body is not buried anywhere because it was cremated. The ashes are in a favorite Grecian urn of his, and the urn is in Golder's Green Cemetery in London.

☞ ☜

**FALLACY:** Sitting Bull, who defeated Custer at the Little Big Horn, was the most important of the Apache war chiefs.

**FACT:** In his own language, the man's name was Tatanka Iyotake. A Sioux chief, not an Apache chief, he was the medicine chief—not the war chief—at the Battle of the Little Big Horn. His body was buried at Post Cemetery, Fort Yates, North Dakota. The epitaph on the stone was *Chief of the Hunkpapa Sioux.* His remains were stolen from there in 1954 and reburied in Sitting Bull Park in Little Eagle, South Dakota.

☞ ☜

**FALLACY:** The Empire State Building can survive lightning strikes, but if it were struck by an airplane, it would break like a tree.

**FACT:** The Empire State Building can survive lightning strikes with no major problem because the building is one huge lightning rod. Even if it were struck by a large plane it wouldn't break, and that's not just theory. On 28 July 1945, a U.S. Army B-25 bomber took off from Bedford, Massachusetts, headed for Newark, New Jersey. Flying through fog, it crashed into the Empire State Building's seventy-ninth floor. Fourteen people, including the three on the plane, were killed; the death toll was so low because 28 July 1945 was a Saturday. There was severe damage to several floors, but the Empire State Building is much too massive and strongly supported by its steel framework to break. Remember, it supported Skull Island's most famous resident and his friend: King Kong and Fay Wray.

☞ ☜

**FALLACY:** Wyatt Earp, Doc Holliday, and Bat Masterson died in shootouts.

**FACT:** Wyatt Berry Stapp Earp died of natural causes in 1929. John Henry "Doc" Holliday—a dentist, not a physician—died of tuberculosis. William Barclay "Bat" Masterson was a sports writer for the New York *Morning Telegraph* from 1902 until he died of a heart attack in 1921.

☞ ☜

**FALLACY:** The French and Indian War was between the French and the Indians.

**FACT:** The French and Indian War was between the French and the British. It was the last of a series of four North American wars that were part of the much larger ongoing war as European nations were establishing colonial empires. The first, from 1689 to 1697, was known in the colonies as King William's War and in Europe as part of the War of the League of Augsburg. Queen Anne's War, from 1702 to 1713, was part of the War of the Spanish Succession. King George's War, from 1744 to 1748, was part of the War of the Austrian Succession. The fourth, from 1754 to 1763 and called the French and Indian War by the colonists, was thought of in Europe as part of the Seven Years' War. In the North American part of the empire game, ended by the Treaty of Paris, France lost. Britain received France's North America territories, kept Canada and the lands east of the Mississippi, then traded Spain the Louisiana territory west of the Mississippi and New Orleans, for Spanish Florida. Why do we know the war by the name "French and Indian" if it was between the French and the British? Native Americans were enlisted by both sides, but it was the British who won the war and got to name it; they were fighting both French and Indians.

☞ ☜

**FALLACY:** Airports, for obvious reasons, are never named for people who died in an airplane crash.

**FACT:**  Airports, for obvious reasons, are *almost* never named for people who died in an airplane crash. There's a notable exception at Oklahoma City, Oklahoma. Will Rogers Airport is named for the famous humorist despite the fact that he died in an airplane crash near Point Barrow, Alaska, in 1935. As for other airport disasters, Amelia Earhart's luggage still hasn't been found.

☞ ☜

**FALLACY:**  Bucephalus was an ancient Greek male sex god.

**FACT:**  Bucephalus may have been a sex god to some four-footed Greeks, but probably not to most two-footed Greeks. He was definitely real, though, and definitely male. Bucephalus, a stallion, was Alexander the Great's war horse.

☞ ☜

**FALLACY:**  "Old Ironsides" was one of the first American ironclad ships.

**FACT:**  The first battle between American ironclads was on 9 March 1862, between the *Monitor* and the *Virginia* (called the *Merrimack* before it was rebuilt as an ironclad). The frigate *Constitution,* launched in 1797 and still fully commissioned by the U.S. Navy, earned the nickname "Old Ironsides" in the War of 1812 when some British cannonballs bounced off her sides. Old Ironsides's sides aren't made of iron, though; they're made of oak. After the most recent renovation was completed in 1994, only about 10 percent of the original ship remains. "New Ironsides"?

☞ ☜

**FALLACY:**  Learned Hand, Mother Jones, and Carry Nation were fictional characters.

**FACT:**  Learned Hand, a strong defender of free speech, was a federal judge from 1909 to 1951. His opinions were held in such high regard that he was often referred to as "the tenth justice of the Supreme Court." Mother Jones was Mary Harris Jones, an Irish-born American labor leader and one of the founders of the Industrial Workers of the World. Carry (not Carrie) Moore Nation was a hatchet-toting teetotaler and intemperate temperance crusader; pushing prohibition, she used her hatchet to smash bottles and chop up furniture in saloons.

☞ ☜

**FALLACY:** Dinosaurs couldn't have lived in Antarctica because it's too cold.

**FACT:** Antarctica is cold now because of where it is, but it wasn't always there, and it wasn't always cold. The continents have drifted considerable distances over time; Antarctica was once far north of its present location and enjoyed a much more temperate climate. Dinosaur fossils were first discovered on James Ross Island near the Antarctic Peninsula in 1986 and tested out at 75 to 80 million years old. The second discovery, in 1991, was on Mount Kirkpatrick, about 400 miles from the South Pole and 2,000 miles from James Ross Island; those fossils are 200 million years old.

☞ ☜

**FALLACY:** The electric blanket was invented in the United States in the 1950s.

**FACT:** The electric blanket was invented longer ago than you might think, and not in the United States. The original electric blanket is credited to C. T. Snedekor of England, who called it a thermogen. His invention was tested and reported upon very positively by the British medical journal *Lancet,* which was in turn quoted by the American journal *Scientific American* in its issue of August 1894.

☞ ☜

**FALLACY:** The greatest extinction of life on Earth occurred about 65 million years ago, when the dinosaurs suddenly died off.

**FACT:** The dinosaurs didn't die off all at once, but most of the remaining ones became extinct roughly 65 million years ago during a mass extinction at the end of the Cretaceous period. We know of at least five mass extinctions, however—during the Ordovician, Devonian, Permian, Triassic, and Cretaceous periods—and the dinosaur-deadly extinction at the end of the Cretaceous was not even close to being the most extensive. At the end of the Permian period, about 250 million years ago, up to 90 percent of the forms of life on Earth became extinct.

☞ ☜

**FALLACY:** The Kingsford charcoal briquette company was started by a man named Kingsford.

**FACT:** That's half right. The company that today is the Western Hemisphere's largest maker of charcoal briquettes was started by a man named Ford. Henry Ford, to be exact. His cars contained a lot of wood, which meant a lot of wood scraps. Never one to overlook a money-making opportunity, Ford turned these scraps into charcoal and sold them under the name Ford Charcoal Briquettes. As the charcoal company changed hands, the name was changed to Kingsford Products Company; Kingsford is now owned by Clorox Company. Toss that one on the barbie.

☞ ☜

**FALLACY:** The Liberty Bell cracked on 4 July 1776 while being rung to announce the Declaration of Independence.

**FACT:** Although the words "Proclaim Liberty throughout all the Land" appear on the bell, there was no Liberty Bell in 1776. Originally called the Province Bell and ordered from the Whitechapel Foundry in London to commemorate the fiftieth anniversary of the Commonwealth of Pennsylvania, it arrived in Philadelphia in August 1752. It cracked while being rung the following month, was recast by Pass and Stow of Philadelphia with an unfortunate-sounding mix of metals, and therefore recast again. Recasting involves breaking a bell into pieces, melting the pieces, and pouring the molten metal into a new mold. The resulting bell was finally hung in the tower of the State House in June 1753. It was officially called the State House Bell, but was sometimes referred to as the Great Bell or the Old One, until renamed the Liberty Bell in the mid 1800s by abolitionists, referring to liberty for slaves; the State House, meanwhile, had become Independence Hall. Although the State House Bell was rung to announce the first public reading of the Declaration of Independence, that event was on 8 July 1776, not 4 July. A major crack appeared in the bell on 8 July 1835 while it was being tolled for the death of Chief Justice John Marshall; the bell was muffled and tolled again in 1841 for the death of President William Henry Harrison. To reduce potential vibration damage when the bell was rung to commemorate Washington's birthday in 1846, the original crack was deliberately widened into the famous crack seen today. A new crack, much smaller and narrower and extending up and to the right from the top of the old one, appeared in the Liberty Bell in 1907. Interestingly, on the original order for this bell ordered by Pennsylvania, and on the bell itself, the word *Pennsylvania* is misspelled *Pensylvania*.

☞ ☜

**FALLACY:** The first aerial photograph was taken during World War I.

**FACT:** The first aerial photograph was taken considerably before the outbreak of World War I in 1914. It was also taken considerably before the Wright brothers' flights on 17 December 1903. The first aerial photograph was taken by Gaspard Tournachon near Paris, in 1858—from a balloon. And that's not just a lot of hot air.

☞ ☜

**FALLACY:** Captain Bligh of the *Bounty* was set adrift by mutineers and was never heard from again.

**FACT:** Cruel Captain William Bligh commanded the *Bounty* on a round trip between England and Tahiti. In April 1789, on the return trip, the crew mutinied and set Bligh and eighteen other men adrift in a small boat. Two months later the boat reached Timor, a large island east of Java. In 1805, Admiral Bligh was appointed governor of New South Wales, Australia, and apparently governed there as he had governed on the *Bounty*: there was a rebellion in 1808, and Bligh was imprisoned. Ultimately retired in England, he died in 1817, and was never heard from again.

# ⑥

# Humans and Other Sports

**FALLACY:** A person who plays a calliope is a callipygian.

**FACT:** A calliope, best known from circuses, is a loud organlike instrument that plays steam whistles from a keyboard. Calliope, from Greek mythology, is the muse of poetry. A callipygian, from the Greek words for beauty and buttocks, is a person with beautiful buttocks.

☞ 🕮

**FALLACY:** Newt Gingrich was born in Georgia.

**FACT:** Representative Newt Gingrich, Republican from Georgia elected as Speaker of the House in 1995, was born on 17 June 1943 in Harrisburg, Pennsylvania.

☞ 🕮

**FALLACY:** There used to be only one football Bowl game, the Rose Bowl; now there are abut a dozen.

**FACT:** Now there are about two dozen. The Rose Bowl was the granddaddy of them all, starting in 1902 when Michigan beat Stanford 49-0, but it didn't become an annual event until 1916 (Washington State 14, Brown 0). Listing some but by no means all of the football Bowl games: the Alamo Bowl, the Aloha Bowl, the California Raisin Bowl, the Carquest Bowl (known as the Blockbuster Bowl until 1993), the Citrus Bowl, the Copper Bowl, the Cotton Bowl, the Fiesta Bowl, the Freedom Bowl, the Gator Bowl, the Hall of Fame Bowl, the John Hancock Bowl (known as the Sun Bowl in its precommercial days), the Heritage Bowl, the Holiday Bowl, the Hula Bowl, the Independence Bowl, the Las Vegas Bowl, the Liberty

Bowl, the Orange Bowl, the Peach Bowl, the Rose Bowl, the Senior Bowl, the Sugar Bowl, the Super Bowl, and the Ty-D-Bol.

☞ ☜

**FALLACY:**   If you're half as old as someone else, you'll always be half as old as they are.

**FACT:**   If you're half as old as someone else you when you're ten and they're twenty, a decade later you'll narrow the gap and be two-thirds as old as they are. A decade after that you'll narrow the gap even more and be three-fourths as old as they are. A decade after that you'll get even closer and be four-fifths as old as they are. And so it goes. You'll never be as old as they are, though, so you may as well stop aging right now.

☞ ☜

**FALLACY:**   Airplanes are almost always late.

**FACT:**   Only half of all airplanes are almost always late. Here's the way it works: the airplane you're on is almost always late, but your connecting flight is almost always right on time.

☞ ☜

**FALLACY:**   Only mammalian embryos develop inside a fluid-filled amniotic sac.

**FACT:**   The embryos of mammals, including humans, develop while floating in amniotic fluid inside an amniotic sac formed by a membrane called the amnion. We mammals share this trait with birds and reptiles.

☞ ☜

**FALLACY:**   Pelé is the first name of that famous soccer star, not his last name.

**FACT:**   Internationally famous Brazilian soccer star Pelé was appointed in 1995 to the cabinet position of special secretary for sports, by President Fernando Henrique Cordoso. Neither his first name nor his last name is Pelé. Edson Arantes do Nascimento's nickname is Pelé.

☞ ☜

**FALLACY:**   Humans belong to the anthropod group of animals.

**FACT:**   There are anthropoids and there are arthropods, but there are no anthropods. *Anthropoid* means "resembling a human" and refers to the

Pongid family of great apes, which includes chimpanzees, gorillas, and orangutans. The phylum Arthropoda includes arachnids (mites, scorpions, spiders, ticks), crustaceans (barnacles, crabs, lobsters, shrimp), insects (beetles, bees, butterflies, crickets, flies, mosquitoes), and myriapods (centipedes, millipedes). The arthropod phylum is neither small nor insignificant: more than 80 percent of all animal species are arthropods. Humans, who belong to the phylum Chordata, are the only remaining species of the genus Homo.

☞ ☜

**FALLACY:** Neither President Clinton nor Hillary Rodham Clinton was born in Arkansas.

**FACT:** Hillary Rodham wasn't born in Arkansas; she was born on 26 October 1947 in Chicago, Illinois. Bill Clinton was born in Arkansas, on 19 August 1946 in the town of Hope. Daughter Chelsea was born on 27 February 1980 in Little Rock, Arkansas.

☞ ☜

**FALLACY:** In a ball game, the team that's on the offense has control of the ball.

**FACT:** In most ball games, the team that's on the offense has control of the ball. Soccer, for example, and football and basketball. In baseball, though, the team that's on the defense has control of the ball.

☞ ☜

**FALLACY:** The president of the United States threw out the first ball at the first major-league night baseball game.

**FACT:** The first major-league night baseball game was played on 24 May 1935. The president of the United States was Franklin D. Roosevelt. The game was between the Cincinnati Reds and the Philadelphia Phillies, at Cincinnati's Crosby Field. The Reds won 4–1. Roosevelt did not attend the game, but he did something that made the game possible: throwing a switch at the White House, he turned on the lights.

☞ ☜

**FALLACY:** Because of the pounding it takes, a basketball is "bounced out" after one professional game.

**FACT:** Depends on how long the game is. According to basketball-maker

Spalding, the life of an average National Basketball Association ball ends with its 10,000th bounce. It isn't the people who play the game who should be making millions, it's the people who count all those bounces.

☞ ☜

**FALLACY:** The longest basketball field goal was about seventy-five feet.

**FACT:** It was a game to remember, that 25 February 1989 contest in Erie, Pennsylvania, between Fairview High and Iroquois High. The game had gone into overtime, and overtime was running out with the score tied. Christopher Eddy threw the ball just as time expired; it sailed down the court and into the basket, winning the game for Fairview, 51–50. That field goal was measured at 90 feet, 2.25 inches.

☞ ☜

**FALLACY:** A biretta is a pistol.

**FACT:** A biretta is a stiff square cap with three or four ridges on top, and should not be confused with a bireme, which was an ancient galley with two banks of oars on each side. A Beretta, often of the 9-millimeter persuasion, is a pistol.

☞ ☜

**FALLACY:** Joe Louis still holds the record for successful defenses of a boxing title.

**FACT:** Joe Louis, born Joseph Louis Barrow, turned professional in 1934 and won the world heavyweight boxing title in 1937. He successfully defended his title 25 times, including 21 knockouts, making a total of 26 undefeated title fights. Joe Louis retired, still holding the title, in 1949. In December 1993, at Puebla, Mexico, Julio Cesar Chavez successfully defended his World Boxing Council super lightweight title for the 26th time, making a total of 27 undefeated title fights. A round begins or ends when the bell rings, but a boxing ring is not round.

☞ ☜

**FALLACY:** The odds against dealing all the cards of a suit to each of four poker players are about a trillion to one.

**FACT:** If anyone offers you those odds to try, don't take them, but if anyone accepts those odds to try it, definitely make the bet.

The odds against dealing all thirteen cards of a suit to each of four poker players are more than two octillion to one. If you have a lot of numbers you want to use up, another way of writing that is 2,000,000,000,000,000,000,000,000,000,000 to 1.

☞ ☜

**FALLACY:** Buckshot is a whole lot of very small pellets in a shotgun shell.

**FACT:** Birdshot is a whole lot of very small pellets in a shotgun shell. Buckshot, used for killing adult males (bucks) of various species, is a few relatively large pellets in a shotgun shell, ranging from about ¼ inch to ⅓ inch in diameter. If you used birdshot on a buck, he'd take off and you'd never see him again. If you used buckshot on a bird, you'd probably miss the bird because there are so few pellets in the pattern; if you managed to hit it, there'd be nothing left to see. Buckshot is for shooting bucks, and birdshot is for shooting birds; a third type, larger than buckshot and called a slug, is not used for shooting slugs.

☞ ☜

**FALLACY:** The higher brain functions are in the cerebellum.

**FACT:** The cerebellum is a three-lobed part of the brain that takes care of posture and coordinates voluntary muscle movements. The cerebrum is the largest part of the brain, divided into right and left hemispheres linked by the corpus callosum. The cerebral cortex is the outer-layer "gray matter" covering the hemispheres of the cerebrum. The higher brain functions are in the cerebral cortex. All of us, though, have occasionally received this message when we're trying to think of something: "The brain you have reached is not in service at this time."

☞ ☜

**FALLACY:** *Fat* and *slim* are opposites.

**FACT:** Sometimes they're opposites, as in the diet world, and sometimes they're the same, as in "slim chance," which means not much of a chance, and "fat chance," which means not much of a chance.

☞ ☜

**FALLACY:** The military rank *colonel* was originally spelled *kernel*.

**FACT:** Although many people who hold the rank of colonel consider themselves the indispensable kernel of their organization, that's not where the word came from. It came from the Latin *columna,* "column," and meant merely the leader of a column of soldiers.

☞ ☜

**FALLACY:**  The word *conjugal* means "sexual."

**FACT:**  The word *conjugal* refers to marriage or the relationship of spouses, and does not specifically mean sexual. Community property, for example, is a conjugal right under the laws of some states. As many married people will attest, marriage and sex definitely do not mean the same thing. Having more than one spouse probably wouldn't help; the plural of spouse is not spice.

☞ ☜

**FALLACY:**  The maximum distance a cow chip can be thrown is about a hundred feet.

**FACT:**  You have to step very carefully around this topic because there are so many qualifications. Speaking of totally natural, unmodified cow chips, Steve Urner on 14 August 1981 at the Mountain Festival at Tehachapi, California, managed to throw one 266 feet. There is no record of the name of the other vital member of the team, without whom this feat could not have been accomplished: the bovine artist who crafted the chip.

☞ ☜

**FALLACY:**  Joe DiMaggio hit some of his most memorable World Series home runs at Yankee Stadium.

**FACT:**  Couldn't have been all that memorable. None of the record books remember them. Joe DiMaggio, who played his entire career with the New York Yankees, never hit a single World Series home run at Yankee Stadium. He did, however, hit a total of 361 home runs.

☞ ☜

**FALLACY:**  One cent, doubled every day for a month, would amount to several thousand dollars.

**FACT:**  One cent, doubled very day for a thirty-one day month, would amount to considerably more than several thousand dollars. Starting off the first day as 1¢, the second day it would amount to 2¢, the third day to 4¢, and the seventh day of the first week to 64¢. On the last day of the second week it would amount to 8,192¢. On the last day of the third week it would amount to 1,048,576¢. On the 31st day it would amount to 1,073,741,824¢, or more than $10.7 million. Start saving those pennies.

☞ ☜

**FALLACY:**  Humans can move their ears, but not for any useful purpose.

**FACT:**  When humans move their ears intentionally, the purpose is usually to amuse themselves or others. When their ears move automatically, often without their conscious knowledge, it's usually for one of two quite useful purposes: either the ear has been irritated and it's trying to get rid of the irritation, or the ear is moving like a directional antennae, aiming toward a sound. In the aural cacophony of a city the antenna effect is overwhelmed, but if you pay attention in a quiet countryside you can feel the ear on one side of your head move to focus on a sound in that direction.

☞ ☜

**FALLACY:**  ESPN stands for Entertainment SPorts Network.

**FACT:**  Pesky *P*, isn't it? ESPN actually stands for Entertainment and Sports Programming Network.

☞ ☜

**FALLACY:**  The Green Monster is a character on Sesame Street.

**FACT:**  The Cookie Monster is a character on Sesame Street. The Green Monster is the short left-field fence at Boston's Fenway Park; that base-ball-park fence was named by pitchers who saw some of their best pitches batted over it. Probably the best-remembered homer over the Green Monster is Carlton Fisk's in the bottom of the twelfth inning of game six of the 1975 World Series. Despite it, though, the National League Cincinnati Reds beat the American League Boston Red Sox 4–3 in that World Series.

☞ ☜

**FALLACY:**  To avoid sexism, the word *fireman* should be replaced with *firefighter*.

**FACT:**  In some cases that's true; both men and women belong to fire departments and fight fires. In some cases that's not true; on railroad locomotives, the job of the fireman is to maintain a fire for the engine, not to fight the fire—to avoid sexual overtones, use the word *stoker*.

☞ ☜

**FALLACY:**   There are only two types of football: real football and soccer.

**FACT:**   There are at least half a dozen types of football. To most of the world, "real football" means soccer, officially called Association football. What people in the United States call football, the rest of the world calls American football. Other types include Australian Rules football; Canadian football; Gaelic football; and rugby football, also called rugger.

☞ ☜

**FALLACY:**   An American football field is 5,000 square yards: 100 yards long by 50 yards wide.

**FACT:**   A U.S. football field is 5,333 square yards. Although it is 100 yards long, it is 53⅓ yards wide. A Canadian football field, just as American as a U.S. football field, is 7,150 square yards: 110 yards long and 65 yards wide.

☞ ☜

**FALLACY:**   When someone says "I'm closer to forty than I am to thirty," it means that they're in their late thirties.

**FACT:**   Either that, or it means that they're displaying the proverbial wisdom that comes with age: they'd also be closer to forty than they are to thirty if they were fifty.

☞ ☜

**FALLACY:**   Lou Gehrig's first name was Louis.

**FACT:**   Nope, and it wasn't Lou, either. Nicknamed the Iron Horse, he was the American League's Most Valuable Player four times during the fourteen seasons he played for the New York Yankees. He played in 2,130 consecutive league games and seven World Series, hit 493 home runs, and had a lifetime batting average of 0.340. At the age of thirty-seven he died of amyotrophic lateral sclerosis, sometimes called Lou Gehrig's disease. His name was Henry Louis Gehrig.

☞ ☜

**FALLACY:**   The longest hole in the golf world is at the course run by the St. Andrews club in Scotland.

**FACT:**   The full name of that famous golf institution near St. Andrews in Fife, eastern Scotland, is the Royal and Ancient Golf Club of St.

Andrews. The golf world's longest hole is not in Scotland, however; geographically speaking, it's about as far from Scotland as you can get. On the other side of the world, and in the Southern Hemisphere, the 948-yard, par-7, sixth hole of Western Australia's Koolan Island Golf Course is the longest hole in the golf world.

☞ ☜

**FALLACY:** *Grampus* comes from *Gramps,* which comes from *Grandfather.*

**FACT:** I'm not saying it's impossible that your grandfather was a grampus, but it's highly improbable. A grampus, *Grampus griseus,* is a cetacean related to dolphins. Even if you have such a relative you may not want to call him by the English version of the original Latin words, which translate as "fat fish."

☞ ☜

**FALLACY:** *Habeas corpus* does not refer to a human body.

**FACT:** Unlike *corpus delicti,* which does not refer specifically to a human body but to the body of evidence in a crime, *habeas corpus* does refer specifically to a human body. A Constitutional right, writs of habeas corpus require that a person held in custody be brought before a court, which will determine whether or not the person is being held legally. The name comes from the fact that the first words of such a writ are "Habeas corpus." Literally, habeas corpus means "you should have the body" (of the prisoner).

☞ ☜

**FALLACY:** The Ivy League of colleges was established in the 1800s when the colleges were founded.

**FACT:** Only one of the colleges was founded in the 1800s: Cornell, in 1865. Harvard was founded in 1616, Yale in 1701, Pennsylvania in 1740, Princeton in 1746, Columbia in 1754, Brown in 1764, and Dartmouth in 1769. The Ivy League itself, which regulates intercollegiate sports, wasn't formally established until 1956.

☞ ☜

**FALLACY:** Jersey Joe Walcott's real name was Joseph Walcott.

**FACT:** In addition to winning the heavyweight boxing crown several times, the first in July 1951 in a bout against Ezzard Charles, Jersey Joe Walcott lost six heavyweight title fights, more than any other boxer. Two of those losses were to Joe Louis, in December 1947 and June 1948, and one was to Rocky Marciano, in September 1952. Jersey Joe is in boxing's Hall of Fame; his real name was Arnold Raymond Cream.

☞ ☜

**FALLACY:** A man who is intestate can't produce children.

**FACT:** Sure he can. So can a woman who is intestate. The word has nothing to do with nether nubbins. It means someone who hasn't made a legal will.

☞ ☜

**FALLACY:** Jimmy the Greek was named James by his parents.

**FACT:** Jimmy the Greek, famous Las Vegas oddsmaker, isn't called "the Greek" for nothing. His original first name was Dimitrios; his original last name was Synodinos. He changed his name to James Snyder. Although President Gerald Ford's pardon of Richard Nixon was his most famous (or infamous), he also granted a pardon to Jimmy the Greek for gambling violations.

☞ ☜

**FALLACY:** Lacrosse was invented in France.

**FACT:** That stick-and-ball game was invented in North America, by Native Americans. The original name has been lost; it was named *la crosse* by French-speaking European immigrants who learned the game long ago in what is now Canada.

☞ ☜

**FALLACY:** If you're going to bet, your best odds are with a government lottery.

**FACT:** A lottery is simply a tax on people who don't understand statistics. If you're going to bet in a government lottery, the overwhelming odds are that you're going to lose. The people who control government gambling take their profit off the top. Shoot craps in Las Vegas or pump coins into a slot machine in Atlantic City and you'll get better odds. Odds for the big prize in government lotteries run from 20 million to 50 million against you. If you really want to give your money to the government, let the IRS fill out your tax forms.

☞ ☜

**FALLACY:** Legally, manslaughter is one type of murder.

**FACT:** Legally, there are four types of homicide: accidental, justifiable, manslaughter, and murder. A doctor's killing someone during an attempt to save the person's life would be accidental homicide. A government-approved execution would be justifiable homicide. Neither accidental homicide or justifiable homicide is a criminal offense; both manslaughter and murder are criminal offenses. What distinguishes manslaughter from murder is that in manslaughter there is no malice or premeditation; the killing is without "malice aforethought." Killing someone in an automobile accident is an example of involuntary manslaughter; killing someone "in the heat of passion" is an example of voluntary manslaughter. Legally, both manslaughter and murder are types of homicide, but manslaughter is not a type of murder.

☞ ☜

**FALLACY:** The marathon race in the Olympic Games is twenty-six miles long because that's the distance from Marathon to Athens.

**FACT:** The marathon race in the Olympic Games commemorates the feat of Pheidippides, a runner who in 490 B.C. took news back to Athens of the Greek victory over the Persians at Marathon. The Battle of Marathon was a major event because it ended the First Persian War. There are two problems with the twenty-six-mile distance. First, Athens isn't that far from Marathon. Second, the Olympic Games marathon race is not 26 miles long, but 26 miles, 385 yards; no, that doesn't come out to an even number in the metric system: 42 kilometers, 195 meters. The marathon was included in the first modern Olympic Games in 1896, and the distance was standardized at the 1908 Games in London. Twenty-six miles, 385 yards, is the distance between the stadium where the games were held and the Queen's residence at Windsor Castle.

☞ ☜

**FALLACY:** There is no way to know where in the body the mind lives.

**FACT:** The way to narrow it down is deduction. If a person loses both arms and both legs, the mind is still there. If a person receives transplants of heart and liver and lungs and intestines and pancreas and kidneys and whatever, the mind is still there. If a person loses eyes, ears, nose, and parts of the skull, the mind is still there. The only thing that cannot be lost is the brain, and even parts of the brain can be lost without losing the mind. Adding all those together and subtracting them from the body narrows the search considerably.

☞ ☜

**FALLACY:** The female form of *master* is *mistress.*

**FACT:** Technically correct, but sometimes the term is not used. When top-rated European female golfers competed in a tournament sponsored by an automobile company, for example, the company decided to call the contest the BMW Masters rather than the BMW Mistresses.

☞ ☜

**FALLACY:** Stan Musial is the only baseball player to win Most Valuable Player awards in two different positions.

**FACT:** Stan Musial, who is in baseball's Hall of Fame, did win Most Valuable Player awards in two different positions, but he is not the only player to do so. Hank Greenberg did, too, and is also in the Hall of Fame. Robin Yount, who retired in 1994 before the beginning of the season, was a shortstop when he won MVP in 1982, and a centerfielder when he won another MVP in 1989.

☞ ☜

**FALLACY:** A major-league pitcher who has a no-hitter going is rarely replaced.

**FACT:** Depends on how the major-league pitcher is accomplishing that feat. If he has a no-hitter going because he's striking out all the opposition batters, he'll rarely be replaced. If he has a no-hitter going because he's walking them all, he's gone.

☞ ☜

**FALLACY:** The Olympic bronze, silver, and gold medals are made of bronze, silver, and gold.

**FACT:** Originally true, but no longer. The first break from that tradition was at the 1992 Winter Games in Albertville, France, where the medals were made of crystal. The 1994 Winter Games in Lillehammer, Norway, continued the trend by awarding medals of stone fringed with bronze, silver, or gold.

☞ ☜

**FALLACY:**  The Ouija board originated more than a thousand years ago in the Orient as a method of contacting the supernatural.

**FACT:**  The Ouija board, as accurate as any other method of contacting the supernatural, goes back just over a century. It was created as a commercial board game and was first patented in 1892 not in the Orient, but in the United States. The trademarked name Ouija is a combination of the French and German words for "yes": *oui* and *ja.*

☞ ☜

**FALLACY:**  We're genetically closer to our children than we are to our brothers and sisters or our parents.

**FACT:**  Each of our parents has a separate gene pool; we inherit half of our gene pool from each of them. We and our mates have separate gene pools; our children inherit half of their gene pool from each of us. Our brothers and sisters inherit their gene pool from the same parents that we do; we are therefore genetically closer to our brothers and sisters than we are to our children or our parents. Some teenagers and their parents swear that they're not related, but it only seems that way.

☞ ☜

**FALLACY:**  Rocky Marciano was born in Italy.

**FACT:**  Rocky Marciano, the oldest of six children born to parents who came to the United States from Italy, was born in Brocktown, Massachusetts. He was not only the only heavyweight boxing champion but also the only world champion in any weight class to win every fight of his professional career—forty-nine of them, from the beginning in 1947 until he retired undefeated in 1956. His name wasn't always Rocky Marciano; when he was born in 1923, his parents named hm Rocco Francis Marchegiano.

☞ ☜

**FALLACY:**  Every Rose Bowl game has been played on New Year's Day in Pasadena, California, because that's where the Rose Bowl is.

**FACT:**  That's definitely where the Rose Bowl is, but not every Rose

Bowl game has been played in the Rose Bowl. During World War II, the 1942 game was played at Durham, North Carolina, home of Duke University; Oregon State outscored Duke 20–16. That was the only Rose Bowl game not played in Pasadena. Although the Rose Bowl parade and game are traditionally held on New Year's Day, that isn't always true, either, because of another tradition: Never on Sunday. In 1995, for example, New Year's Day fell on a Sunday, so the game was played on Monday. Penn State, which hadn't been in the Rose Bowl since 1923 (Southern California 14, Penn State 3), won over Oregon, which hadn't been in the Rose Bowl since 1958 (Ohio State 10, Oregon 7), by a score of 38–20, making coach Joe Paterno the only coach to win in all four of the traditional major bowls (Cotton, Orange, Rose, and Sugar), and giving him a record sixteen bowl victories.

☞ ☜

**FALLACY:**   Truth serum makes a person tell the truth.

**FACT:**   The truth of the matter is that there's no such thing as a truth serum. The traditional "truth serums" are scopolamine and thiopental sodium (also known as sodium pentothal), the main effect of which is to make a person less inhibited, much as alcohol does. As anyone who has listened to drunken ramblings realizes, an uninhibited imbiber will often talk on at great length about all manner of things. Some of what is said will be true; some will be partly true, partly false, and partly imaginary; some will not have even a nodding acquaintance with either truth or reality.

☞ ☜

**FALLACY:**   Although there were women in the armed forces during the Vietnam War, they weren't allowed to go to Vietnam.

**FACT:**   Some 265,000 women were in the armed forces during the Vietnam War, and 11,500 of them were sent there. Women weren't allowed to engage in combat, but they were allowed to go to Vietnam.

☞ ☜

**FALLACY:**   An athlete is never featured twice on a Wheaties cereal box.

**FACT:**   The marketing people at Wheaties know a good thing when it happens to them. If the picture of a particular athlete boosts sales, they often feature that athlete again. And again. Chicago Bulls basketball star

Michael Jordan graced the Wheaties box a record twelve times; he was so good for sales that his twelfth appearance came after he had retired—temporarily—from basketball.

☞ ☜

**FALLACY:** Teenagers are too young and inexperienced to play in baseball's World Series.

**FACT:** Fred Lindstrom didn't think so. He was an eighteen-year-old New York Giant when he played in all seven games of the 1924 World Series. It wasn't his fault that American League Washington beat National League New York 4–3.

☞ ☜

**FALLACY:** The heaviest professional wrestler weighed about 400 pounds.

**FACT:** *Half of* the heaviest professional wrestler weighed about 400 pounds. William J. Cobb, known professionally as Happy Humphrey, weighed more than 800 pounds; how much more probably depended on who he'd eaten before being weighed.

☞ ☜

**FALLACY:** Among trucks, a rig can be called either a trailer or a semi.

**FACT:** A rig is the whole outfit, including both the tractor and the trailer or semi. A trailer carries its full weight on its own wheels. A semi, short for semitrailer, has only rear wheels, and rests its front end on the fifth-wheel coupling with the tractor. A double semitrailer doesn't add up to one trailer; it's a rig with one semi attached to the rear of another semi.

☞ ☜

**FALLACY:** Submarines, for obvious reasons, don't have sails.

**FACT:** Submarines do have sails, but not the kind you're probably thinking of. The conning tower of a submarine is called its sail.

☞ ☜

**FALLACY:** In a deck of cards, half of the face cards face right, half face left.

**FACT:** Using a deck of Bicycle Playing Cards as an example, the one-eyed jack of spades faces left, and the queen of spades, king of spades, and jack of clubs also face left. The one-eyed jack of hearts faces right, and so do the queen and the king of hearts. Both the king and queen of clubs face right, along with the jack, queen, and one-eyed king of diamonds. Two-thirds of the twelve face cards face right.

☞ ☜

**FALLACY:** Golf clubs are numbered according to the weight of the head.

**FACT:** Golf clubs are numbered according to the *loft* of the head—the angle of the backward slant on the face of the club that determines how high the ball will go. The higher the loft, the higher the number of the club. In addition to the numbered woods and irons, there are special clubs such as the putter, the sand wedge, and the pitching wedge—which is handy for angry golfers looking for something to pitch.

☞ ☜

**FALLACY:** The Canadian Football League is a league of Canadian football teams.

**FACT:** On 7 July 1993 the Gold Miners opened their season by playing the Rough Riders in Ottawa, Canada's capital; that's the Gold Miners of Sacramento, California, the first U.S. franchise in the Canadian Football League. On 17 July 1993 the Calgary Stampeders played the Gold Miners at Sacramento State University's Hornet Field, marking the first time that a CFL game had been played between a Canadian team and a host team in the United States. Being the hosts, it was only proper for the Gold Miners to let the Stampeders win, 38–36. Since then there have been more below-the-border franchises, including Las Vegas and Baltimore—neither of which is notably Canadian.

☞ ☜

**FALLACY:** Two brothers have played in baseball's major leagues, and so have three brothers, but never four brothers.

**FACT:** At least fifteen families have provided three brothers to baseball's major leagues, and at least one family provided four. The record, though, goes to the Delahanty family. The Delahanty brothers who played in baseball's major leagues: Ed, Frank, Jim, Joe, and Tom.

☞ ☜

**FALLACY:**  More collect calls are made on the day that colleges open than any other day.

**FACT:**  Well, first off, there is no one day on which colleges open. Second, college students usually arrive with what they think will be enough money for the semester; it isn't until that money runs out a few weeks later that they call home. According to AT&T, more collect calls are made on Father's Day in June than any other day.

☞ ☜

**FALLACY:**  California's schools are financed with profits from the state lottery.

**FACT:**  That's what many Californians thought would happen, and that's why many Californians voted to allow this form of state gambling—but that's not how it worked out. Although $2 billion a year is taken in by the lottery, its contribution to California's schools amounts to less than 3 percent of the state's education budget.

☞ ☜

**FALLACY:**  Schools haven't banned long hair for males since the 1960s.

**FACT:**  There were many battles in the 1960s over the right of male students, as well as female students, to decide for themselves how long they wanted their hair. Students claimed their hair was theirs, giving them the right to grow it as long as they wanted to; school disciplinarians claimed that if males were allowed to have long hair, it would be detrimental to academic standards and discipline. In a long and expensive series of court cases, the students won. In the 1980s, the same battle was fought over students' rights to have short hair or no hair at all. Coming full circle, in June 1994 a judge ruled that a school district's ban on long hair for male students was vital to promoting safety and high academic standards. Considering the state of education today, it's surprising that in some places there is more concern about what goes on on the outside of a student's head than on the inside. Sanity may yet prevail, but it's definitely a hairy problem.

☞ ☜

**FALLACY:**  If you fly thousands of miles, you're going to get jet lag.

**FACT:**  The main effects of jet lag are caused by changing time zones, thereby confusing your body's clock. Not only are there ways of alleviating jet lag when traveling thousands of miles, there's a way of avoiding it all together. Flying from Hawaii to California you change time zones twice; flying from Hawaii to Tahiti, a roughly equivalent distance, you don't change time zones at all. The secret to avoiding jet lag is to travel only north-south, never east-west.

☞ ☜

**FALLACY:**  Baseball's Hall of Fame includes all National League players who have won the MVP award with a unanimous vote.

**FACT:**  Here is the complete list of National League players who have won the Most Valuable Player award with a unanimous vote: Orlando Cepeda. The year was 1967. Although he played the first eight years of his major-league career with the Giants, he was playing for the St. Louis Cardinals when he won all 280 votes of the Baseball Writers Association of America for Most Valuable Player. He retired in 1974. In 1993, for the fourteen year, Cepeda was on the ballot for baseball's Hall of Fame. He received 252 votes from members of the BWAA; 381 votes were needed that year. In 1994, his final year of regular eligibility for the Hall of Fame, he received 335 of the 342 votes needed from members of the association. The official word is that his being continually passed over has nothing to do with his having been arrested in Puerto Rico in 1975 for picking up a package of marijuana at the airport.

☞ ☜

**FALLACY:**  Ping-Pong is the real name of the game; calling it table tennis is just an affectation.

**FACT:**  Table tennis is the real name of the game, which was devised as an indoor version of lawn tennis. Ping-Pong is a registered trademark of one company that makes table tennis equipment.

☞ ☜

**FALLACY:**  The bayonet was named for the man who invented it.

**FACT:**  The name of the man who invented the bayonet is not known, for which he should be grateful. The weapon got its name from the place where it was first made, Bayonne. No, not the one in northeastern New Jersey near Upper New York Bay; the one in southwestern France near the Bay of Biscay.

☞ ☜

**FALLACY:**  Some professional football teams have lost games on three different TV networks, a few have lost on four networks, but none has lost on more than four.

**FACT:**  Many professional football teams have lost games on three different TV networks, some have lost on four networks, and a few have lost on five. When the Denver Broncos lost an exhibition game to the San Francisco 49ers in August 1994, though, they made football history by becoming the first team to lose on six different TV networks. That game was the first under the Fox Network's new National Football League broadcasting contract. The other five networks on which the Denver Broncos lost games were ABC, CBS, ESPN, NBC, and TNT.

☞ ☜

**FALLACY:**  The Black Sox scandal involved the Chicago Black Sox.

**FACT:**  The Black Sox scandal occurred at the 1919 World Series between Chicago and Cincinnati. After eight members of the Chicago team were investigated for accepting bribes to fix the game, Baseball Commissioner Kenesaw Lewis banned them from professional baseball for life. The eight players were pitcher Eddie Cicotte, center fielder Happy Felsch, first baseman Chick Gandil, left fielder "Shoeless" Joe Jackson, utility man Fred McMullin, shortstop Swede Risberg, third baseman Buck Weaver, and pitcher Clause Williams. The Cincinnati team was the Reds. The Chicago team was the White Sox; the name Black Sox comes from an allusion to the scandal having blackened the team's name. The Cincinnati Reds won the 1919 World Series 5–3; the Chicago White Sox have not won a World Series since 1917.

☞ ☜

**FALLACY:**  Gertrude Ederle was the first person to swim across the English Channel.

**FACT:**  When Gertrude Caroline Ederle swam across the English Channel on 6 August 1926, she not only became the first woman to swim the channel, she also set a new record of 14 hours and 39 minutes. The first known person to swim across the English Channel was Matthew Webb. He began from Dover at 12:56 P.M. on 24 August 1875, swam through the afternoon, the night, and into the next day, landing at Calais Sands 21 hours and 45 minutes after he began. On 27 September 1994, Chad

Hundeby swam from Dover, England, to Cap Gris-Nez, France, in 7 hours 17 minutes.

☞ ☜

**FALLACY:** A codpiece is a piece of cod.

**FACT:** There was always something fishy about a codpiece, but it had nothing to do with a codfish. Middle English *cod* meant "bag" or "scrotum." In the fifteenth and sixteenth centuries, European men's trousers were tight fitting, leaving only a frontal opening for some very important parts; a codpiece (*codpece*) was a bag or pouch used to conceal the family jewels. Many a man stuffed the contemporary equivalent of tissues into his codpiece to increase the apparent size of his jewelry collection.

## 7

# International

**FALLACY:**  Budapest, Hungary, is an ancient city.

**FACT:**  Budapest, the capital and largest city of Hungary in the north-central part of the country, didn't exist until 1873. The ancient city of Buda was in the hills on the west bank of the Danube River. The modern city of Pest grew up on the east bank. In 1873 they were joined in holy municipality to form Budapest.

☞ ☜

**FALLACY:**  The arch was invented by the Romans.

**FACT:**  The arch was invented long before the Romans. The Assyrians used it, the Babylonians used it, the Egyptians used it, and the Greeks used it. The classic Roman semicircular arch was borrowed from their predecessors in Italy, the Etruscans.

☞ ☜

**FALLACY:**  Smith is the most common family name.

**FACT:**  Purely a matter of perspective. Smith is the most common family name only in English-speaking countries; in the United States, for example, there are more than 2 million Smiths. The four most common surnames in China are Li, Liu, Wang, and Zhang. It has been estimated that there are more than 130 million Zhangs.

☞ ☜

**FALLACY:**  The first British colony in Australia was established in the late 1800s.

**FACT:**  The first British colony in Australia was New South Wales, a penal colony, established on 26 January 1788 where Sydney now stands. The 26th of January is Australia Day, a public holiday. Australia Day is not considered a holiday by the aboriginal people already there when the British arrived.

☞ ☜

**FALLACY:**  Australia became a country about the same time the United States became a country.

**FACT:**  The United States became a country on 4 July 1776 when delegates of the thirteen colonies adopted the Declaration of Independence, separating the colonies from Great Britain and joining them into the United States. Australia became a country on 1 January 1901 when the Commonwealth Act of 1900 went into effect, joining the separate colonies into the Commonwealth of Australia.

☞ ☜

**FALLACY:**  Paris is the most populous French-speaking city in the world; Marseille is second.

**FACT:**  Paris is not the most populous French-speaking city in the world and Marseille isn't second. The largest isn't Lyon or Toulouse, Nice, Nantes, Strasbourg, or Bordeaux. Marseille, with a population of about 800,000 is the third most populous French-speaking city. Paris, with a population of about 2 million, is the second largest. The largest French-speaking city, with a population of about 3 million, is Montreal, Canada.

☞ ☜

**FALLACY:**  The word *barbecue* comes from the brand of an Old West cattle ranch, the Bar-B-Q.

**FACT:**  So far as is known, there was never an Old West cattle ranch with that brand. The word *barbecue* entered American English from American Spanish *barbacoa*. The Spanish took the word from the Taino, an Arawak people of the Bahamas and the Greater Antilles (including Cuba, Jamaica, Hispaniola, and Puerto Rico). The Taino became extinct under Spanish rule during the sixteenth century.

☞ ☜

**FALLACY:** The world's largest bar is in New York City.

**FACT:** The world's largest bar is the Mathäser, at Bayerstrasse 5, München (Munich), Germany. It seats 5,500 people, and serves more than 10,500 gallons of beer per day.

☞ ☜

**FALLACY:** Brazil is so large that it shares a border with six other countries.

**FACT:** Brazil is so large that it shares a border with ten other countries: Argentina, Bolivia, Columbia, French Guiana, Guyana, Paraguay, Peru, Suriname, Uruguay, and Venezuela. The only two South American countries with which Brazil does not share a border are Chile and Ecuador.

☞ ☜

**FALLACY:** Buckingham Palace belongs to the British people.

**FACT:** Buckingham Palace, along with Windsor Castle—the largest castle in England—Balmoral Castle in Scotland, and a huge amount of other real estate, belongs to the world's richest woman: Queen Elizabeth II. If Parliament should abolish the monarchy, the castles and palaces—and even the crown jewels—would remain the property of Elizabeth Windsor's family. Family jewels, indeed.

☞ ☜

**FALLACY:** New York City has a larger population than Canada.

**FACT:** New York City is extremely densely populated, with 24,327 people per square mile. Canada, leaving some elbow room for its citizens, has a population density of seven per square mile. Even at that ratio of 3,475-to-1, however, Canada's population of 28 million is four times that of New York City's 7 million. There are 18 million people in all of New York State, for a population density of 384 per square mile. Although no U.S. city has a larger population than Canada, the state of California does, with 31 million people and a population density of 198 per square mile.

☞ ☜

**FALLACY:** Canada's first female prime minister was very popular with the voters.

**FACT:** Kim Campbell, Canada's first female prime minister, was elevated to that post by her Progressive Conservative Party in June 1993; the voters had their first chance to give their opinion in October. The Progressive Conservative Party held 154 seats in the House of Commons before the election; after the election it held two. The voters were expressing their opinion of the prime minister and her Conservatives, not of female prime ministers. Campbell resigned as leader of the party on 13 December 1993.

☞ ☜

**FALLACY:** Portland cement was created in Portland, Oregon.

**FACT:** When Portland cement was created in 1824, there was no Portland, Oregon; that town wasn't founded until 1845. The patent was issued to Joseph Aspdin of Leeds, England, for a process of grinding and heating a combination of clay and limestone. He called it Portland cement because it looked like the stone quarried at Portland, Dorset County, in southern England. Today it's simply called cement.

☞ ☜

**FALLACY:** Black is the color of mourning and death.

**FACT:** Black is the color of mourning and death in some cultures, but that tradition is far from universal. In China and some other parts of Asia, which includes a large percentage of the human race, the color of mourning and death is white.

☞ ☜

**FALLACY:** The Doomsday Book was about the end of the world.

**FACT:** The landed gentry may have thought so when William the Conqueror had it compiled in 1086. It was a census of landowners and a survey of the property they owned, to make sure William was getting all of his taxes. It covered the area south of the Ribble and Tees Rivers, with the exception of London and Winchester. The actual name of the work was Domesday Book, but that's merely a Middle English spelling of doomsday, which means judgment day.

☞ ☜

**FALLACY:** Dresden china is made in Dresden, Germany.

**FACT:** Dresden was virtually destroyed in 1945 by World War II bombing raids, though that's not why Dresden china isn't made in Dresden.

Dresden china has been made in Meissen, a town near Dresden, since the early 1700s. Meissen china, Meissen porcelain, Meissen ware, or Dresden china—it's called all of those—was the first true porcelain made in Europe.

☞ ☜

**FALLACY:**   Daylight Saving Time begins in April and ends in October.

**FACT:**   In the United States, Daylight Saving Time begins on the first Sunday in April and ends on the last Sunday in October. Has been that way since 1987, when the beginning was moved up from the last week in April. Tinkering with time to "save" daylight is not an exclusively American strangeness, however. Many nations do it. China first went on Daylight Saving Time in May 1986. Seasons in the Southern Hemisphere are the reverse of those in the Northern Hemisphere, so it wouldn't make much sense to start Daylight Saving Time in April when the days are getting shorter. In Brazil, among other nations, Daylight Saving Time begins in October. Remember the adage: "A day without sunshine is like a night."

☞ ☜

**FALLACY:**   The capital of Japan was moved to Tokyo from the ancient capital, Edo.

**FACT:**   Edo, founded as a coastal village in the twelfth century and the capital of the shogunate from 1603 to 1868, became the imperial capital in 1868 and was renamed Tokyo.

☞ ☜

**FALLACY:**   Gandhi's full name was Mahatma Gandhi.

**FACT:**   *Mahatma* is not a name but a title of respect for someone with great knowledge and love of humanity. It comes from the Sanscrit *maha,* "great" plus *atma,* "life." Gandhi's full name was Mohandas Karamchand Gandhi. Born in 1869, he used passive resistance for decades to gain India's freedom from Great Britain in 1947, and was murdered by a religious fanatic in 1948.

☞ ☜

**FALLACY:**   Because the U.S. invasion of Grenada was such a small operation, no medals were awarded.

**FACT:** The entire nation of Grenada is less than half the size of New York City. According to historian Arthur Schlesinger Jr., although we never had more than 7,000 troops on that small island in that small operation, the U.S. military awarded 8,612 medals.

☞ ☜

**FALLACY:** The Tower of London is a tower.

**FACT:** The Tower of London is not a tower, but a walled fortress on the north bank of the Thames River begun by the Normans in the eleventh century. Within the fortress were built the Beauchamp tower, the Bell Tower, the Bloody Tower, the Malmsey Tower, the Wakefield Tower, and the oldest of them all, the White Tower, built in 1078. There is no tower called the Tower of London in the Tower of London.

☞ ☜

**FALLACY:** The famous photo of the raising of the American flag on Iwo Jima during World War II was of the actual event.

**FACT:** That famous photo, of the raising of the American flag on Mount Suribachi on Iwo Jima, largest of the Volcano Islands, was of a reenactment of the actual event. It was staged so that the photographer, Joe Rosenthal, could get just the right picture. Taken in March 1945, the photo won a Pulitzer Prize. Iwo Jima was returned to Japan in 1968.

☞ ☜

**FALLACY:** Japan and the United States signed a peace treaty at the end of World War II in 1945.

**FACT:** Japan surrendered on 14 August 1945. No peace treaty was signed in 1945—or in 1946, 1947, 1948, 1949, or 1950. A peace treaty was signed by Japan, the United States, and forty-seven other countries in San Francisco on 8 September 1951, restoring Japan's sovereignty as of 28 April 1952.

☞ ☜

**FALLACY:** Karachi is the capital of Pakistan.

**FACT:** Karachi, in southeastern Pakistan on the Arabian Sea near the delta of the Indus River, is the nation's largest city, its main seaport and commercial center, and the capital of Sind province. Karachi was the national capital from 1947, when Pakistan became independent, until

1959, when Rawalpindi became the capital for a transitional time. The capital of Pakistan today is the city built especially for that purpose: Islamabad.

☞ ☜

**FALLACY:**  Seoul is the oldest city in Korea.

**FACT:**  There's no denying that Seoul, the capital of South Korea, is old. It was founded in 1392 and served as the capital of the Yi dynasty until 1910—but the capital of North Korea is older. Pyongyang, which legend says was founded in 1122 B.C., served as the capital of the Chosen kingdom in the third century B.C. Pyongyang is the oldest city in Korea.

☞ ☜

**FALLACY:**  Lichtenstein is a fictional land.

**FACT:**  Lichtenstein, first name Roy, is internationally known for his American Pop Art. Liechtenstein, on the other hand, is a principality on the Rhine River, in the Alps between Austria and Switzerland. It is slightly over sixty square miles in size, making it the world's fourth-smallest country, and is so closely associated with Switzerland that its currency is the Swiss franc.

☞ ☜

**FALLACY:**  The word *England,* like the word *China,* came from the name of one of its earliest rulers.

**FACT:**  The word China did come from the name of one of its earliest rulers, Qin (Ch'in, Chin) Shihuangdi, who founded the first dynasty to rule over a united China. The word England, though, came from *Engle,* "The Angles." Those were the Angles of Anglo-Saxon fame. The Latin name for England was Anglia. England = Angland = land of the Angles.

☞ ☜

**FALLACY:**  *Mesopotamia* is an ancient Mesopotamian word whose meaning is unknown.

**FACT:**  *Mesopotamia* is a Greek word. Just as *hippopotamus* comes from Greek roots meaning "horse" and "river," *Mesopotamia* comes from Greek roots meaning "between" and "rivers." Mesopotamia is the area between the Euphrates and Tigris Rivers in what is today Iraq. It was home to the first historic civilization, Sumer, and later to Akkad, Babylonia, and Assyria.

☞ ☜

**FALLACY:**   More Cubans live in Havana than in any other metropolitan area; Santiago de Cuba is second.

**FACT:**   More Cubans live in Havana than in any other metropolitan area, and Santiago de Cuba is Cuba's second largest city. The metropolitan area with the largest Cuban population after Havana, though, is Miami, Florida.

☞ ☜

**FALLACY:**   The world's tallest manmade monument is the Great Pyramid.

**FACT:**   The world's tallest manmade monument is not the Great Pyramid of Cheops (Khufu) at Giza, which stands at 480 feet. It isn't the Washington Monument, either, although that is the world's tallest obelisk at 555 feet. The world's tallest manmade monument is the Gateway to the West arch in St. Louis, Missouri. Completed in 1965, the arch is as tall as it is wide: 630 feet.

☞ ☜

**FALLACY:**   The Nobel Prize for Peace has been awarded every year since 1901.

**FACT:**   The first Nobel Prizes were awarded in 1901 for five fields: chemistry, literature, peace, physics, and physiology or medicine. Not all prizes are awarded every year. Peace prizes were awarded from 1901 through 1913, but not from 1914 through 1916 (World War I), 1923 or 1924, 1928, 1932, 1939 through 1943 (World War II), 1955 or 1956, 1966 or 1967, or 1972. None of the five prizes has been awarded every year, but physics comes closest, skipping only 1916, 1931, 1934, and 1940 through 1942. No prizes at all were awarded from 1940 through 1942.

☞ ☜

**FALLACY:**   Oxbridge is a town in England.

**FACT:**   Oxbridge isn't a town anywhere. It's a collective term for Oxford University and Cambridge University, often referring to the academic, economic, or social atmosphere of the universities, as in "He has an Oxbridge accent."

☞ ☜

**FALLACY:** Heidelberg, Germany, was virtually destroyed by British bombers during World War II.

**FACT:** In an odd outbreak of sanity in the midst of the insanity of World War II, Britain and Germany had one very civilized agreement: the British would not bomb the university towns of Heidelberg and Göttingen, and the Germans would not bomb the university towns of Cambridge and Oxford.

☞ ☜

**FALLACY:** Palmyra is a resort island.

**FACT:** Well, there's Palmyra and then there's Palmyra; both hot, in very different ways. One was a desert oasis town northeast of Damascus, Syria, that controlled trade routes to Babylonia and the Persian Gulf. At the peak of its power in the third century, it was the most important town in the eastern part of the Roman Empire. The other is an uninhabited atoll a thousand miles south of Hawaii. It was claimed by the United States in 1912, and although privately owned, it is administered by the U.S. government. Definitely not a resort island, Palmyra since 1986 has been a nuclear waste dump.

☞ ☜

**FALLACY:** Someone is gored to death every few years during the Running of the Bulls in Pamplona, Spain.

**FACT:** Surprisingly few people have been gored to death during the annual running of the Bulls in Pamplona, Spain; in July 1995, Matthew Tassio of Illinois became the thirteenth person gored to death since 1924. The runs, which occur daily and last about two minutes, are part of the weeklong San Fermin Fiesta in July. There are sometimes hundreds of injuries, but very few of them are caused by the bulls; it's the wild partying that takes the toll. The bulls run half a mile from their pens to the city's bullring, where they are killed in bullfights that evening.

☞ ☜

**FALLACY:** The water in the Panama Canal is ocean water.

**FACT:** Not only is the water in the Panama Canal not ocean water, it isn't even salty. The canal has three pairs of locks along its fifty-one-mile length, allowing ships to go in both directions simultaneously. From Pacific to Atlantic, these are the Miraflores locks, the Pedro Miguel locks—both of which are near the Pacific end—and the Gatún locks near the Caribbean end. The Panama Canal crosses artificial lakes, the largest of which is Gatún Lake, formed by a dam on the Chagres River. It is from streams and these lakes that the canal gets its water. Fresh water flows out of the canal into the Atlantic and Pacific Oceans, not salt water into it from them. Panama takes over operational control of the Panama Canal in the year 2000.

☞ ☜

**FALLACY:** The capital of Portugal has always been in Portugal.

**FACT:** Not only has the capital of Portugal not always been in Portugal, it has not always been in Europe or even on the Eurasian continent. King João VI fled in 1807 when Portugal was successfully invaded by France during the Napoleonic Wars. In 1808 he established a new Portuguese capital at Rio de Janeiro, Brazil. When King João VI returned to Portugal in 1820 to suppress a revolution, he left his son as regent. Bad move. On 7 September 1822, his son declared Brazil independent of Portugal and himself Pedro I, emperor of Brazil.

☞ ☜

**FALLACY:** The wave of emigration from Ireland in the 1800s was caused by overpopulation.

**FACT:** The wave of emigration from Ireland in the mid-1800s was caused by a combination of *Phytopthora infestans* and greedy foreigners. *Phytopthora infestans,* a fungus better known as potato blight, struck from 1845 to 1847, virtually destroying Ireland's potato crop. The Irish had been reduced to a subsistence diet under the rule of absentee English landlords; because potatoes were the staple food of that diet, widespread starvation resulted. One million people died, and another million fled the country. Between 1845 and 1851, Ireland's population dropped by nearly one-fourth. More interested in profit than in people, the absentee landlords continued to export food from Ireland throughout the famine.

☞ ☜

**FALLACY:** Britain was the first nation to recognize the independence of the United States, after Cornwallis's surrender at Yorktown.

**FACT:** In 1781, British General Charles Cornwallis moved his 6,000 troops to Yorktown, Virginia, on Chesapeake Bay. A French fleet under François de Grasse blockaded Chesapeake Bay; 8,846 American troops under George Washington and 7,800 French troops under Rochambeau set up a land blockade. The siege began on 6 October. Cornwallis surrendered on 19 October 1781, but Britain did not recognize the United States as an independent country until well after the Treaty of Paris negotiations got underway in April 1782. An agreement was reached in November, but it wasn't signed until 3 September 1783, and it wasn't ratified by Congress until 14 January 1784. France recognized the independence of the United States on 17 December 1777, and signed a treaty of aid with the new nation on 6 February 1778.

☞ ☜

**FALLACY:** President Franklin Delano Roosevelt's getaway, Campobello, is in New York State.

**FACT:** President Franklin Delano Roosevelt's getaway, Campobello, is not in New York State, or anywhere else in the United States. Campobello, on Campobello Island, is in the Bay of Fundy off the far-eastern coast of Maine, in the Canadian province of New Brunswick.

☞ ☜

**FALLACY:** Canada's largest metropolitan area is its capital, Ottawa.

**FACT:** Ottawa is Canada's capital, but not its largest metropolitan area. The Ottawa-Hull metropolitan area has a population of about 920,000. Vancouver has a population of about 1.6 million. Montreal has a population of about 3.1 million. Toronto, Canada's largest metropolitan area, has a population of about 3.8 million. Ottawa-Hull is Canada's fourth-largest metropolitan area.

☞ ☜

**FALLACY:** The world's longest railway is the Orient Express.

**FACT:** The Orient Express made its first run in 1883. Although it is a train rather than a railway, its route is indeed long, running between Paris and Istanbul, Turkey. The world's longest railway, though, is the Trans-Siberian Railway. Construction started in 1891 and was completed with a link around Lake Baikal in the year of the Russian Revolution, 1917. The Trans-Siberian Railway runs 5,800 miles between Moscow in the west and Vladivostok on the Sea of Japan.

☞ ☜

**FALLACY:** Tobago and Trinidad are two of the smallest nations in the Caribbean.

**FACT:** There is no nation of Tobago in the Caribbean, and no nation of Trinidad. These two West Indies islands near Venezuela's northeast coast were combined politically in 1888 and gained independence from Britain on 31 August 1962. In 1976 the nation became a republic with the official name Republic of Trinidad and Tobago.

☞ ☜

**FALLACY:** The European headquarters of the United Nations is in Brussels, Belgium.

**FACT:** The European headquarters of the United Nations is not in Belgium, or in any other member country of the United Nations. It is located in Geneva. Switzerland, because of its historical neutrality when it comes to the affairs of other countries, has not joined the United Nations.

☞ ☜

**FALLACY:** The United States has a larger population than Uruguay, but Uruguay has a larger population than any single U.S. state.

**FACT:** California has a larger population than Uruguay. New York has a larger population than Uruguay. Indiana has a larger population than Uruguay. Uruguay does have a larger population than Delaware, Kansas, or Rhode Island. To put things in perspective, Uruguay has a population of about 3.2 million; Los Angeles has a population of about 3.5 million.

☞ ☜

**FALLACY:** The world's smallest republic is Vatican City.

**FACT:** Vatican City is not a republic; its system of government might best be described as a theocratic monarchy. Until 1968, the world's smallest republic was twenty-four-square-mile San Marino, in central Italy, known officially as Serenissima Repubblica di San Marino (Most Serene Republic of San Marino). On 31 January 1968, Nauru, an eight-square-mile island just south of the Equator in the western Pacific Ocean, became an independent republic—and the world's smallest.

☞ ☜

**FALLACY:** The Eiffel Tower, although massive, is not notably tall.

**FACT:** The Eiffel Tower, designed and built by Alexandre Gustave Eiffel, was begun in 1887. It opened in 1889, which was fortunate because it was built for the Paris Exhibition of 1889. The open iron framework on four huge masonry piers sits by the River Seine on the Champs de Mars. Not only is it massive, it is 300 meters (984 feet) tall. Take note of that notable height. The Eiffel Tower was the tallest building in the world from 1889 until 1930.

☞ ☜

**FALLACY:** Istanbul's original name was Constantinople.

**FACT:** Istanbul, Turkey's largest city and main seaport, was originally named neither Constantinople nor Istanbul. It wasn't until 1930 that its official name became Istanbul, changing it from Constantinople. Constantine, emperor of the Eastern Roman Empire, had modestly named it after himself in the year 330. Now the capital of Istanbul Province in northwestern Turkey and spread to both sides of the Bosporus Strait, it was founded on the western side in 660 B.C. by the Greeks; the inlet that forms Istanbul's harbor is called the Golden Horn. The city's original name was Byzantium.

☞ ☜

**FALLACY:** The Aswan Dam on the Nile River was completed in 1970.

**FACT:** The Aswan Dam on the Nile River was completed in 1902 and enlarged in 1934. The Aswan High Dam, south of the Aswan Dam, was completed in 1970. The Aswan High Dam is 375 feet high and 11,811 feet wide, creating a reservoir called Lake Nasser.

☞ ☜

**FALLACY:** The correct name for Niagra Falls is Horseshoe Falls.

**FACT:** There are several correct names for the falls. The Niagara River falls from Lake Erie to Lake Ontario at the Canadian–U.S. border, between Niagara Falls, New York, and Niagara Falls, Ontario, creating Niagara Falls. The river is split by Goat Island into two waterfalls, officially named American Falls and Canadian Falls; because of its shape, Canadian Falls is popularly known as Horseshoe Falls. The Niagara River between the two Great Lakes was created about 10,000 years ago when the North American ice sheet began to melt; as the river eroded away soft stone, the falls were formed. Because the vast majority of the river's water flows over Horseshoe Falls, it is eroding upstream much faster than is American Falls.

☞ ☜

**FALLACY:** "Hawaii" is the modern name given to the islands by Europeans.

**FACT:** Hawaii is the name given to the islands by Polynesians, who arrived there more than 1,250 years ago. The English sailors who arrived about 215 years ago named them the Sandwich Islands, not because they thought that the natives were cannibals, but in honor of the Earl of Sandwich who was, not coincidentally, the first lord of the admiralty at the time.

☞ ☜

**FALLACY:** "Mutton Snappers" is an impolite nickname for the fancy-dress guards at Buckingham Palace.

**FACT:** The fancy-dress guards at Buckingham Palace are called "Beefeaters," which historically was an impolite reference to the fact that they were well-fed policemen for the rich while the rest of the citizenry went hungry. Beefeaters in the fifteenth century, and in the twentieth, are not only Yeomen of the Guard at Buckingham Palace, but also Warders of the Tower of London. Mutton Snappers are a whole different kettle of fish. Specifically, they're *Lutjanus analis,* denizens of the western Atlantic Ocean, available in your local fish store as snappers.

☞ ☜

**FALLACY:** Australia's original settlers were British prisoners.

**FACT:** Australia's original British settlers, most of them prisoners being exiled from Great Britain, arrived in 1788. That made them about 50,000 years too late to be Australia's original settlers. The ancestors of the people often called Aborigines, but many of whom call themselves Koori, arrived on the continent long before there was a Britain, great or otherwise.

☞ ☜

**FALLACY:**   Indira Gandhi and Golda Meir were the first democratically elected female heads of state.

**FACT:**   Both Indira Gandhi and Golda Meir were prime ministers, not heads of state; they were appointed to the post of prime minister, not elected. The first democratically elected female head of state was Vigdis Finnbogadóttir, elected president of Iceland in 1980.

☞ ☜

**FALLACY:**   In World War II, the Allies' D-Day landing sites were code named Omaha Beach and Utah Beach.

**FACT:**   On 6 June 1944, in a campaign code named Operation Overlord, an Allied force of 130,000 landed on the coast of Normandy, France. Five landing sites were designated along a fifty-mile stretch of coast. The beaches assigned to British and Canadian forces were code named Gold, Juno, and Sword; the beaches assigned to U.S. forces were code named Omaha and Utah.

☞ ☜

**FALLACY:**   Greenland is a Danish colony.

**FACT:**   Greenland became a Danish colony in 1721. On 1 May 1979, however, it was granted home rule. Greenlanders elect their own Provincial Council, which in turn sends two members to the Danish Parliament. Another thing that changed when Greenland came under home rule was it dropped the name Greenland. Its official name since then has been Kalaallit Nunaat; now you know why many people still call it Greenland. Kalaallit Nunaat's capital is Nuuk.

☞ ☜

**FALLACY:**   The islands of Sardinia and Corsica are part of Italy.

**FACT:**   Sardinia is more than twice as large as Corsica, and more than twice as far from the Italian mainland; Sardinia is part of Italy. Corsica is about twice as far from the French mainland as it is from the Italian mainland; Corsica is part of France.

☞ ☜

**FALLACY:**   Dublin is the Irish name for Ireland's capital.

**FACT:**   Dublin is the English name for Ireland's capital. The Irish Gaelic name of this largest city in Ireland, located at the mouth of the River

Liffey (River of Life) on the coast of the Irish Sea, is Baile Átha Cliath. The English name of the country is Ireland; the Irish name is Eire.

☞ ☜

**FALLACY:**  Auschwitz is in Germany.

**FACT:**  Auschwitz, site of the infamous Nazi extermination camp, was never in Germany and is nowhere anymore. The name was changed to Oswiecim. Oswiecim is west of Cracow in southwestern Poland.

☞ ☜

**FALLACY:**  The scarlet costumes worn by English fox hunters are called their hunting scarlets.

**FACT:**  The scarlet costumes worn by English fox hunters are called their hunting pinks. They're named not for their color, but for a London tailor named Pink who designed them. Oscar Wilde's description of fox hunting: "The English country gentleman galloping after a fox—the unspeakable in full pursuit of the uneatable."

☞ ☜

**FALLACY:**  The Amazon River was named for a South American tribe of women warriors.

**FACT:**  The Amazon River was named for a tribe of women warriors, but they didn't live on that continent, or in the 1500s when the river received that name. A Spanish explorer fighting native people along the river noted that the women fought along with the men, and he named it the Amazon River because of a Greek myth he'd learned back in Spain. In Greek mythology, the Amazons were a nation of female warriors who removed their right breasts so they wouldn't interfere with archery or swordplay. Don't know what left-handers did, but this is definitely worse than cutting off your nose to spite your face.

☞ ☜

**FALLACY:**  Thanks to new laws, most of the world's major cities now meet the minimum clean-air standard of the United Nations World Health Organization.

**FACT:**  Would that that were true. The fact is that of the world's cities with the highest populations, not one of the top twenty meets the World Health Organization's minimum clean-air standard.

☞ ☜

**FALLACY:** Turquoise is found only in Mexico and the southwestern United States.

**FACT:** Turquoise, which is basically copper and aluminum, was known in Old French as *la pierre turqueise,* "Turkish stone." That's where the name comes from. Whether the stone first came from Turkey or just passed through Turkey on its way to Europe, nobody knows.

☞ ☜

**FALLACY:** The stones that make up London's Tower Bridge were moved to Arizona and reassembled there.

**FACT:** Tower Bridge, named for the nearby Tower of London, is still in London. The bridge moved to Lake Havasu City, Arizona, and officially opened there in 1971, was London Bridge. Moving the stones of Tower Bridge somewhere else and reassembling them wouldn't be of much use. The stones are just a facade to make the bridge, which was opened in 1894, look like an ancient stone bridge. The functional bridge itself, cloaked by the stonework, consists of a steel frame and steel cables.

☞ ☜

**FALLACY:** The Chinese have less trouble with duplicate names because they put the family name first.

**FACT:** In official lists, almost everyone puts the family name first. That doesn't help much if both the family name and the personal name are common. There are just as many *Johnson, Williams* in Bakersfield or Baltimore or Boise as there are *William Johnsons.* According to a recent census in Beijing, there were 13,000 *Wang Shuzhens,* and there would have been just as many *Shuzhen, Wangs.*

☞ ☜

**FALLACY:** Bermuda is the main island of the Bahamas.

**FACT:** The Bahamas include about 700 islands and 2,000 islets extending more than 750 miles from the southeastern coast of Florida southeast to Hispaniola. Over 75 percent of the more than 250,000 inhabitants live on either Grand Bahama or New Providence. Columbus first landed in the Western Hemisphere on San Salvador (Watling) Island, which was inhabited by the Arawak. Colonized by Britain in 1647, the Bahamas became a British Crown Colony in 1717. Since 1973, however, it has been an independent country, with its capital at Nassau on New Providence; the other major city is Freeport, on Grand Bahama. The official name of the country is Commonwealth of the Bahamas. Bermuda is a self-governing British dependency made up of several hundred small coral islands, about 575 miles east of Cape Hatteras, North Carolina. The capital is Hamilton, on Great Bermuda, the largest of the twenty inhabited islands.

☞ ☜

**FALLACY:**   Brazil is the only Latin American nation where Spanish is not the common language.

**FACT:**   The common language in eighteen Latin American countries is Spanish. Brazil, where Portuguese is the common language, is not the only exception, however. The "Latin" in Latin America refers to languages that developed from Latin. The common language in Haiti is French. Other countries south of the United States, although they are not Latin American nations, also have a common language other than Spanish: Belize, Jamaica, Guyana, and Trinidad and Tobago, for example, where the common language is English. In Suriname, the common language is Dutch.

☞ ☜

**FALLACY:**   The permanent members of the United Nations Security Council are Britain, France, Germany, Russia, and the United States.

**FACT:**   The United Nations Security Council consists of fifteen members, ten of which are elected by the General Assembly. The other five members of the Security Council are permanent members. Because the composition of the Security Council was determined in 1945 at the end of World War II, two of the world's current major economic powers, Germany and Japan, were not included as permanent members. The permanent members are Britain, China, France, Russia (which took the seat of the Soviet Union), and the United States. Procedural matters can be passed by a vote of any nine of the fifteen members. For all other matters, those nine votes must include all five permanent members; this is the "veto power" of the permanent members.

☞ ☜

**FALLACY:**   The tunnel under the English Channel, nicknamed the Chunnel, is the world's longest railroad tunnel.

**FACT:**   One portal of the Channel Tunnel is at Cheriton, near Folkestone, England; the other portal is at Fréthun, near Calais, France. The distance between the two portals is 31 miles, with 24 of those miles underwater. That's long, but not long enough to be the longest. The world's longest railroad tunnel is the Seikan Rail Tunnel between the Japanese islands of Honshu and Hokkaido; total length is 33.5 miles, with 14.5 of them underwater beneath the Tsugaru Strait. The Chunnel does, however, include the world's longest *underwater* railroad tunnel.

☞ ☜

**FALLACY:**   Rio de Janeiro is Brazil's capital and largest city.

**FACT:**   Official name of the country is República Federativa do Brasil (Federative Republic of Brazil). Rio de Janeiro (River of January), on the Atlantic coast's Guanabara Bay, is neither Brazil's capital nor its largest city. Since 1960 the capital has been inland on the central plateau: the federal district of Brasília, with a population of about 2 million. Rio de Janeiro has a population of about 10 million. São Paulo, with a population of about 15 million, is Brazil's largest city.

☞ ☜

**FALLACY:**   The German town of Baden-Baden was given that name because of the bad-water springs nearby.

**FACT:**   The town of Baden-Baden in southwestern Germany, in the state of Baden-Württemberg near the French border, was established in the third century as a Roman garrison town. Located in the Rhine River Valley, on the edge of the Black Forest, Baden-Baden has for centuries been among Europe's most popular spas because of its warm mineral springs. It was indeed named for its waters, but they aren't bad: the German verb *Baden* translates into English as "bathe." Don't forget to wash between your ears.

# 8

# Language

**FALLACY:**  The word *capella* means singing without a band.

**FACT:**  Capella is a double star in the constellation Auriga, approximately forty-six light-years from Earth. The name is the diminutive of the Latin word *caper,* "goat." All things considered, saying that someone was singing like a goat might not be taken kindly. *A cappella,* on the other hand, means singing not just without a band but without any musical accompaniment at all.

**FALLACY:**  A bugbear is a small species of bear.

**FACT:**  A bugbear is a bugaboo, an imaginary and frightening creature. Typical use of a bugbear is when foolish adults tell children: "If you aren't good, the boogeyman will get you." As anyone who remembers childhood knows, children already have enough fears to deal with.

**FALLACY:**  Jason and the Argonauts sailed on the *Argos.*

**FACT:**  They would have to have been flea-sized people. In the Greek legend, Jason and the Argonauts went looking for the golden fleece on a ship named the *Argo,* hence the name Argonauts. Argos was Odysseus's dog in Homer's *The Odyssey.*

**FALLACY:**  Hippies of the 1960s made up the word *OM* for chanting; it doesn't actually mean anything.

**FACT:**  Well, for one thing it actually means a river in Russia that joins the Irtysh River at Omsk. Far older than the name of the Om River, or the 1960s, is the Sanscrit syllable *om,* made up of the three sounds *a, u,* and *m,* and therefore sometimes spelled *aum.* In Hindu religious tradition that syllable was used as a mantra to begin and end prayers, to aid in contemplation of reality, and to invoke supernatural power. When drawn out, the *m* sound sets up a resonance in the human head, which may be why so many heads enjoy it.

☞ ☜

**FALLACY:**  The word *booze* comes from E. G. Booze, a Philadelphia distiller in the 1800s.

**FACT:**  Although there was a Philadelphia distiller by the name of E. G. Booze in the 1800s, the best bet is that the modern English word *booze* comes from the older word *bouse,* also meaning liquor. *Bouse* came from Middle English *bousen,* meaning to drink to excess, which came from Middle Dutch *busen.* This information should win you a free drink on a bar bet.

☞ ☜

**FALLACY:**  Although rivers sometimes meander, the word *meander* has nothing specific to do with rivers.

**FACT:**  The spelling of the word has meandered over time as much as the river that was its source. The ancient Greeks took note of a wandering river in Phrygia, Asia Minor, and called it *Maiandros,* which turned up in Latin as *Maeander,* which is where we got the word *meander.* The name of the river has kept on meandering and is now *Menderes.*

☞ ☜

**FALLACY:**  Clothing that comes in twos, such as pants and socks, is called "a pair of."

**FACT:**  Some is, but not all. Panties and shoes and earmuffs and shorts are called "a pair of." Coming from a root word which means "upper arms," though, a brassiere is surprisingly singular.

☞ ☜

**FALLACY:**  Anything that has buoyancy will float on water.

**FACT:**  It depends on the type of buoyancy. Put something underwater and let go. If it has positive buoyancy, it will rise; if it has neutral buoyancy, it will stay where it is; if it has negative buoyancy, it will sink. Buoyancy counts in air, too; a lead balloon, for example, has negative buoyancy.

☞ ☜

**FALLACY:** In Louisiana, a Cajun is someone whose ancestors were French or Spanish colonial settlers along the Gulf Coast.

**FACT:** In Louisiana, a Creole—not a Cajun—is someone whose ancestors were French or Spanish colonial settlers along the Gulf Coast or in the West Indies. A Cajun, coming from the other direction, is someone whose ancestors were settlers from the French colony of Acadia, Canada. The British took over Canada after the French and Indian Wars, and expelled many of the French between 1755 and 1758. Much of what was Acadia is now Nova Scotia.

☞ ☜

**FALLACY:** *Fauna* is the plural of *faunus.*

**FACT:** Fauna refers to a complete group of animals, such as the fauna of Australia or the fauna of the Cretaceous period; the similar word for plants is flora. Both flora and fauna are plural; neither has a singular. Linnaeus chose the words from Roman mythology. Fauna was the sister of Faunus, the god of animals who was half human and half goat; Flora was the goddess of flowers.

☞ ☜

**FALLACY:** Capital C or small c, calorie is a Calorie is a calorie.

**FACT:** What a difference a C makes. A calorie, also called a gram calorie, is the amount of energy needed to raise the temperature of one gram of water by one degree Celsius. In the International System, one calorie is 4.187 joules. A Calorie, also called a kilogram calorie or a kilocalorie, is 1,000 calories. It's the capital-C Calorie that Calorie counters count so carefully, but in common usage it's not capitalized.

☞ ☜

**FALLACY:** The expression "It worked like a charm" means something worked very well.

**FACT:**  That's what people generally mean when they use that expression, but think about it: charms don't work.

☞ ☜

**FALLACY:**  Concrete and cement are different words for the same thing.

**FACT:**  You make cement without concrete, but you don't make concrete without cement. Cement is a cooked combination of limestone and clay. Add water, sand, and gravel to cement and you have concrete.

☞ ☜

**FALLACY:**  The word *deadline* came from the fact that if your project hadn't crossed the line by that time, it was dead.

**FACT:**  That would be bad enough, but the word deadline actually came from the fact that if *you* crossed that line, *you* were dead. It was originally a boundary line around or within prisons. Prisoners who crossed the line were shot. Writers sometimes feel that the original meaning hasn't changed much.

☞ ☜

**FALLACY:**  Denim was named by Levi Strauss, who invented that type of cloth.

**FACT:**  Denim was named long before Levi Strauss made his first pair of Levi's, which were pants made of heavy denim. Denim is a type of twilled serge cloth. The southern French city of Nîmes became so famous for making this type of serge that the cloth became known as *serge de Nîmes,* "serge from Nîmes." Over time that became shortened to "de Nîmes," and then to "denim."

☞ ☜

**FALLACY:**  The word *dingbat* was invented by the writers of the TV show *All in the Family.*

**FACT:**  There were dingbats before Archie called Edith that. Use of the word goes back to at least 1901, when it meant a typographical symbol or ornament such as * or #. Other meanings include a scatterbrained person (a.k.a. a ding-a-ling), a thrown object, and a whatchamacallit.

☞ ☜

**FALLACY:**  *Fahrenheit* is a German word meaning "temperature."

**FACT:** Fahrenheit is definitely a German word. The Fahrenheit temperature scale was named after the German physicist who invented it, Gabriel Daniel Fahrenheit. Gesundheit, Gabe.

☞ ☜

**FALLACY:** A hush puppy is a quiet dog.

**FACT:** A hush puppy, or hushpuppy, is a ball of cornmeal dough fried in deep fat, popular in the South. Origin of the term is unknown, but it likely comes from the fact that more than one hushpuppy has been given to a loud dog with the admonition, "Hush, puppy!"

☞ ☜

**FALLACY:** Fluorescence is the modern word for what used to be called phosphorescence.

**FACT:** A fluorescent bulb is not a phosphorescent bulb. Fluorescence refers to the emission of electromagnetic radiation, such as light, by a substance that is absorbing energy. When the energy source is removed—turning off the electricity to a fluorescent bulb, for example—fluorescence ends. Phosphorescence, on the other hand, refers to the emission of light even after the energy source—usually light—has been removed. A common phrase for phosphorescence is "glow-in-the-dark."

☞ ☜

**FALLACY:** *Fragile, fragible,* and *frangible* mean the same thing.

**FACT:** Two of those are words; fragible is not. *Fragile* means both breakable and delicate; spun glass is fragile. *Frangible* means breakable, but not fragile; most children's toys are frangible.

☞ ☜

**FALLACY:** San Francisco's Golden Gate was named that because it was the gateway to the gold fields.

**FACT:** Gold was discovered at John Augustus Sutter's mill in 1848; because it took a while for news to travel in those days, the California Gold Rush began the following year with the '49ers. The entrance into San Francisco Bay, now spanned by the Golden Gate Bridge, was named the Golden Gate by John C. Fremont in 1846, two years before the gold fields were discovered. It reminded him of the Golden Horn, an inlet of the Bosporus Strait in northwestern Turkey that forms the harbor for Istanbul.

☞ ☜

**FALLACY:** Aside from infinity, which is not a number, the largest number with a name is a googol.

**FACT:** A googol is $10^{100}$: the number 1 followed by 100 zeros. A septendecillion is $10^{102}$: the number 1 followed by 102 zeros. An octodecillion is $10^{108}$; a novemdecillion is $10^{114}$; a vigintillion is $10^{120}$. A centillion is $10^{600}$: the number 1 followed by 600 zeros. A googolplex is $10^{googol}$: the number 1 followed by $10^{100}$ zeros.

☞ ☜

**FALLACY:** Hansom cabs, invented in New York City, were originally called handsome cabs.

**FACT:** Although hansoms, also called hansom cabs, are best known from New York City's Central Park, they weren't invented in that city. A hansom is a two-wheeled, covered, horse-drawn carriage with the driver's seat elevated behind the passenger area, giving the passengers a clear view ahead. It was invented in the mid-1800s by London architect Joseph Aloysius Hansom.

☞ ☜

**FALLACY:** An organism with the sexual characteristics of both sexes can be called either a hemimorphite or a hermaphrodite.

**FACT:** An organism with the sexual characteristics of both sexes is a hermaphrodite. Hermaphroditus was the son of Hermes and Aphrodite; he and the nymph Salmacis ended up sharing one body. Hemimorphite is a mineral, $Zn_4Si_2O_7(OH)_2 \bullet H_2O$, one of the zinc ores. A more common name for hemimorphite is calamine, as in "an ocean of calamine lotion."

☞ ☜

**FALLACY:** *Admiral* was originally a French word.

**FACT:** The English did get the word from French, but it didn't originate there. The French got the word from Latin, but it didn't originate there, either. The Romans got the word from Arabic *'amir a 'ali,* "high commander."

☞ ☜

**FALLACY:**   A hogshead is exactly that, the head of a hog.

**FACT:**   A hogshead is exactly that, but it is not the head of a hog. The head of a hog is a hog's head. A hogshead is a unit of volume, anywhere from sixty-three to 140 gallons depending on whom you ask. The most common hogshead in the United States is sixty-three gallons. A barrel that holds a hogshead also is called a hogshead, showing a higher regard for truth-in-advertising than the ten-gallon hat.

☞ ☜

**FALLACY:**   The prefix *in,* as in "inactive," means "not."

**FACT:**   That's what *in* means in "inactive," and in "inadequate," "incapable," "incredible," and "indirect." That's not what it means, though, in "inflammable," "infuriate," "initiate," "inside," or "intestine." The incompatibility between those lists may inchoately appear incomprehensible, but it's indisputable.

☞ ☜

**FALLACY:**   *Cab* is a shortened form of *taxicab.*

**FACT:**   That's putting the cart before the horse; *cab* came first. The English word was derived from the French *cabriolet,* a one-horse, two-wheeled, two-seat carriage with a folding top. The trail from there leads back through Italian to the Latin word *caper,* "goat," which some modern taxicabs smell like. Where did *taxicab* come in? It's a shortened form of *taximeter cab,* a cab equipped with a meter to compute the fare (tax).

☞ ☜

**FALLACY:**   You can use a question mark at the end of a sentence, or you can use an exclamation point, but you can't use both.

**FACT:**   You can use whatever you want—it's a free country. Strict grammarians may want to limit you to either a *?* or an *!* at the end of a sentence, but some statements seem to require both. "You're going to do what" obviously needs a question mark, but "You're going to do WHAT" also needs an exclamation point. Many of us would use both, but that leaves the problem of whether to put the *?* or the *!* first. There is now a punctuation mark, called an interrobang, which solves the problem: "You're going to do what?"

☞ ☜

**FALLACY:** Lord Kelvin's family name was Kelvin.

**FACT:** Aristocracies are almost as strange as people who consider themselves aristocrats. "Lord Kelvin," a major nineteenth-century researcher in the field of thermodynamics, gave us the Kelvin temperature scale. The man's title was Lord Kelvin; his name was William Thomson.

☞ ☜

**FALLACY:** A maelstrom is a violent storm.

**FACT:** A maelstrom is not a storm, violent, or otherwise. *Maelstrom* comes from Dutch words for "grinding/whirling stream," and means a large, powerful, violent whirlpool that draws in such things as people and ships.

☞ ☜

**FALLACY:** At its root, the word *democracy* means "mob rule."

**FACT:** At its root, the word *democracy* means "rule by the people." The root word of democracy is the Greek *demos,* "people." The root word of ochlocracy, sometimes called mobocracy or mob rule, is the Greek *okhlos,* "crowd" or "mob."

☞ ☜

**FALLACY:** Morse code has all the letters of the alphabet, but the only punctuation code is the word *stop.*

**FACT:** In addition to all the letters of the alphabet, Morse code has codes for accented letters in French, German, and Spanish; it also has codes for each number from 0 through 9. Among the punctuation codes available are:

| | |
|---|---|
| colon | − − − • • • |
| comma | − − • • − − |
| hyphen | − • • • • − |
| period | • − • − • − |
| question mark | • • − − • • |
| semicolon | − • − • − • |

☞ ☜

**FALLACY:** *Libel* and *slander* are different words for the same thing.

**FACT:** Libel and slander are different words because they mean different things. *Libel* refers to publication of false information about someone that maliciously damages their reputation; *slander* refers to oral communication of false information about someone.

☞ ☜

**FALLACY:** *Odds and ends,* like *flotsam and jetsam,* are different.

**FACT:** Flotsam and jetsam are different. Flotsam is floating debris from a shipwreck or sunken ship; jetsam is material that has been thrown overboard—jettisoned. Odds and ends are a different matter. Imagine a box of odds and ends. Remove one item, then another, then another, until there's only one item left in the box. Is it an odd or an end? The fact is, it isn't either. *Odds and ends* is a plural noun, not two plural nouns.

☞ ☜

**FALLACY:** A palindrome is a ten-letter word, *palindrome* being a perfect example.

**FACT:** Palindrome is not a palindrome, but the number of letters in it has nothing to do with that fact. A palindrome is a word, phrase, or sentence spelled the same way from the left or the right. The word "madam," for example, or the apocryphal comment from Napoleon referring to his place of exile: "Able was I ere I saw Elba."

☞ ☜

**FALLACY:** Hogwash, literally, is what hogs are washed with.

**FACT:** Washing hogs with hogwash wouldn't do much for getting them clean. Hogwash, literally, is garbage fed to hogs, also called slop or swill. Figuratively, hogwash is balderdash or nonsense; a political speech, for example.

☞ ☜

**FALLACY:** The word *pencil* is derived from the word *pen.*

**FACT:** The word pencil is not derived from the word pen; the words come from completely different roots. Pen comes from the Latin *penna,* "feather." Pencil comes from the Latin *penis,* "brush," "penis," or "tail."

☞ ☜

**FALLACY:**   The original Pennsylvania Dutch were Dutch.

**FACT:**   German-speaking immigrants from Germany and Switzerland settled in Pennsylvania during the seventeenth and eighteenth centuries. The German word for German is *Deutsch,* which is how they became known as the Pennsylvania Dutch. Not a wooden shoe or a tulip among them.

☞ ☜

**FALLACY:**   The study of pens, from fountain pens to ballpoints, is called penology.

**FACT:**   The study of pens, from fountain pens to ballpoints, is called the study of pens. Penology, from the Greek *poine,* "penalty," is the study of prisons. Not by coincidence, another of our words also derives from *poine:* pain.

☞ ☜

**FALLACY:**   Mocha, as a name for coffee, was invented by jazz musicians in the 1920s.

**FACT:**   Mocha, as a name for coffee, was invented centuries before the 1920s. It refers specifically to a rich, dark, pungent, high-quality Arabian coffee. A flavoring made from very strong coffee mixed with cocoa or chocolate also is called mocha. The name comes from the town of Mocha, Yemen. The modern Monday-morning instruction is: "Instant human: just add coffee."

☞ ☜

**FALLACY:**   Anyone who can read English can figure out Old English.

**FACT:**   Old English, the Germanic-based English language from the mid-fifth century until the Norman Conquest, was the language of the Anglo-Saxons. It has nothing to do with such modern concoctions as "Ye Olde English Shoppe." The most famous work written in Old English is the 3,182-line epic poem *Beowulf,* composed about the eighth century. Here's a selection translated into modern English:

> Also he saw a standard worked in gold hanging high over the hoard,
> greatest of hand-made wonders, woven by skill of limbs.

Here's the same selection—lacking one letter that doesn't exist in modern English—in Old English:

> Swylce he siomian geseah segn eall-gylden heah ofer horde,
> hond-wundor maest gelocen leoo-craeftum.

Anyone who can read English can figure out Old English?

☞ ☜

**FALLACY:**  A red drum is a drum.

**FACT:**  A red drum, known to its friends as *Sciaenops ocellata,* is a fish found in the waters off the east coast of North America. Other names for red drum are channel bass and redfish. According to those who have tasted it, it can't be beat.

☞ ☜

**FALLACY:**  The Roaring Forties came after the Gay Nineties and the Roaring Twenties.

**FACT:**  The Gay Nineties and the Roaring Twenties got their names from the spirit of those decades. The most significant event of the 1940s was World War II. The Roaring Forties, in fact, don't refer to the calendar at all. Strong prevailing winds called the westerlies occur in both the Northern Hemisphere and the Southern Hemisphere, between latitudes 30° and 60°. They're stronger in the Southern Hemisphere because there is more open ocean there, and they're strongest of all between the latitudes 40° and 50°—the Roaring Forties.

☞ ☜

**FALLACY:**  *Sacher torte* is a legal term referring to a specific type of wrongful act.

**FACT:**  Sacher torte is a culinary term referring specifically to an apricot-jam-filled chocolate cake with chocolate icing. The name comes from *Sacher,* an Austrian family who ran restaurants, and *torte,* a cake made with a lot of eggs. The legal term is *tort.*

☞ ☜

**FALLACY:**  A presbyope is an official of the Presbyterian Church.

**FACT:**  There's no reason why a presbyope couldn't be an official of the Presbyterian Church, but there's no connection between the two. A presbyope is someone with presbyopia, a common condition of the eye often first noticed in middle age. As the lens becomes increasingly less elastic, a person finds it increasingly difficult to focus on nearby objects such as reading material. "My eyes are fine, it's just that my arms are too short."

☞ ☜

**FALLACY:**   SASE is an acronym for Send A Stamped Envelope.

**FACT:**   No, and it doesn't stand for Self-Absorbed Stomped Elephant, either. SASE stands for Self-Addressed Stamped Envelope. FUBAR and SNAFU are also acronyms; in polite company they stand for Fouled Up Beyond All Recognition, and Situation Normal—All Fouled Up.

☞ ☜

**FALLACY:**   *Scotophobia* is a fear of Scots.

**FACT:**   Even Scotsmen and Scotswomen sometimes suffer from scotophobia, but that doesn't mean that they're afraid of themselves. Scotophobia is fear of darkness; the word comes from the Greek *skotos,* "darkness." Most Scots, by the way, don't use the adjective "Scotch" when referring to themselves. It's an English contraction of "Scottish" that so distresses some Scots that it sends them in search of a drop of Scotch whiskey.

☞ ☜

**FALLACY:**   *Archimedean screw* is a vulgar expression that has nothing to do with Archimedes.

**FACT:**   An Archimedean screw would be out of place in a magazine called *Sex for Fun and Profit.* Also known as Archimedes' screw, it is a simple mechanical device used for raising water. Think of a large screw inside a tight-fitting cylinder, with the bottom end of the cylinder in a river. As the screw is turned, water is raised to the top of the cylinder by the spiral threads. Must have been a good invention; it's been in use since it was invented by Archimedes in the third century B.C.

☞ ☜

**FALLACY:**   The obverse side of a coin is the back side.

**FACT:**   The obverse side of a coin is the front side: the side with the main picture or design. The back side is called the reverse. When flipping a coin, heads is the same as obverse, and tails is the same as reverse.

☞ ☜

**FALLACY:** *Kick over the traces* means to hide the traces of a crime.

**FACT:** Kicking something over the traces of a crime would help to hide them, but the phrase "kick over the traces" has nothing to do with hiding the crimes of two-footed animals. Traces are side straps that connect a draft animal to a vehicle. The word comes from Latin *tractus,* which comes from *trahere,* "to haul." To kick over the traces means to break free of restraints.

☞ ☜

**FALLACY:** President Harry Truman originated the expression, "If you can't stand the heat, get out of the kitchen."

**FACT:** President Truman did say, "If you can't stand the heat, get out of the kitchen," but he didn't originate the expression. It was said *to* President Truman by another Harry, his old friend Harry Vaughan. Truman used the expression as his reason for not running for reelection in 1952. A memorandum he wrote to himself on 16 April 1950 probably comes closer to the true reason he refused to run:

> In my opinion eight years as President is enough and sometimes too much for any man to serve in that capacity. There is a lure in power. It can get into a man's blood just as gambling and lust for money have been known to do.

☞ ☜

**FALLACY:** *Grog,* the name of an alcoholic drink, is a shortened form of the word *groggy.*

**FACT:** In 1740, a British admiral named Edward Vernon ordered that watered rum be served to his sailors. Because Vernon frequently wore a grogram cloak, his nickname was Old Grog. That's where grog got its name. *Groggy,* which came from *grog,* is what you become if you drink too much watered rum.

☞ ☜

**FALLACY:** *Tyrannosaurus rex* is the Latin name of that dinosaur.

**FACT:** The people who named that carnivorous dinosaur of the Cretaceous period may have had one too many literary libations, because they came up with a mixed-language name. *Tyrannosaurus* comes from the Greek words for "tyrant" and "lizard." *Rex* is the Latin word for "king."

☞ ☜

**FALLACY:** A tepee, also called a wickiup or a wigwam, is covered with hides.

**FACT:** Although similar, a tepee, a wickiup, and a wigwam are not the same. Native Americans of the Great Plains used tepees, cone-shaped tents of hides. Wickiups, frame huts oval at the bottom and covered with mats of grass or reeds or other vegetation, were used as temporary shelters by nomadic peoples in the dry West and Southwest. Wigwams, arched frameworks of poles covered with bark, hides, or mats, were used from the Great Lakes eastward.

☞ ☜

**FALLACY:** A woodwind instrument, by definition, must be made of wood.

**FACT:** Many woodwind instruments, such as bassoons, clarinets, and oboes, are made of wood; many flutes, which are woodwinds, are not. Recorders, also woodwind instruments, are often made of plastic, and saxophones are always made of metal.

☞ ☜

**FALLACY:** *Zymurgy* is the last word in the dictionary.

**FACT:** Depends entirely upon the dictionary. The last word in the 1993 *Merriam Webster's Collegiate Dictionary* is "zymosan." The last word in the 1992 *American Heritage Dictionary of the English Language* is "zyzzyva." Those are the last defined words, but there are sections following the main part of the dictionaries. The actual last words in each of those dictionaries, not counting the covers, are, respectively, "Massachusetts" and "London."

☞ ☜

**FALLACY:** The name *Podunk* was made up by comedians to mean any small, isolated town or region.

**FACT:** The name Podunk was not made up by comedians to mean any small, isolated town or region. There are two very real such places in New England, one in Connecticut and the other in Massachusetts. The word is of Algonquin origin.

☞ ☜

**FALLACY:** Currants—used in desserts, drinks, jams, and jellies—got their name from a Native American word.

**FACT:** The origin of our word "currant" goes back a long way, through Middle English to Anglo-Norman to Latin to Greek. The Greeks called the city-state of Corinth *Korinthos*, the Romans called it *Corinthus*, in Anglo-Norman it was *Corauntz*, and in Middle English it was *Coraunte*. In languages before modern English the fruits of the plant were called "raisins of Corinth," which became shortened to our current "currant."

☞ ☜

**FALLACY:** The apex of a pyramid is the point opposite to its vertex.

**FACT:** The apex of a pyramid is its highest point. The vertex of a pyramid is its highest point. With pyramids as with mountains, apex and vertex are the same: the point farthest from and opposite to the base.

☞ ☜

**FALLACY:** The word *smith* is a short form of *blacksmith*.

**FACT:** The word *blacksmith* came from the word *smith*, not the other way around. A smith is someone who works with metal; a blacksmith is someone who works with "black metal"—iron. A whitesmith is someone who works with "white metal"—tin. A smithy is the place where a smith works. Since a blacksmith is by definition also a smith, Henry Wadsworth Longfellow was correct when he used both names for the same person in his poem *The Village Blacksmith*:

> Under the spreading chestnut tree
> The village smithy stands;
> The smith, a mighty man is he,
> With large and sinewy hands;
> And the muscles of his brawny arms
> Are strong as iron bands.

☞ ☜

**FALLACY:**  A *Pooh-Bah* was the head of an ancient culture: a king.

**FACT:**  A Pooh-Bah, as defined by the inventors of the word, was not a king; he was the Lord-High-Everything-Else. The inventors of the word were W. S. Gilbert and Arthur Sullivan, who created the Pooh-Bah as a character in *The Mikado*. The ancient culture was Japan, and the head of the culture was a mikado: an emperor.

☞ ☜

**FALLACY:**  The larger the number, the more Roman numerals you need to write it.

**FACT:**  Doesn't work quite that way. Would be closer to the truth to say that the more numbers other than 0, the more Roman numerals you need to write it. The year 1999, for example, is MCMXCIX. All you need for the year 2000 is MM. The first year of the next century, which is also the first year of the next millennium, is MMI.

☞ ☜

**FALLACY:**  Before indoor plumbing, people used to keep nightjars under their beds.

**FACT:**  Possibly, but they wouldn't have gotten much sleep. A nightjar, any of several birds of the family Caprimulgidae, is called that because of the jarring sound it makes at night. Nighthawks and whippoorwills are nightjars. Nightjars are also called goatsuckers, from the old belief that they sucked milk from goats' udders. Before indoor plumbing, to avoid taking long walks in the wee hours of the night, people used to keep chamber pots under their beds.

☞ ☜

**FALLACY:**  *DOS HIGH* is computer drug slang.

**FACT:**  Might look that way if you've been smoking one of those funny cigarettes. DOS stands for Disk Operating System. When you turn your computer on, so to speak, DOS is loaded into memory. There's a limited amount of conventional memory, so if possible you load DOS into high memory with the command DOS=HIGH. Another common computer code is ERROR: Unable to locate COFFEE.CUP—Operator Halted.

☞ ☜

**FALLACY:**   The word *kilometer* should be pronounced kil-OM-eter.

**FACT:**   If you pronounce the word *kilometer* kil-OM-eter, it's only logical to pronounce the word *centimeter* cen-TIM-eter, which nobody does. According to the National Metric Council, *centimeter* should be pronounced the way it almost always is, CENTI-meter, and *kilometer* should be pronounced KILO-meter.

☞ ☜

**FALLACY:**   Patent leather can be any color, but it's not leather.

**FACT:**   Patent leather comes in any color you want, so long as you want black. That's the only color it comes in. It's made by finishing black leather to a hard, smooth, glossy surface with a once-patented process, hence the name.

☞ ☜

**FALLACY:**   *Ishkabibble* is a nonsense word meaning nonsense.

**FACT:**   Two words: Ish Kabibble. He was a comic trumpeter with Kay Kyser's band, the Kollege of Musical Knowledge, during the height of the Big Band era. He took his name from the lyrics of one of his trademark songs. His real name was Merwyn Bouge.

☞ ☜

**FALLACY:**   An "arctophile" is someone who loves the Arctic.

**FACT:**   The word may look as if that's what it means, and there is a connection, but an arctophile is someone who loves bears. The root is a Greek word, *arktos,* "bear." The Arctic got its name from the constellation Ursa Major, or Great Bear, the most prominent constellation in the far northern sky. Ursa Major includes the seven stars that make up the Big Dipper; the last two stars in the handle of the Big Dipper point toward Polaris, the North Star.

☞ ☜

**FALLACY:**   *Apian* refers to apes, *caprine* refers to the island of Capri, *murine* refers to eyes, and *vulpine* refers to vultures.

**FACT:**   *Apian* comes from the same root as apiary and refers to bees. *Caprine* comes from the same root as Capricorn and refers to goats. *Murine* comes from the same root as the name of the biological family

Muridae and refers to mice and rats. *Vulpine* comes from the same root as the name of the constellation Vulpecula and refers to foxes.

☞ ☜

**FALLACY:**  The partridge was named for the person who discovered it.

**FACT:**  The partridge wasn't named for a person, but for a sound. The word comes from Greek *perdix,* which comes from the root *perd,* "fart." The partridge was named for the rushing-wind sound it makes when it takes off.

☞ ☜

**FALLACY:**  The process for making suede leather was invented in the American Old West.

**FACT:**  Suede is leather with a fuzzy, napped surface. The Americans got the word for that type of leather from the English, who got the word from the French, who shortened it from the phrase *gants de Suède,* "Swedish gloves." That may be a clue as to where the process for making suede was invented.

☞ ☜

**FALLACY:**  The tuxedo originated in England.

**FACT:**  Hard as it is to believe when looking at that uncomfortable costume, the tuxedo was created as semiformal wear without tails to replace the formal wear with tails that originated in England. The tuxedo originated at a country club in Tuxedo Park, Westchester County, New York.

☞ ☜

**FALLACY:**  The word *news* is an acronym of north, east, west, south.

**FACT:**  Although the first letters of north, east, west, south do spell "news," that's not where the word came from. The modern English word *news* came from Middle English *newes,* the plural of *newe,* which came from Old English *niwe.* And that's the news.

☞ ☜

**FALLACY:**  Black ice is black-colored ice.

**FACT:**  Black ice is ice, as anyone who has hit a patch of it and gone skidding is well aware, but it isn't black. Black ice is a thin, transparent layer of regular ice; because it's transparent, it allows the color of the road to show through, making the ice itself virtually invisible. Black ice was named when most paved roads were black. With today's concrete freeways, the term white ice would be just as appropriate, and just as wrong.

☞ ☜

**FALLACY:** *Penultimate* means "final."

**FACT:** Penultimate means "next to last." It comes from Latin root words meaning "almost" and "last." The last of something, such as the last word in this sentence, is not penultimate, but ultimate.

☞ ☜

**FALLACY:** English is relatively easy to learn because it has regular, logical rules.

**FACT:** Learning the rules of the English language ranks right up there with chicken pox and the onset of puberty as one of the joys of child-hood. Once the rules have been mastered, of course, you've got them for life. Who could ever forget *e before i except after y,* or *i before e except after c*—or however that goes? Then there's the rule for pro-nouncing words that end in *ough,* such as borough, bough, chough, cough, dough, enough, furlough, plough, rough, slough, sough, thorough, though, through, tough, trough—and the ever-popular hiccough. Easy as 3.14159265358979323846264335.

# 9

# Medicine

**FALLACY:** You should never wake a sleepwalker.

**FACT:** You should never use a firecracker to wake a sleepwalker who has a weak heart, but other than that, there's no reason not to wake one. If someone is about to sleepwalk naked out the front door, it might be a good idea to rouse him or her. This superstition comes from the old belief that a sleepwalker's spirit leaves the body and might not make it back if the person is wakened.

☞ ☜

**FALLACY:** Men have one less rib than women.

**FACT:** Ah, yes, the old Adam's Rib problem. Adam's Bridge is a chain of shoals running between India and Sri Lanka, which according to Hindu tradition was built for Rama to rescue his wife from the demon king. Then there's Adam's Peak, a place of pilgrimage by Buddhists, Hindus, and Muslims, on Sri Lanka. Scientists haven't found anything supernatural about Adam's Bridge or Adam's Peak, but scientific method is meant for dealing with the natural, not the supernatural. Numbers, for example. There are twenty-four ribs in a male human's body. There are twenty-four ribs in a female human's body. Who's got the barbecue sauce?

☞ ☜

**FALLACY:** The air in commercial airliners is always fresh because it comes in from outside.

**FACT:** The air outside is quite cold, and therefore needs to be heated before it can be breathed. Planes built before the 1980s replaced the air in the cabin every three minutes. To reduce fuel costs, planes built since the 1980s replace the air every six to seven minutes. At that replacement rate, only about 50 percent of the air in an airliner is fresh; the rest is recycled. Whether or not that causes an increase in the incidence of airborne diseases among passengers and crew is a matter of debate among airlines, insurance companies, and their horde of lawyers.

☞ ☜

**FALLACY:** A beer puts the least amount of alcohol into the blood-stream, a glass of wine puts more, and a shot of whiskey puts most.

**FACT:** An average twelve-ounce beer, a five-ounce glass of wine, and a one-and-a-half-ounce shot of eighty-proof whiskey have about the same amount of alcohol and therefore put the same amount of alcohol into the bloodstream. The main difference is in how rapidly the alcohol gets there. The more diluted the alcohol, the slower it's absorbed. On the other hand, the sooner the alcohol gets into the bloodstream and is processed by the liver, the sooner it's burned up. The alcohol from a shot of whiskey will get into the bloodstream and be processed fastest, the same amount from a glass of wine will take a bit longer, and the same amount from a beer will take longest. As a rough rule of thumb, the liver processes one drink per hour; if you drink more than that, the excess alcohol builds up in your bloodstream, raising both your blood alcohol level and the height of tomorrow's hangover.

☞ ☜

**FALLACY:** Antigens are one of the body's defenses against invaders.

**FACT:** Antigens are the invaders. They cause the body to produce anti-bodies, one of the body's defenses against invaders. When antigens such as bacteria, toxins, viruses—or transplanted tissues—get inside the body, white blood cells called lymphocytes produce proteins to protect against them. This process is part of the body's immune system.

☞ ☜

**FALLACY:** The largest vein in the body is the jugular vein.

**FACT:** There is no one vein called the jugular vein. The word *jugular* refers to the throat or neck; there are several large veins on each side of the neck that drain blood from the head and can be referred to as jugular veins. The largest vein in the body, which carries blood from the lower body to the right atrium of the heart, is the inferior vena cava.

☞ ☜

**FALLACY:**   People who are blind can hear better than people who aren't.

**FACT:**   Lack of sight has no effect on the physical apparatus of hearing. People who are blind hear as variably as people who aren't—some better than average, some worse. People who have problems with one sense will put more emphasis on the other senses. Although people who are blind cannot hear better than people who aren't, they pay more attention to what they hear, so it appears that they can hear better.

☞ ☜

**FALLACY:**   If Teflon comes off a pan and gets into your food, you digest it.

**FACT:**   Teflon is a trademark for a fluorocarbon resin, more specifically an inert polymer of tetrafluoroethylene. Because it is inert, it does not react with food, or with your gastrointestinal tract, or with much of anything else. If a gram of Teflon came off a pan and got into your food, a gram of Teflon would come out the other end. Alimentary, my dear Watson.

☞ ☜

**FALLACY:**   Karen Ann Quinlan was in a coma longer than any other person.

**FACT:**   On 14 April 1975, after ingesting a combination of alcohol, Darvon, and Valium, Karen Ann Quinlan went into a coma. The respirator helping her to breathe was removed in 1976, but she was in what is called a persistent vegetative state—her body stayed alive, but she never regained consciousness before her death in 1985. Elaine Esposito went into a coma during an appendectomy in 1941. She died in 1978, still in the coma.

☞ ☜

**FALLACY:**   The backbone is the largest bone in the human body.

**FACT:**   The backbone, spinal column, spine, or vertebral column, is not one single bone. It is made up of 7 cervical vertebrae, 12 thoracic vertebrae, 5 lumbar vertebrae, 5 fused sacral vertebrae, and 5 fused caudal vertebrae (the coccyx), for a total of 34. The largest bone in the human body is the femur or thighbone.

☞ ☜

**FALLACY:** The cotton in the top of a bottle of pills should be put back in the bottle to keep the pills sanitary.

**FACT:** Exactly the opposite. Once the bottle is opened, the cotton should be discarded. When the cotton has been handled it is no longer sanitary, and replacing it in the bottle could contaminate the pills. The cotton is there to keep the pills from rattling around in a too-big bottle during shipment, reducing themselves to fragments; that won't happen in your home unless you live on top of the San Andreas Fault.

☞ ☜

**FALLACY:** Hundreds of allergic Americans die each year from insect bites.

**FACT:** Not even *one* hundred Americans die each year from insect bites. According to the U.S. Office of Disease Prevention and Health Promotion, the average annual human toll in the battle between bugs and Americans is forty. No estimate of insect casualties was given.

☞ ☜

**FALLACY:** All condoms are effective against sexually transmitted diseases such as AIDS.

**FACT:** The U.S. Food and Drug Administration sent letters to manufacturers of natural-skin condoms, requiring them to state on their products that they are ''intended to prevent pregnancy and do not protect against HIV infection and other sexually transmitted diseases.'' HIV is the virus that causes AIDS. *Latex* condoms do provide protection against sexually transmitted diseases such as AIDS, chlamydia, gonorrhea, hepatitis, herpes, and syphilis; natural-skin, or lamb-skin, condoms do not. Using a vaginal spermicide containing nonoxynol-9, in addition to nonoxynol-9-impregnated latex condoms, considerably improves protection against both pregnancy and sexually transmitted diseases. Heterosexual, homosexual, bisexual, or trisexual, everyone should be aware of this.

☞ ☜

**FALLACY:** A communicable disease is not the same as a contagious disease.

**FACT:** A communicable disease is one that can be spread by direct or indirect contact. A contagious disease is one that can be spread by direct or indirect contact. The agent of a communicable disease, such as a bacterium or a virus, is called a contagium.

☞ ☜

**FALLACY:** The best thing to drink if you're cold is alcohol.

**FACT:** One of the worst things to drink if you're cold is alcohol. Alcohol makes you feel warmer, but it's an illusion. When your skin is warm, you feel warm. Alcohol dilates the blood vessels near the skin, warming it. What this is actually doing, though, is bringing your body's inner warmth to the surface, There it is lost. The best thing to drink if you're cold is something hot. What's that you say? A hot toddy?

☞ ☜

**FALLACY:** Exercising specific areas of the body can reduce the amount of fat there.

**FACT:** Exercising can burn fat. Exercising the muscles in specific areas of the body can increase the muscle mass in those areas. When the body burns fat, it burns the most easily available fat. Exercising specific areas of the body does not specifically reduce the amount of fat there. Situps can reduce your overall body fat, but won't selectively remove fat from your Bay Window; squeezing a spring with your knees won't remove fat just from Thunder Thighs; butt clenching won't transform a gluteus maximus into a gluteus minimus.

☞ ☜

**FALLACY:** The disease known long ago as *pox* left disfiguring pockmarks on the face, but it was not life threatening.

**FACT:** "A pox upon thee!" was no small curse. Many epidemic diseases were called poxes, but two stood out. Greatpox, caused by the spirochete *Treponema pallidum,* is what we today call syphilis; smallpox, caused by a poxvirus, is what we today call smallpox. Of the two, in those days it was far better to have smallpox. With smallpox you either died, or survived with disfiguring pock marks and a lifelong immunity to smallpox; in either event, it was over. With greatpox, once you caught it, you had it the rest of your life. The primary stage was a minor skin ulcer at the point of infection that soon disappeared, and all seemed well. The secondary stage, which appeared several weeks later, involved fever, ulcers on the skin and mucous membranes, and inflammation of the bones, eyes, and central nervous system. These symptoms, too, disappeared over time, and again all seemed well. The tertiary stage might not strike for a decade, but when it did it caused skin ulcers that would not heal, damage to the aorta and to the heart itself, irreversible degeneration of the central nervous system, and death. Syphilis is no longer a greatpox because it can be cured with penicillin; the symptoms of untreated syphilis, however, have not changed. The U.N. World Health Organization declared smallpox extinct in nature as of 1980. Smallpox virus is now known to exist only at the Research Institute for Virus Preparations in Moscow, and the Centers for Disease Control and Prevention (CDC) in Atlanta. Scientists are working to sequence smallpox's DNA and store it on computer.

☞ ☜

**FALLACY:**   About the only plastic surgery that men use is a facelift.

**FACT:**   An uplifting thought, but not true. Many plastic surgeons claim they can make you look like a movie star. Technically, they're not lying; the movie star is Frankenstein's monster. According to an advertisement in a major-city newspaper from an organization specializing in plastic surgery for men, they routinely perform: Cheek Implants, Circumcision, Chin Implants, Ears-Nose, Eyelids-Browlift, Facial Implants, Facelift, Liposuction, Pec-Calf Implants, Penile Enlargement, Penile Lengthening, Penile Implant, and the ever-popular Tummy Tuck. There's apparently no limit to what either women or men will lift in an attempt to lift their spirits.

☞ ☜

**FALLACY:**   When it comes to teeth, *plaque* and *tartar* are different words for the same thing.

**FACT:**   When it comes to teeth, plaque is a thin film of mucus and bacteria. The bacteria break down carbohydrates, which is good, but they also secrete an acid that attacks tooth enamel; plaque keeps the bacteria from being washed away. Tartar, which commonly forms along the gum line when plaque is not removed, is a hard, yellowish deposit composed of salivary secretions, food residue, and salts such as calcium carbonate.

☞ ☜

**FALLACY:**   The iron in red blood cells is called hemoglobin.

**FACT:**   Red blood cells are red because of their iron-containing component, hemoglobin. Hemoglobin is red because of its iron-containing component, heme. Heme makes up about 6 percent of hemoglobin; the other 94 percent is globin. Heme is a dark red substance: $C_{34}H_{32}N_4O_4Fe$. The iron in red blood cells, which is the Fe in heme, is called iron.

☞ ☜

**FALLACY:** The average adult human brain weighs about a pound.

**FACT:** Although relatively small, the average adult human brain contains a lot of heavy thoughts; it weighs about 2.75 pounds.

☞ ☜

**FALLACY:** There's an antibiotic in honey that kills germs.

**FACT:** There's no antibiotic in honey that kills germs. Germs can't survive in honey, though. The same process occurs as in sugar-cured foods such as ham. Sugar, including that in honey, is extremely hydrophilic, absorbing any water it comes in contact with. Any germs that get into honey are dehydrated: sugar-cured to death.

☞ ☜

**FALLACY:** Cracking your knuckles causes you to have large knuckles.

**FACT:** Knuckle cracking is a harmless pastime. It does not cause the knuckles to grow larger; it does not lead to any medical problem. When you separate the two bones of a knuckle it causes a pressure drop in the synovial fluid that lubricates the joint. Gas dissolved in the fluid comes out and forms a bubble, which immediately collapses, causing the popping noise. Many people crack their hand knuckles; quite a few crack their toe knuckles. Not many people know, though, that by standing a couple of feet from a wall and leaning forward, one hand on top of the other, you can also crack your elbow knuckles. Now you know.

☞ ☜

**FALLACY:** The left half of the brain controls the left half of the body.

**FACT:** The two halves of the cerebrum, divided by the longitudinal cerebral fissure, are connected at the bottom by the corpus callosum. The cerebral hemisphere to the right of the corpus callosum, also called the right brain, controls the left half of the body; the cerebral hemisphere to the left of the corpus callosum, the left brain, controls the right side of the body. Which means, of course, that only left-handed people are in their right mind.

☞ ☜

**FALLACY:** The liver cleans the blood.

**FACT:** The liver has many functions, including secreting bile that helps to emulsify fat, changing the dangerous protein-metabolite ammonia into urea, creating blood proteins, converting sugars into glycogen, and aiding in the metabolism of carbohydrates, fats, and proteins. The basic blood cleaner is not the liver, but the kidneys. They filter the blood to remove metabolic waste products, which are sent on to the urinary bladder for excretion.

☞ ☜

**FALLACY:** Unrefrigerated mayonnaise will cause food poisoning.

**FACT:** Basic mayonnaise is whipped vegetable oil, to which has been added a small amount of egg yolk, vinegar, and sometimes lemon juice. One of the best known commercial brands lists these ingredients: soybean oil, partially hydrogenated soybean oil, whole eggs, vinegar, water, egg yolks, salt, sugar, lemon juice. This concoction is sufficiently acidic to retard the growth of most food-poisoning bacteria. The oil in mayonnaise may become rancid, but what's more likely to lay you low in that chicken salad or egg salad or potato salad or tuna salad is the chicken or egg or potato or tuna; not only are those ingredients happy breeding grounds for bacteria, they also lower the protective acidity of the mayonnaise.

☞ ☜

**FALLACY:** A crepuscule is a skin eruption commonly called a pimple.

**FACT:** A crepuscule is not a skin excrescence, eruptive or otherwise. Crepuscule is another word for twilight, as in the title of that great unwritten work *Crepuscule of the Gods.*

☞ ☜

**FALLACY:** German measles is far more dangerous to children than regular measles.

**FACT:** German measles is a viral disease, rubella. Although rubella can cause birth defects in the fetus of a woman who contracts it during her first three months of pregnancy, in children it causes only mild, short, and uncomplicated fever and rash. Regular measles is also a viral disease, rubeola. Complications, especially secondary infections, are far more common with rubeola than with rubella. German measles is far less dangerous to children than regular measles.

☞ ☜

**FALLACY:** For obvious reasons, only women get breast cancer.

**FACT:** Although most of breast cancer's victims are women, men can get it too. In a typical year, about 180,000 females in the United States are stricken with breast cancer, and about 46,000 die of it; about 1,000 males are stricken with breast cancer, and about 300 dic of it. A disease that occurs in men with about the same frequency that breast cancer occurs in women, but which women do not get for obvious reasons, is prostate cancer. About 200,000 men develop prostate cancer each year, and about 38,000 die of it.

☞ ☜

**FALLACY:** You should never look directly at the Moon during a lunar eclipse because it could damage your eyes.

**FACT:** Because the Moon's surface is made of dark material, it reflects only a small percentage of the Sun's light; overall, the Moon's surface is as dark as asphalt. At no time, lunar eclipses and full Moons included, could the light reflected from the Moon harm your eyes. However, looking at the Sun during a solar eclipse is a different matter. The light of the Sun, even when diminished by a partial eclipse, can cause both temporary and permanent damage to your eyes.

☞ ☜

**FALLACY:** A pacemaker is an implanted artificial heart regulator.

**FACT:** A pacemaker is a very natural part of the body. It is the mass of cardiac muscle fibers of the sinoatrial node, the back wall of the heart's right atrium. The pacemaker generates the electrical impulses that cause the heart to beat regularly. The artificial heartbeat regulator, which may be implanted or may be external, was named after the natural pacemaker.

☞ ☜

**FALLACY:** Each human body gets one and only one bladder.

**FACT:** Most people think of the urinary bladder when they hear the word "bladder" but seldom think of the gallbladder, which stores bile from the liver until it is needed in the intestine for digestion of fats.

☞ ☜

**FALLACY:** The Pap test is named for Dr. Pap, the man who developed it.

**FACT:** The Pap test is named for the Greek-American doctor who developed the test in 1943, but his full name was George Papanicolaou, not Pap. The full name of the method for detecting uterine cancer is not the Pap test, but the Papanicolaou test.

☞ ☜

**FALLACY:** Humans can catch parotitis from parrots.

**FACT:** Parrot fever, also called psittacosis, is a disease of parrots and their near relatives caused by the bacterium *Chlamydia psittaci;* parrot fever is communicable to humans. Parotitis, on the other wing, has nothing to do with parrots. It refers to an inflammation of the parotid glands— salivary glands near the ears. The best known cause of parotitis is the unpopular and preventable childhood disease called mumps, which is caused not by a bacterium but by a paramyxovirus.

☞ ☜

**FALLACY:** The pelvis is a large bone just below the waist.

**FACT:** There is no single bone called the pelvis. In humans, the pelvis is made up of the ilium, the ischium, the pubis, the sacrum, and the coccyx.

☞ ☜

**FALLACY:** *Arteriosclerosis* is a misspelling of *atherosclerosis.*

**FACT:** Arteriosclerosis is a thickening of the walls of arteries; it is commonly called hardening of the arteries. Blood flow is reduced because the arteries have lost elasticity. Atherosclerosis is a type of arteriosclerosis where plaque, containing cholesterol and lipids, builds up on the interior walls of arteries, reducing their diameter and therefore the blood flow. Complete blockage can result in heart attack or stroke.

☞ ☜

**FALLACY:** Phloem is produced in the mucous membranes.

**FACT:** Phloem is a plant tissue made up of fibers, parenchyma cells, sclereids, and tubes, used to carry food from the leaves to the rest of the plant. Phlegm, made up of things best not dwelled on at great length, is produced in the mucous membranes of the respiratory tract.

☞ ☜

**FALLACY:** Pneumonia is caused by a virus.

**FACT:** Pneumonia has no one cause. The word comes from Greek roots meaning nothing more specific than "lung disease," and refers to a disease characterized by inflammation of the lungs. Causes range from bacteria such as *Streptococcus pneumoniae,* through viruses and other microorganisms, to chemical or physical irritants. Lung disease caused specifically by dust, such as asbestosis or black lung disease or silicosis, is called *pneumoconiosis,* form the Greek roots meaning "lung" and "dust."

☞ ☜

**FALLACY:** *Prophylactic* means "condom."

**FACT:** Although all condoms are prophylactics, not all prophylactics are condoms. *Prophylactic* means a defense or preventative. The Greek roots of the word translate as "before" and "guard." Childhood immunizations are prophylactics, and so are boots and galoshes and rubbers.

☞ ☜

**FALLACY:** Proteins are the basic building blocks of life.

**FACT:** Carbon, hydrogen, nitrogen, and oxygen are the basic building blocks of life. They form organic (carbon-based) molecules. Amino acids, sugars, and fatty acids, which are organic molecules called monomers, link together to form long molecules called polymers. Nearly all proteins, which are polymers, are derived from twenty amino acids.

☞ ☜

**FALLACY:** *Gonads, loins,* and *pubes* are different words for the same things.

**FACT:** "Gird thy loins!" makes it as a well-known expression, but "Gird thy gonads!" doesn't. Three different words, three different meanings. Gonads are organs that produce eggs or sperm, such as ovaries and testicles. The loin is the part of the lower back between the ribs and the hips; the loins, plural, include the area of the torso near the hips, both front and back, including anything dangling down. The pubes encompass the area of the lower abdomen, surrounding but not including the genitals, specifically including the hair there. This may or may not have any connection to the expression *hair trigger.*

☞ ☜

**FALLACY:** Rabies is mainly a dog disease; cats rarely get it.

**FACT:** Rabies is a much bigger problem among cats than dogs. Since 1981, more cats than dogs have had rabies. In part that's because there are more cats than dogs in the United States; in much larger part that's because more cats than dogs are allowed to run loose. As for the danger to humans, if a dog bites someone its license tag leads to the owner who can be asked about rabies vaccination; in many areas, cats are not licensed.

☞ ☜

**FALLACY:** The Red Cross was founded by a nurse during World War I.

**FACT:** Clara Barton, a nurse who worked with the International Red Cross during the Franco–Prussian War, organized the American Red Cross in 1881. The International Red Cross was founded by the terms of the Geneva Convention of 1864, long before World War I. The driving force behind the International Red Cross, and behind the Geneva Convention itself, was Jean Henri Dunant of Switzerland. In 1901, Dunant shared the first Nobel Peace Prize with Frederic Passy.

☞ ☜

**FALLACY:** Homosexuals do unnatural things that heterosexuals don't.

**FACT:** Nature, not moralists, determines what's natural. As for who does what with whom, with the exception of vaginal intercourse, heterosexuals and homosexuals do the same things. As Marlene Dietrich said, "In America, sex is an obsession; in the rest of the world, it is a fact."

☞ ☜

**FALLACY:** Rheumatism is a disease of the joints.

**FACT:** There is no one disease called rheumatism. The word refers to any of many problems in bones, joints, ligaments, muscles, nerves, or tendons that cause inflammation, pain, and stiffness.

☞ ☜

**FALLACY:** We're each born with one set of tonsils, but they're not good for anything.

**FACT:** We're each born with several sets of tonsils. These masses of lymphoid tissue, part of the lymphatic system, are very good for filtering out disease organisms. The ones most commonly called "the" tonsils are the palatine tonsils, on each side of the throat. The pharyngeal tonsils, between the back of the nose and the throat, are commonly called the adenoids. A third pair, the lingual tonsils, are on the back of the tongue.

☞ ☜

**FALLACY:** Most of a tooth is made up of enamel.

**FACT:** Very little of a tooth is made up of enamel. The innermost core is made up of pulp, but by far the greatest amount of a tooth is made up of dentin. Enamel is just a hard coating on the crown (the above-gum part) of a tooth.

☞ ☜

**FALLACY:** Pork has to be cooked to "well done" or it will give you trichinosis.

**FACT:** Trichinosis is caused by the nematode worm *Trichinella spiralis*. Once a major threat in this country, trichinosis has been virtually eliminated by the pork industry. It used to be considered necessary to cook pork to a well-done (and somewhat dry and chewy) 170° Fahrenheit (77° Celsius) to get rid of the nasty nematode, but it is now known that a moist and tender 160° F (71° C) is sufficient.

☞ ☜

**FALLACY:** Although a human body contains a lot of liquid, it's basically a solid.

**FACT:** A human body is basically a waterproof package of seawater that allows us to walk on the small percentage of Earth that is land. The density of the planet we live on is 5.520 grams per cubic centimeter (g/cm$^3$). The density of pure water is 1.00 g/cm$^3$. The density of seawater is 1.025 g/cm$^3$. The density of a human body is 1.030 g/cm$^3$—although some of us are denser than others.

☞ ☜

**FALLACY:** A man who has had a vasectomy can no longer produce semen.

**FACT:** *Vasectomy* is the surgical procedure removing part or all of the vas deferens, the main tube through which sperm is carried from the testicles to the ejaculatory duct. A man who has had a vasectomy still produces sperm, it just doesn't reach the ejaculatory duct. A sperm is a gamete, a male sex cell, and extremely small; even in huge numbers, sperm occupy very little space. Semen is the total volume of fluid in an ejaculation, including sperm from the testicles, fluid from the seminal vesicles, and fluid from the prostate gland. Sperm makes up such a tiny fraction of semen that a man who has had a vasectomy should notice no difference in the amount of semen he produces.

☞ ☜

**FALLACY:** Glucose and dextrose are different names for table sugar.

**FACT:** Glucose is a monosaccharide, $C_6H_{12}O_6$; table sugar is sucrose, a disaccharide, $C_{12}H_{22}O_{11}$. Dextrose, also called dextroglucose, is the dextrorotary form of glucose; the levorotary form is levulose, also called fructose. Glucose is the main sugar in human blood.

☞ ☜

**FALLACY:** Cooties were made up by children; there's no such animal.

**FACT:** There actually is such an animal. It's as widespread as humans—and quite fond of them. "Cootie" is probably a derivative of the Malaysian word *kutu.* Cooties are body lice.

☞ ☜

**FALLACY:** The best way to avoid catching a cold is to keep away from people who have a cold.

**FACT:** It's not necessarily easier to catch a cold by being in a room with someone who has one than it is by being in a room by yourself. The only way to catch a cold is by catching the viruses that cause it. Those viruses can live for several hours outside a host—on the handset of a telephone, for example, or a door handle, or the handle of a supermarket cart. When you touch something that has the viruses and then rub your eyes, rub or pick your nose, or bite your nails, you offer them a route into your body. Hands down, the best ways to avoid catching a

cold are to keep your hands away from your face and to wash your
hands whenever you've handled something that might have been handled
by someone with a cold.

☞ ☜

**FALLACY:** Those thick areas of skin on the feet are called *galluses.*
**FACT:** Galluses perform an entirely different lower-body function; also
called braces or suspenders, they keep pants from falling down. The
word galluses comes from *gallowses,* a plural of gallows. Those thick
areas of skin on the feet are called calluses.

☞ ☜

**FALLACY:** Saltwater fish are high in sodium because they're high in salt.
**FACT:** Saltwater fish are not high in sodium. Their blood is about a third
as salty as the water they swim in, making it similar in sodium content to
human blood. Although an ocean fish takes in a lot of sodium in the saltwater it takes in, neither its blood nor its flesh is high in sodium because it
excretes sodium at a much higher rate than does a human.

☞ ☜

**FALLACY:** The flu is a major nuisance, but it's not life threatening.
**FACT:** Influenza is caused by strains of a myxovirus belonging to the
family Orthomyxoviridae. Most cases of flu are not life threatening, except to those with immune systems weakened by age or illness. Some
strains of influenza are more virulent, though, than the ones we've experi-
enced in the last three-quarters of a century. The strain that ran rampant
in the winter of 1918–1919 killed more than 20,000,000 people. In the
United States alone, more than 550,000 people died—more than all the
American military personnel who died in World War I and World War
II, combined. We have vaccines today that we didn't have then, but they
work only to prevent the flu; we still have no cure for influenza.

☞ ☜

**FALLACY:** *Piloerection* is a sexual term.
**FACT:** Including "piloerection" on a list of sexual responses wouldn't
raise even an eyebrow, but it is not a sexual term. Piloerection refers to
your hair standing up, as commonly happens when you get goose bumps.
Being bumped by a goose won't cause it, but being goosed may. The

difference between erotic and kinky is the difference between using a goose feather and using the whole goose.

☞ ☜

**FALLACY:** If you're bitten by a snake, you should take an antivenom.
**FACT:** There is no such thing as an antivenom. There *is* such a thing as an *antivenin,* an antitoxin to the venom of an insect, snake, spider, or other venomous creature. And what is an antitoxin? A toxin causes an animal to produce an antibody capable of neutralizing that specific toxin. That antibody is an antitoxin, and if it's an antitoxin to a venom, it's an antivenin.

☞ ☜

**FALLACY:** *Electrolysis* means "hair removal."
**FACT:** Electrolysis means passing an electric current through an electrolyte, a substance in which the current is carried by ions rather than by free electrons. The most common use of electrolysis is electroplating—depositing a thin layer of metal on an object. Galvanizing iron or steel with a layer of zinc, for example, to prevent oxidation. Using electric current to destroy living tissue, such as hair roots so as to permanently remove unwanted hair from a body part, is also called electrolysis. Electroplating the body part would work, too, but is not recommended.

☞ ☜

**FALLACY:** The endocrine gland is small but vital.
**FACT:** There are endocrine glands, but there is no endocrine gland. Also called ductless glands because they secrete hormones directly into the bloodstream, endocrine glands are scattered throughout the body, and include the adrenal glands, ovaries, pancreas, pituitary gland, testes, thymus, and thyroid.

☞ ☜

**FALLACY:** British-born Florence Nightingale was a famous nurse in World War I.
**FACT:** Florence Nightingale was born in 1820 in Florence, Italy, and died in 1910; World War I didn't begin until 1914. A world-famous British hospital reformer and considered the founder of modern professional nursing, she organized a group of thirty-eight nurses at Scutari

after the 1854 battle of Alma during the Crimean War and went on from that beginning to upgrade the quality of nursing, public health, and sanitation throughout the British empire. In 1860 she established her renowned nursing school at St. Thomas's Hospital in London.

☞ ☜

**FALLACY:**   We have to cut our hair because it keeps growing; it even keeps growing for a while after we die.

**FACT:**   Some hair on the human body grows to great lengths unless cut; some doesn't. Not many people regularly trim their arm or leg hair, or their eyelashes. Human scalp hair usually stops growing when it reaches about three feet, but considering how many humans there are, it's not surprising that there are exceptions. One of those exceptions is Mata Jagdamba, whose hair is nearly fifteen feet long. As for hair growing after a person has died, it doesn't. What gives it that appearance is the drying and shrinking of the body, which causes more of the hair shaft to show.

☞ ☜

**FALLACY:**   *Ptomaine poisoning* is another term for food poisoning.

**FACT:**   You may get food poisoning at Terry's Ptomaine Parlor, but it's unlikely to be ptomaine poisoning. Ptomaine is a product of bacterial putrefaction of protein, which gives off a very strong smell; our word comes from the Greek ptoma, "corpse." The most common source of food poisoning is another type of bacteria, salmonella.

☞ ☜

**FALLACY:**   Jock itch is caused by bacteria thriving in a warm, moist place.

**FACT:**   The formal name for jock itch is *tinea cruris*. Tinea is any of several fungal, not bacterial, skin infections. Tinea cruris literally means tinea of the leg, but that's close enough. Equally popular are tinea barbae (beard), and tinea capitis (head). Ringworm is a tineal infection; when ringworm occurs on the foot (tinea pedes), it is called athletes foot. Although athletes often get athlete's foot, astronauts rarely get missile toe.

☞ ☜

**FALLACY:**   *Stomatitis* means an inflammation of the stomach.

**FACT:**   Stomatitis might be a warning that you're heading for an upset stomach, but that's not what it means. An inflammation of the stomach is gastritis. Stomatitis comes from the Greek word *stoma,* "mouth"; stomatitis is an inflammation of the mucous lining of the mouth. Words of wisdom: a closed mouth gathers no feet.

# Science

**FALLACY:** *Multitasking* is a complicated computer procedure.

**FACT:** Not at all. People were multitasking long before computers existed. Walking and chewing gum at the same time, for example, or reading in the bathroom.

☞ ☜

**FALLACY:** Alpha, beta, and gamma rays can penetrate most materials.

**FACT:** Natural radioactivity produces three types of radiation: alpha particles, beta particles, and gamma rays. An alpha particle is the nucleus of a helium atom, consisting of two neutrons and two protons, and is therefore positively charged. Alpha particles cannot penetrate even Madonna's clothing. A beta particle is a high-energy electron, and is therefore negatively charged; it can penetrate not only clothing, but wooden walls. Gamma rays, which are essentially high-energy x-rays, have no charge, and are highly penetrating. Gamma radiation has the shortest wavelength and highest frequency of the electromagnetic spectrum—it does it until it hertz.

☞ ☜

**FALLACY:** NASA was created near the end of World War II.

**FACT:** The National Aeronautics and Space Act created NASA. It was signed into law by President Dwight D. Eisenhower on 29 July 1958, more than a decade after the end of World War II.

☞ ☜

**FALLACY:**  Even when full, the Moon produces only about one-thousandth as much light as the Sun.

**FACT:**  The Moon produces no light at all. Even the brightest moonlight is sunlight reflected from the Moon's surface. If you look carefully, you can often see the dark part of the Moon. That's because of earthshine: sunlight reflected from Earth to the Moon, then back to Earth. Earthshine is brightest when the Moon is darkest, because just as a full Moon sees a new Earth, a new Moon sees a full Earth. Then there's the fact that Earth in the Moon's sky is four times as large as the Moon in Earth's sky. Moonlight and earthshine come in photons; moonshine comes in quarts.

☞ ☜

**FALLACY:**  It's difficult to memorize more than a few numbers of the numerical value of pi.

**FACT:**  James Hopwood Jeans, British astronomer, mathematician, and physicist, thought the same thing, so he simplified matters by coming up with a mnemonic. Remember this and you'll have the first fifteen numbers of pi: "How I want a drink, alcoholic of course, after the heavy chapters involving quantum mechanics." The number of letters in each word gives you 314159265358979—all you have to do is put a decimal point after the first one. Using decimals is easy, but beware of ratios when dealing with complicated numbers because nineteen out of seventeen people get them wrong.

☞ ☜

**FALLACY:**  Although there is zinc in pennies now, a penny is still mostly copper.

**FACT:**  Although there is copper in pennies now, a penny is mostly zinc. Pennies minted since 1982 are basically zinc coins with a copper coating. The new pennies are 97.5 percent zinc and only 2.5 percent copper. Some people contend that there is no longer a use for pennies, a contention of which the zinc industry is not fond. George Willig would agree that pennies can be very useful. On 26 May 1977, he was arrested for climbing the outside of the 110-floor World Trade Center in New York City. The district attorney decided that it was a crime worth prosecuting. The judge took a lighter view of the matter, and fined George a penny a floor.

☞ ☜

**FALLACY:**  Acid rain is common, but snow is pure so there's no such thing as acid snow.

**FACT:**  The major causes of acid rain are sulfur dioxide and nitrogen oxides. These chemicals combine with moisture in the atmosphere to form acidic compounds, which can then fall as acid precipitation. Acid precipitation includes acid rain and, if it freezes, acid snow. Another form of acidic atmospheric moisture, which forms near ground level, is acid fog. If someone tells you they're as pure as the driven snow, they're giving you a snow job.

☞ ☜

**FALLACY:**  Yuri Gagarin was the first human to escape Earth's gravity.

**FACT:**  On 12 April 1961, Yuri Gagarin became the first human to orbit Earth, but Earth's gravity was holding *Vostok 1* in that orbit. The first humans to escape Earth's gravity were William Anders, Frank Borman, and James Lovell: the crew of *Apollo 8*. In December 1968 they reached the point where the gravitational pull of Earth and that of the Moon are equal, then continued on into the Moon's gravitational field and, on 24 December, went into orbit around the Moon. Picky people might want to argue that they were still in Earth's gravitational field because the Moon orbits Earth, but that line of argument wouldn't end there because Earth orbits the Sun and the Sun orbits the center of the Milky Way Galaxy.

☞ ☜

**FALLACY:**  The temperature scale that used to be called Celsius is now called Centigrade.

**FACT:**  Centigrade is a logical name for that temperature scale because centi-grade refers to 100 gradations between the freezing and boiling points of water. It was originally called Centigrade, but to avoid confusion between the temperature scale and a hundredth part of a grade, the name was officially changed in 1948 to Celsius, honoring Anders Celsius. Many people who aren't worried about their grades still call it Centigrade.

☞ ☜

**FALLACY:**  The only solar system bodies that have an atmosphere are Venus, Earth, Mars, Jupiter, Saturn, Uranus, and Neptune.

**FACT:**  Each of those does have an atmosphere, but those are only seven of the twelve solar system bodies with an atmosphere. Pluto has an atmosphere, leaving Mercury as the only planet that does not. Saturn's fourteenth and largest moon, Titan, has an atmosphere; Jupiter's ninth moon, Io, has an atmosphere; and Neptune's second moon, Triton, has an atmosphere. The last of the twelve has, by far, the largest atmosphere of any body in the solar system: the Sun.

☞ ☜

**FALLACY:** Each state could issue about a hundred million unique seven-character auto license plates if they used all twenty-six letters and all nine single numbers.

**FACT:** First off, ten single numbers are possible: 0 through 9. Using all combinations of those numbers and the twenty-six letters of the English alphabet, each state could issue more than 78 *billion* unique seven-character auto license plates. If you want a larger selection, go to Cambodia: the Khmer alphabet has seventy-four letters.

☞ ☜

**FALLACY:** Almost all background radiation comes from uranium and other natural radioactive materials in the ground.

**FACT:** Some background radiation does come from natural radioisotopes in the rocks and soil, as well as in the atmosphere. Some comes from radioactive materials we've put into the air and soil from nuclear power plants and nuclear weapons testing. Some comes from cosmic radiation—high-energy particles and gamma rays that arrive on Earth from all directions.

☞ ☜

**FALLACY:** It's difficult to remember both the freezing point of a substance and its melting point.

**FACT:** If you remember one, it's not difficult to find the other. The freezing point of water, for example, is 0° Celsius (32° Fahrenheit); the melting point of water is also 0° Celsius. The freezing point and the melting point of a substance are the same point; what you call that point depends on whether you're working your way up the temperature scale, or down.

☞ ☜

**FALLACY:** Hydrogen has the lowest boiling point of any element.

**FACT:** In addition to being the most abundant element in the universe, hydrogen is the lightest of the elements and therefore might be thought to have the lowest boiling point. It doesn't. Although hydrogen's boiling point at atmospheric pressure is extremely low at −252.87° Celsius (−423.17° Fahrenheit), helium's is even lower: −268.93° C (−452.07° F). Helium has the lowest boiling point of any element.

ɪ☞ ☜ɪ

**FALLACY:** Boiling water makes the most noise just after it reaches a full boil.

**FACT:** As water heats, it boils first on the bottom of the pan where it's hottest, forming water-vapor bubbles. It doesn't look as if the water is boiling because the bubbles don't make it to the top; the cooler water above them causes them to shrink and pop. Water makes more and more noise as it heats because there are more and more bubbles forming and popping. When all the water in the pan gets hot enough to allow the bubbles to reach the top and escape, the level of noise drops quickly. Boiling water makes the least noise just after it reaches a full boil— exactly the opposite of most humans.

ɪ☞ ☜ɪ

**FALLACY:** The British thermal unit originated as part of the metric system.

**FACT:** The British thermal unit (Btu) originated not as part of the metric system, but as part of the old system of Imperial units. One Btu was defined as the amount of heat needed to raise one pound of water one degree Fahrenheit at a pressure of one atmosphere. Another way of putting that is that one Btu is ¹/₁₈₀th the amount of heat required to raise one pound of water from 32° Fahrenheit to 212° Fahrenheit—from the freezing point to the boiling point. In the International System (SI) used today, one Btu is defined as 1055.06 joules.

ɪ☞ ☜ɪ

**FALLACY:** You can see the Big Dipper only half of the year; the other half, you can see Cassiopeia.

**FACT:** Cassiopeia is a constellation between Andromeda and Cepheus. It's shaped like a lazy W, and the sharper of the two Vs in the W points toward Polaris, the North Star. The Big Dipper is comprised of seven bright stars in the constellation Ursa Major or Big Bear; the two bright stars at the front of the cup point toward Polaris. From the midlatitudes of the Northern Hemisphere, unless your horizon is blocked or you're standing next to a very large significant other, you can see both Cassiopeia and the Big Dipper at any time of the year. Find either one, then look across Polaris to the other side of the sky and you'll see the other one.

☞ 🕭

**FALLACY:** Deuterium is similar to uranium.

**FACT:** Deuterium is similar to uranium in name only. Uranium, symbol U, is a metallic element with three naturally occurring isotopes: U-234, U-235, and U-238. Uranium-235 is the one used for nuclear fission. Deuterium, symbol D, is an isotope of hydrogen that, unlike common hydrogen, has a neutron in its nucleus. Deuterium is also known as heavy hydrogen. Deuterium oxide, or heavy water, which is $D_2O$ rather than $H_2O$, is used to slow fast neutrons in nuclear reactions.

☞ 🕭

**FALLACY:** The brightest star in the sky is the North Star.

**FACT:** Polaris, the North Star, is one of the most famous stars in the Northern Hemisphere's sky, but it is not the brightest. The brightest star in the sky is the Sun. The brightest star in the night sky is Sirius, the Dog Star, in the constellation Canis Major.

☞ 🕭

**FALLACY:** One horsepower is the amount of power generated by one average horse.

**FACT:** One horsepower is the energy necessary to raise 33,000 pounds one foot in one minute, or 550 foot-pounds of force per second, or 745.7 watts. If you're going to horse around with the metric system, one horsepower equals 1.0139 metric horsepower. One average horse generates about ⅔ horsepower.

☞ 🕭

**FALLACY:** Eclipses can occur during any phase of the Moon.

**FACT:** First off, there are two kinds of eclipse involving the Sun, Earth, and Moon. When the Moon gets between Earth and the Sun it causes a solar eclipse; when Earth gets between the Sun and the Moon it causes a lunar eclipse. Neither of these is possible except when the Moon crosses Earth's orbital plane at a time when all three bodies are in a line. When the Moon passes between Earth and the Sun, the side facing us is dark because there's no sunlight; that's a new Moon. When the Moon is on the far side of Earth, the side facing us is fully illuminated; that's a full Moon. Solar eclipses, therefore, can occur only at a new Moon, and lunar eclipses can occur only at a full Moon.

☞ ☜

**FALLACY:**  There can be anywhere from no eclipses to twelve eclipses during a year.

**FACT:**  Celestial mechanics has some pretty hard and fast rules about what Earth, Sun, and Moon can do with one another. Counting both solar and lunar eclipses, there can never be more than seven in a year. The minimum number of eclipses during a year is two, and if that's all there are, both have to be solar. Them's the rules.

☞ ☜

**FALLACY:**  A total solar eclipse can last for as long as half an hour.

**FACT:**  It would be interesting if a total solar eclipse could last for half an hour—and even more interesting if it could last for an entire day. Because of the relative sizes and possible locations of the Sun, Moon, and Earth, however, such an eclipse can't last even half an hour. The maximum possible length of a total solar eclipse is seven and a half minutes. If you don't believe me, check it with your sundial.

☞ ☜

**FALLACY:**  Because fiber-optic telephone lines use laser light rather than electrical signals, they're impossible to tap.

**FACT:**  Because fiber-optic telephone lines transmit data on beams of laser light rather than by electrical signals, they're difficult, but not impossible, to tap. Tapping a fiber-optic line does, however, reduce the strength of the signal, which would let the person receiving the call know that the line had been tapped. That much is public knowledge. What new techniques have been developed and kept secret by the people who do such things in the name of the public, is private knowledge. Considering that phone sex is aural sex, does it cause aurgasms?

☞ ☜

**FALLACY:** Another name for the Hunter's Moon is the Harvest Moon.

**FACT:** The Harvest Moon is the full Moon nearest the autumnal equinox. For several nights around this time, the Moon rises just about sunset, providing light for farmers to harvest crops. The Hunter's Moon is the next full Moon after the Harvest Moon. Keep in mind that the seasons are reversed between the Northern Hemisphere and the Southern Hemisphere, so there's a six-month difference between their Harvest Moons.

☞ ☜

**FALLACY:** The official kilogram is a centuries-old piece of iron.

**FACT:** Since the kilogram is part of the metric system, which originated in France in 1799, if the international standard for the kilogram were made of iron, it would have changed constantly for a number of reasons, including rust. In fact, the International Prototype Kilogram is a platinum-iridium cylinder kept at the International Bureau of Weights and Measures at Sèvres, France.

☞ ☜

**FALLACY:** There are hundreds of grooves on a 33 rpm record.

**FACT:** Certainly looks that way, but there aren't. Instead of counting across the record, start at the beginning of the groove and follow it. When you've finished counting that one, turn the record over and count that one. There are only two grooves on a 33 rpm record. If you want a huge number of grooves, break the record in half—then start counting.

☞ ☜

**FALLACY:** It's hard to make gunpowder.

**FACT:** The basic formula for gunpowder, the oldest human-made explosive, has been known since ninth-century China. As most reference works will tell you, it's made of roughly 75 percent potassium nitrate (saltpeter), 15 percent charcoal, and 10 percent sulfur. The percentage of each, and the size of the granules, is a bit more complicated. Muskets, for example, required fine granules for a fast explosion, while cannon required larger granules for a slower explosion. It's easy to make gunpowder; what's hard is making gunpowder without blowing yourself up.

☞ ☜

**FALLACY:** Helium was first observed in Earth's atmosphere.

**FACT:** When helium was first observed, it was not in Earth's atmosphere. The most inert of the chemical elements and the lightest of the noble gases, helium was first observed spectroscopically in the Sun's atmosphere during a solar eclipse in 1868. It was not discovered on Earth until 1895.

☞ ☜

**FALLACY:** Helium is used in blimps and balloons because it is the lightest gas.

**FACT:** Helium is used in blimps and balloons because it is totally inert: it does not form compounds. Helium comes close, but it is not the lightest gas. An atom of helium has two electrons around a nucleus of two protons and two neutrons, and an atomic weight of 4.0026. The lightest gas, and the most abundant element in the universe, is hydrogen, which has one electron around a nucleus of one proton, and an atomic weight of 1.008. Far from being inert, hydrogen is extremely reactive, notably with oxygen with which it forms the compound $H_2O$: water. The reaction of hydrogen with oxygen is combustion, as in the Hindenburg disaster on 6 May 1937 when the hydrogen-filled German dirigible burst into flame and crashed to the ground. Although 60 percent of the people on board survived, hydrogen is nothing to make light of.

☞ ☜

**FALLACY:** The energy of a hydrogen bomb comes from exploding uranium.

**FACT:** A hydrogen bomb is a fusion bomb. The process involves fusing two atoms of hydrogen to make one atom of helium. There is less mass in one atom of helium than in two atoms of hydrogen. Much of the missing mass is transformed into energy. The amount of energy released can be calculated by Einstein's formula $E = mc^2$, where $E$ is energy, $m$ is mass, and $c^2$ is the speed of light squared.

☞ ☜

**FALLACY:** Ice is slippery.

**FACT:** Actually, ice is not slippery. What makes people and other things slip on ice is water. A thin layer of ice melts when pressure is applied to it, and it is this wet layer on top of the ice that is slippery. The more pressure, the better the melt, which is why ice skates work so well: the full weight of the skater's body is concentrated onto two thin blades.

☞ ☜

**FALLACY:** There is no such thing as an "irrational" number.

**FACT:** There are lots of irrational numbers but, irrationally, those quoted by politicians are seldom among them. An irrational number is any number that can't be expressed as the ratio of two whole numbers. Most square roots, including the square roots of 2 and 3, are irrational numbers. Another type of irrational number is represented by pi, which starts out with 3.141592 and goes on forever.

☞ ☜

**FALLACY:** The kilogram is defined as 1,000 official grams.

**FACT:** Just the opposite. The gram is defined as $\frac{1}{1000}$th of the official kilogram. A kilogram in the International System of Units is a mass equal to a platinum-iridium International Prototype Kilogram, kept at Sèvres, France. The basic units of the metric system are the meter and the kilogram, and other units are derived from them.

☞ ☜

**FALLACY:** Because cold water sinks, lakes turn to ice from the bottom up.

**FACT:** As water becomes colder it also becomes denser, and sinks. When it becomes cold enough to turn to ice, though, the ice rises because it is less dense than water. That's why you'll see a thin layer, then a thickening layer, of ice on top of a lake. Lakes turn to ice from the top down.

☞ ☜

**FALLACY:** Only light can travel at the speed of light in a vacuum.

**FACT:** Not only can light travel at the speed of light in a vacuum (roughly 299,792 kilometers, or 186,282 miles, per second), it can't travel either faster or slower. It's not alone, though. All electromagnetic waves, from radio waves through visible light to gamma radiation, travel at the speed of light: 186,282 mps—it's not just a good idea, it's the law.

☞ ☜

**FALLACY:** Marble, regardless of its color, is so hard that it lasts almost forever.

**FACT:** Marble comes in any color you want, so long as you want white. Any colors you see in marble other than white are impurities. Marble is a metamorphic rock, formed by the recrystallization of limestone or dolomite. In a vacuum, marble might last almost forever, but like limestone, marble is dissolved by acids. Acid precipitation, including acid rain, is even now eating away at such marble structures as the Parthenon and the Taj Mahal.

☞ ☜

**FALLACY:** Not counting the Moon, the first bright light you see in the evening sky is a star.

**FACT:**   *Star white, star bright,*
   *First star I see tonight,*
   *I wish I may, I wish I might,*
   *Have the wish I wish tonight.*

The first "star" you see in the evening is probably not a star. Most likely it's a planet, and of the planets, it's most likely Venus. Depending on the locations of Earth and Venus in their orbits, Venus can be either an evening star or a morning star. Other planets in the western sky near sunset can also be bright enough to be visible while the sky is still so light that it blocks out the fainter, real stars.

☞ ☜

**FALLACY:** Madame Curie discovered radioactivity.

**FACT:** Marie Sklodowska married Pierre Curie in 1895. They worked both individually and as a team. Radioactivity was discovered in uranium by Antoine Becquerel in 1896, but extensive research with radioactivity, establishing the field, was done by the Curies. Becquerel and the Curies shared the Nobel Prize for Physics in 1903. Marie Curie continued her research and, in 1910, discovered both polonium (Marie was born in Poland) and radium. Because of these discoveries, Marie Curie was awarded the Nobel Prize for Chemistry in 1911. That made her not only the first person ever to receive Nobel Prizes in two different fields, but the first person ever to receive two Nobel Prizes.

☞ ☜

**FALLACY:**   Metals are solid at room temperature.

**FACT:**   Most metals are solid at room temperature, but not all. The only common metal liquid at room temperature is mercury, also called quicksilver. Mercury's melting point is −39° Celsius (−38.2° Fahrenheit), and its boiling point is 357° C (674.6 F). Mercury is highly toxic in any of its forms and, because it is so difficult to eliminate from the body, it is a cumulative toxin. Speaking of metals, if a tin whistle is made of tin, what is a fog horn made of?

☞ ☜

**FALLACY:**   Meteor showers are caused by material from the asteroid belt.

**FACT:**   Annual meteor showers are named for the place in the sky from which they appear to radiate. Among the most famous are August's Perseids from the direction of the constellation Perseus, December's Geminids from the constellation Gemini, November's Leonids from Leo, May's Eta Aquarids from Aquarius, and October's double-header, the Draconids from Draco and the Orionids from Orion. The material causing these meteor showers is not from the asteroid belt, but from comets. As a comet loops in toward the Sun and then heads back out, it warms, sublimates, and leaves debris in its wake. When Earth crosses the comet's orbit, this debris, burning up in Earth's atmosphere, causes the famous meteor showers. The Perseid meteor shower, for example, is caused by debris from comet Swift-Tuttle, and the Draconid meteor shower occurs when we cross the orbit of comet Giacobini-Zinner. Halley's comet, which was first recorded in 239 B.C. and returns every seventy-six years, provides us with two annual meteor showers: the Eta Aquarid when we cross its orbit in May, and the Orionid when we cross it in October.

☞ ☜

**FALLACY:**   Meteors are bright, but they don't add much mass to Earth.

**FACT:**   Some meteors are bright, but many aren't. Most meteors average about 200 millionths of a meter in diameter—what most people would call dust. As anyone who has gone on safari for the fearsome Dust Bunny knows, large amounts of dust can accumulate rapidly. In the course of an average year, Earth collects about 80,000,000 pounds—40,000 tons— of meteoric mass.

☞ ☜

**FALLACY:** The largest meteorite found on Earth is the Barringer, or Coon Butte, meteorite.

**FACT:** The largest of the more than one hundred meteorite *craters* found on Earth so far is the one near Canyon Diablo in Arizona, between Flagstaff and Winslow. Variously called Barringer Crater, Coon Butte Crater, or Meteor Crater, it is 4,140 feet in diameter; the meteorite that caused it, however, has never been recovered. The largest meteorite found on Earth was discovered at Hoba West, near Grootfontein, Namibia. The Hoba West meteorite measures nine feet by eight feet, and weighs about sixty-five tons.

☞ ☜

**FALLACY:** The pneumatic tire was invented by Charles Goodyear.

**FACT:** Charles Goodyear's claim to fame is that he developed the vulcanization process, taking out a patent on it in 1844. The pneumatic tire was invented in the late 1880s by a Scottish veterinarian, John Boyd Dunlop, reportedly for his son's tricycle.

☞ ☜

**FALLACY:** Wood floats, rocks sink.

**FACT:** Most wood floats, but as many a sunken wooden boat demonstrates, under the right conditions wood can sink. Most rocks sink, but pumice isn't one of them. Pumice is a light igneous rock, full of air pockets, that forms from volcanic froth and floats quite well.

☞ ☜

**FALLACY:** The longest a human has been on the Moon was a couple of hours.

**FACT:** The longest a human has been on the Moon was during the Apollo 17 mission in December 1972, the last manned mission to the Moon. Ronald E. Evans stayed with the mother ship in orbit. Eugene A. Cernan and Harrison H. Schmidt descended and were on the Moon for seventy-five hours, more than forty-four hours of which they spent outside their landing craft.

☞ ☜

**FALLACY:** The different colors of neon lights are caused by different coatings of the inside of the glass tubes.

**FACT:** There is no coating on the inside of the glass tube of a neon light that would cause it to glow a different color. What you are seeing is the neon itself glowing. When neon gas is conducting electricity in a tube, it glows red. Only red. If you are looking at any other color, you are not looking at neon. To get other colors in "neon" signs, other gases are used.

☞ ☜

**FALLACY:** The U.S. nickel coin is made of nickel.

**FACT:** Nickel is a hard, ferromagnetic, silver-white, metallic element. The U.S. nickel coin is a copper-nickel alloy containing 75 percent copper and only 25 percent nickel. That doesn't hold true, of course, for a wooden nickel.

☞ ☜

**FALLACY:** The North Star is part of the Big Dipper.

**FACT:** Ursa Minor, the Little Bear, also known as the Little Dipper, is a ladle-shaped constellation around the north celestial pole. The brightest star in Ursa Minor is the tip of its handle, Polaris, the North Star. Ursa Major, the Great Bear, is a far larger constellation containing the seven stars of the Big Dipper. Among many other names, the Big Dipper is known as Charles's Wain, the Plow, and the Starry Plough. The two stars at the front of the Big Dipper point roughly toward the North Star.

☞ ☜

**FALLACY:** Oxidation, by definition, has to involve oxygen.

**FACT:** Oxidation, by definition, refers to any chemical reaction in which electrons are lost. The reverse of oxidation, a chemical reaction in which electrons are gained, is called reduction. The two processes are complementary, and the number of electrons lost by one substance equals the number of electrons gained by another. Oxygen is a very common oxidant (a substance that gains electrons) but by no means the only one. Chlorine is a strong oxidizing agent; when combined with sodium, a reducing agent, the result is sodium chloride: common table salt.

☞ ☜

**FALLACY:** A year has more than 10,000 hours.

**FACT:** Only seems that way when you aren't having fun. A year has

31,557,600 seconds, which is 525,960 minutes, which is only 8,766 hours. Don't put off having fun a second longer.

☞ ☜

**FALLACY:** It's not easy to remember the order of the planets outward from the Sun.

**FACT:** Remember this mnemoric, and the first letter of each word will tell you the order of the planets outward from the Sun: My very excellent mother just served us nine pizzas. Translation: Mercury, Venus, Earth, Mars, Jupiter, Saturn, Uranus, Neptune, Pluto.

☞ ☜

**FALLACY:** All the planets are named after Greek or Roman gods.

**FACT:** All the planets are named after Greek or Roman gods—except one. Mercury, Venus, Mars, and Jupiter were named after gods. Saturn, Uranus, Neptune, and Pluto were named after gods. Earth wasn't.

☞ ☜

**FALLACY:** The scientific name for salt is sodium chloride.

**FACT:** Salt is a compound formed by the combination of an acid and a base, which neutralize each other as the hydrogen of the acid is replaced by positive ions. Sodium chloride, common table salt, is only one of many, many salts. Another edible salt, often mixed with sodium chloride to make "light" table salt, is potassium chloride.

☞ ☜

**FALLACY:** Ice, water, and water vapor can't all exist at the same temperature.

**FACT:** Ice, water, and water vapor can indeed all exist at the same temperature. The variable that makes it possible is pressure. The temperature and pressure that allow a substance to exist simultaneously as solid, liquid, and vapor is called its triple point. The triple point of water is a temperature of 273.16 kelvins (0° Celsius; 30° Fahrenheit), and a pressure of 611.2 pascals (611.2 newtons per square meter).

☞ ☜

**FALLACY:** Mercury, being closest to the Sun, is the hottest planet.

**FACT:** Mercury, which does not have an atmosphere, is not hot all over. On the night side it gets down to −180° Celsius (−292° Fahrenheit). At the equator on the side facing the Sun it gets up to 427° C (800° F); by comparison, the melting point of lead is 328° C (622° F). Mercury does not hold the Hottest Planet record, though. Venus, because its atmosphere creates a greenhouse effect, has an overall temperature of 460° Celsius (860° Fahrenheit).

☞ ☜

**FALLACY:** Water gas is just water vapor, and therefore harmless.

**FACT:** Water gas and water vapor are two completely different things, and water gas is far from harmless. Composed of about 50 percent carbon monoxide and 40 percent hydrogen, it is made by passing steam over hot carbon such as coal or coke. Because of its components, water gas is a high-energy-content fuel and burns with an intense bluish flame; also because of its components, it is deadly if breathed.

☞ ☜

**FALLACY:** WD-40, which will loosen almost any stuck-together metal parts, got its name from "Will Detach" and the year 1940.

**FACT:** WD-40 was developed in the 1950s to protect missile parts from damage by southern California's coastal fogs. After thirty-nine near misses, Norm Larsen, on his fortieth try, came up with a formula that successfully got under moisture in metal pores and displaced it. Norm Larsen called his success simply Water Displacement—40th formula. WD-40 for short. As many people soon discovered, the petroleum-based product also cleans tools, frees frozen metal parts, and does a host of other things besides protecting metal from moisture by displacing water. The Rocket Chemical Company was formed in 1958 to sell WD-40; since the company sold nothing else, it changed its name in 1959 to WD-40.

☞ ☜

**FALLACY:** Room temperature is whatever temperature a room is.

**FACT:** A room at the geographic South Pole with windows open and no heat would have a year-round average temperature of −49° Celsius, (−56° Fahrenheit). Throughout the course of the year, it would never once reach room temperature. Room temperature, by definition, is from 20° to 25° Celsius (68° to 77° Fahrenheit).

☞ ☜

**FALLACY:** To be a moon, it has to orbit a planet.

**FACT:** Most moons do orbit planets. Not all, though. In 1994, the space probe Galileo discovered that 243 Ida, an asteroid about 52 kilometers (32 miles) long, has a moon. Ida's moon is about 1.5 kilometers (0.9 miles) in diameter, and when Galileo passed, was about 100 kilometers (62 miles) from Ida. In September 1994, Ida's moon was officially named Dactyl.

☞ ☜

**FALLACY:** Since a meter is three feet, a thousand cubic meters is 27,000 cubic feet.

**FACT:** Doesn't work quite that way. A meter is roughly 3.2808 feet. From there on up it goes like this:

$$
\begin{array}{ll}
\text{1 square meter} & = 10.764 \text{ square feet} \\
\text{1,000 square meters} & = 10,764 \text{ square feet} \\
\text{1 cubic meter} & = 35.315 \text{ cubic feet} \\
\text{1,000 cubic meters} & = 35,315 \text{ cubic feet}
\end{array}
$$

☞ ☜

**FALLACY:** Formica is made from formic acid.

**FACT:** This is one of those times when a little knowledge can be a dangerous thing. Formic acid, $CH_2O_2$, got its name from the Latin word *formica,* "ant"; the strong, pungent smell from ants is caused by formic acid. Formica is a trademark for any of several laminated plastic products made of synthetic resin, notably those used as surface finishes on home and restaurant countertops and tabletops. Formica is not made from formic acid.

☞ ☜

**FALLACY:** To see the subtitles on closed-captioned TV programs, you must buy a decoder.

**FACT:** For more than a dozen years you had to buy a decoder to see the subtitles on closed-captioned TV programs. The Television Decoder Circuitry Act of 1990, which took effect on 1 July 1993, requires that all new television sets with screens of 13 inches or larger contain circuitry for decoding and displaying captions. Although originally intended for people with hearing problems, a large percentage of the people who read the captions do so to help them learn English. Captions are now widely available not only on network and cable TV programs, but also on home videos.

☞ ☜

**FALLACY:**  A ton equals 2,000 pounds.

**FACT:**  How much a ton equals depends on where you are and whom you're talking to. The common U.S. ton, also called a short ton, equals 2,000 pounds, or 32,000 ounces. A metric ton (tonne) equals 1,000 kilograms, or 2,204.5855 pounds, or 35,273.3686 ounces. To put that another way, a U.S. ton equals 0.9072 of a metric ton; a metric ton equals 1.1023 U.S. tons. If you're off to have a ton of fun, make it a metric ton.

☞ ☜

**FALLACY:**  The comics section of the Sunday newspaper uses about a dozen different colors.

**FACT:**  Remember mixing blue and yellow to get green when you were a kid? The Sunday comics go in for that process in a big way. All the colors you see are made up of dots of the three primary colors—blue, red, and yellow—plus black.

☞ ☜

**FALLACY:**  Earth's Moon is the largest moon in the solar system.

**FACT:**  Ganymede, largest of Jupiter's moons with a diameter of 3,270 miles, is larger than Earth's Moon, which has a diameter of only 2,160 miles; Ganymede is also larger than the planet Mercury. Earth's Moon doesn't even come in second. The other moons larger than the Moon are Jupiter's Callisto and Io, Saturn's Titan, and Neptune's Triton. Because of Io's blotchy reds and yellows, caused by its active sulfur volcanoes, Io is the moon most likely to hit your eye like a big pizza pie.

☞ ☜

**FALLACY:**  The Moon is only about half as wide as Earth.

**FACT:**  Earth's equatorial diameter is 7,926 miles. The Moon's equatorial diameter is 2,160 miles. That makes Earth 3.67 times as wide as the Moon, or the Moon only 27.25 percent as wide as Earth. To put that in perspective, the Moon isn't even as wide as the United States.

☞ ☜

**FALLACY:**  Scuba gear was invented by the U.S. Navy during World War II.

**FACT:**  Scuba is an acronym for self-contained underwater breathing apparatus. Scuba gear was indeed invented during World War II—but not by the U.S. Navy. Developed by Jacques Yves Cousteau and Émil Gagnan in 1942, it was first successfully tested in 1943.

☞ 🕷

**FALLACY:**  Cosmic rays are rays.

**FACT:**  Primary cosmic rays are high-energy particles, not rays. The highest-energy particles, which come from outside our Milky Way galaxy, are mostly protons—hydrogen nuclei. Lower-energy particles, which probably originate within the Galaxy, are mostly atomic nuclei of elements heavier than hydrogen.

☞ 🕷

**FALLACY:**  A ten-foot sphere has the largest surface area, followed by a ten-foot cube, then a ten-foot pyramid.

**FACT:**  A sphere with a diameter of ten feet has a surface area of 314.159 square feet. A cube ten feet on a side has a surface area of 600 square feet. A ten-foot-high, four-sided pyramid with ten-foot bases, has a surface area of 300 square feet.

☞ 🕷

**FALLACY:**  For obvious reasons, there is no ice on the planet Mercury.

**FACT:**  Ice on Mercury, the planet closest to the Sun, would seem to be in the "snowball in hell" category; daytime temperatures are high enough to melt lead, and the equator reaches 427° Celsius (800° Fahrenheit). There are, however, entire lakes of frozen water on Mercury. Possibly millions of years old, the ice is protected from sunlight in miles-wide polar craters that provide permanent shade. It should be noted that the record low temperature in Hell, Michigan, was −25° Fahrenheit.

☞ 🕷

**FALLACY:**  The boiling point of water is 180° Fahrenheit above its condensation point.

**FACT:**  If you heat water to 100° Celsius (212° Fahrenheit), it will boil into water vapor. If you cool water vapor below 212° Fahrenheit, it will condense into liquid water. The point is that the boiling point and the condensation point are the same point.

☞ ☜

**FALLACY:** The first manmade vehicle to travel on the surface of any celestial body except Earth was the Apollo lunar rover.

**FACT:** Right solar system, right satellite, wrong vehicle. The Apollo lunar rover, also called a Moon buggy and officially called the Lunar Roving Vehicle, was used on the Moon in 1971 and 1972 by Apollo missions 15, 16, and 17. However, the first manmade vehicle to travel on the surface of any celestial body except Earth was the unmanned Luna 17 rover, which traversed about six and a half miles of the Moon's surface during its active life in 1970 and 1971. The Luna 17 rover would creep along in two-week active periods while it had sunlight, sending photos and other data back to Earth. Although the humans who went to the Moon all returned safely, none of the rovers did; they're still on the Moon.

☞ ☜

**FALLACY:** Earth is much closer to Jupiter than it is to the Sun.

**FACT:** One astronomical unit (AU), the mean distance between Earth and the Sun, is 149,597,870 kilometers or 92,955,778 miles. Jupiter orbits at 5.203 AU, which is 778,357,718 kilometers or 483,648,914 miles. The 628,759,848 kilometers or 390,693,136 miles between Jupiter and Earth is 4.203 times the distance between Earth and the Sun.

☞ ☜

**FALLACY:** A minute lasts for sixty seconds—no less, no more.

**FACT:** All minutes are equal, but some are more equal than others. International Atomic Time is extremely accurate because it is determined by the vibrational frequencies of atomic clocks. Universal Time, earlier called Greenwich Mean Time, is determined by the position of stars over Greenwich, England. Because Earth's rotation has been slowing, the International Earth Rotation Service in Paris adds leap seconds on the last day of June or December to keep UT synchronized with IAT. On 30 June 1994, for example, 11:59 P.M. lasted for sixty-one seconds.

☞ ☜

**FALLACY:**  Hydrogen burns cleanly, leaving no combustion products.

**FACT:**  Hydrogen by itself will not burn. When hydrogen burns, it is actually oxidizing: combining with oxygen very rapidly. The space shuttle uses hydrogen and oxygen as fuel at liftoff. Two of the combustion products are heat and light. Those huge white clouds the shuttle produces are made of another combustion product of combining hydrogen with oxygen: water vapor.

☞ ☜

**FALLACY:**  Because numbers are the same everywhere, a billion is a billion no matter where you are.

**FACT:**  The problem lies not in the numbers, but in the names for the numbers. In Britain, France, and the United States, a million is 1,000,000. Then things get a bit more complicated. In Britain and France a billion is a million million: 1,000,000,000,000; in the United States, though, a billion is only a thousand million: 1,000,000,000. What people in the United States call a billion, people in Britain and France call a milliard. From there on up, it's downhill all the way.

☞ ☜

**FALLACY:**  "The dog days of summer" got their name from the fact that dogs lay around during the height of summer heat.

**FACT:**  Astrologers in the Middle Ages believed that when the brightest star, Sirius, was in the same part of the sky as the Sun, the combined heat caused the hottest days of summer. Sirius is 8.6 light-years (50.6 trillion miles) from Earth and provides no additional heat, but the astrologers didn't know that. Sirius, which shares the Northern Hemisphere's daytime summer sky with the Sun, is in the constellation Canis Major, or Greater Dog, and is also called the Dog Star. Put all those facts together and you know where "the dog days of summer" got their name. Halfway around the year, as the night sky of winter wheels overhead, the faithful Dog Star follows Orion the Hunter as he chases the Pleiades, also known as the Seven Sisters, the daughters of Atlas. All that probably has nothing to do with this newspaper ad about dogs in the PETS section: "Great Dames for sale."

# 11

## United States

**FALLACY:** The only presidents who wore a beard while in office were Abraham Lincoln and Ulysses S. Grant.

**FACT:** There are five presidents in the bearded bunch, so far. In addition to Lincoln and Grant, the presidents who chose not to shave either the top or the bottom of their head were Rutherford B. Hayes, James A. Garfield, and Benjamin Harrison.

☞ ☜

**FALLACY:** The U.S. $100 bill is the only bill that's still a Silver Certificate.

**FACT:** Federal Reserve Notes are backed only by the full faith and credit of the government of the United States, not by gold or silver. All US. currency backed by gold or silver has been withdrawn. The U.S. $100 bill—the largest denomination now being printed—is a Federal Reserve Note. Suggesting that the government of the United States has no faith in Federal Reserve Notes of any denomination, these words have been added to all of them: IN GOD WE TRUST.

☞ ☜

**FALLACY:** Aaron Burr's only real claim to fame was being the first American executed for treason.

**FACT:** Aaron Burr was not the first American executed for treason, and his claims to fame are many. He distinguished himself in the Revolutionary War, and from 1791 to 1797 was a U.S. Senator from New York. In the election of 1800, he and Thomas Jefferson each received seventy-three Electoral College votes for the presidency. It was so close between them that the House of Representatives had to vote thirty-six times before deciding to make Jefferson president and Burr vice president. In 1804 Burr lost the race for governor of New York, in large part because of the efforts of his longtime foe, Alexander Hamilton. On 11 July 1804, Vice President Burr and General Hamilton fought the famous duel that ended Burr's political career and Hamilton's life. Burr then became involved in a complicated conspiracy with American General James Wilkinson and others to establish an independent nation in Mexico and the Southwest to be allied with Spain. He was tried for treason in 1807. This may put a burr under your saddle, but he was not executed, for the simple reason that he was acquitted—not convicted—of treason.

☞ ☜

**FALLACY:** George Bush didn't talk about sex in his speeches.

**FACT:** Well, seldom intentionally. He did get off a classic in 1988 at the College of Southern Idaho, referring to his relationship with Ronald Reagan: "For seven and a half years I've worked alongside him, and I'm proud to be his partner. We've had triumphs, we've made mistakes, we'd had sex." As soon as he realized what he'd said, he changed it to, "Setbacks. We've had setbacks."

☞ ☜

**FALLACY:** The first African-American member of the U.S. Cabinet was appointed shortly after the Civil War.

**FACT:** Secretary of Housing and Urban Development Robert C. Weaver was the first African-American to serve as a member of the U.S. Cabinet. He was appointed by President Lyndon Johnson in 1966, considerably after the Civil War.

☞ ☜

**FALLACY:** There are no age or language requirements for becoming a U.S. citizen.

**FACT:** Applicants for U.S. citizenship must be at least eighteen years old. They must be able to read, write, and speak words in common usage in the English language unless they are either physically unable to or they are over fifty-five years of age and have lived in the United States as legal permanent residents for at least fifteen years.

☞ ☜

**FALLACY:** The first president to live in the White House was the first president, George Washington.

**FACT:** George Washington never lived in the White House, because it wasn't completed until after he'd retired from the presidency. The first president to live in the White House was the second president, John Adams. Third fact is that the fourth president wasn't the first to bring a fifth into the White House.

☞ ☜

**FALLACY:** The Civil War was fought in the South because the Confederacy was unable to invade the North.

**FACT:** That would come as a surprise to Indiana, Ohio, and especially to Gettysburg, Pennsylvania.

☞ ☜

**FALLACY:** Massachusetts, where the Pilgrims landed, was the first of the original thirteen American colonies.

**FACT:** Thirteen is a doubly significant number here. Not only were there thirteen original European colonies, but Massachusetts was settled thirteen years too late to be the first. Virginia was settled in 1607; Massachusetts in 1620. The others, in chronological order, were New Hampshire in 1623, New York in 1624, Connecticut and Maryland in 1634, Rhode Island in 1636, Delaware in 1638, New Jersey and North Carolina in 1660, South Carolina in 1670, Pennsylvania in 1682, and Georgia in 1733. However, the order of the original thirteen states is determined by the date on which they ratified the Constitution, that order being: Delaware, Pennsylvania, New Jersey, Georgia, Connecticut, Massachusetts, Maryland, South Carolina, New Hampshire, Virginia, New York, North Carolina, and Rhode Island.

☞ ☜

**FALLACY:** No U.S. president has completed his term, left office, and then been reelected to the presidency.

**FACT:** One did perform that feat. Grover Cleveland was both the twenty-second U.S. president, from 1885 to 1889, and the twenty-fourth, from 1893 to 1897. The twenty-third president, from 1889 to 1893, was Benjamin Harrison.

☞ ☜

**FALLACY:** The Battle Above the Clouds was a battle among warplanes.

**FACT:** It would have been difficult to use warplanes in the Battle Above the Clouds because they hadn't been invented yet. Orville and Wilbur Wright made their famous flights on 17 December 1903. The Battle Above the Clouds, which occurred on 24 November 1863, was part of the Chattanooga campaign during the U.S. Civil War. General Joseph Hooker, making up for his loss to Robert E. Lee at Chancellorsville in May 1863, drove Confederate troops from Lookout Mountain. Despite folklore, incidentally, the nickname "hooker" for a prostitute did not come from the general's name; hookers were called that before the Civil War.

☞ ☜

**FALLACY:** The Stars and Bars, a red flag with crossed blue diagonals, was the official flag of the Confederacy.

**FACT:** The red flag with thirteen white stars on crossed blue diagonals was not the Stars and Bars. A constitutional convention was held in Montgomery, Alabama, on 4 February 1861. The Congress of the Confederate States of America moved to Richmond, Virginia, on 20 July, and in October elected Jefferson Davis as president; he was inaugurated on 22 February 1882. The Congress also adopted an official flag, called the Stars and Bars, but it was not a red flag with crossed blue diagonals. It had three stripes or bars, red-white-red, and a union with a circle of white stars on a blue field.

☞ ☜

**FALLACY:** The first presidential visit to Hawaii came many decades before the first presidential visit to Alaska.

**FACT:** The first presidential visit to Hawaii was by Franklin D. Roosevelt, in 1934. The first presidential visit to Alaska was by Warren Harding, in 1923. Although both belonged to the United States, neither was a state at the time.

☞ ☜

**FALLACY:** Connecticut has a smaller population than any other state except Rhode Island.

**FACT:** Wyoming has a smaller population than Connecticut. Alaska has a smaller population than Connecticut. Vermont has a smaller population than Connecticut. North Dakota has a smaller population than Connecticut. Delaware has a smaller population than Connecticut. South Dakota has a smaller population than Connecticut. Montana has a smaller population than Connecticut. Rhode Island, often used as an example of a small state because of its geographical size, has less than one-third the population of Connecticut—but it has a larger population than any of the other states mentioned above.

☞ ☜

**FALLACY:**   The Constitution went into effect in 1787, when George Washington, President of the United States, sent it to Congress, which approved it.

**FACT:**   George Washington sent the proposed U.S. Constitution to Congress in 1787, but he was not President of the United States; he was President of the Constitutional Convention. After unanimous election by the electoral college, he was inaugurated as President of the United States on 30 April 1789. Congress was not authorized to approve the Constitution, only to submit it to the states for ratification, which it did on 28 September 1787. According to Article VII: "The Ratification of the Conventions of nine States, shall be sufficient for the Establishment of this Constitution between the States so ratifying the Same." The ninth state to do so was New Hampshire, on 21 June 1788. The government, moving about as rapidly as it does today, didn't officially declare the Constitution in effect until 4 March 1789. Definitely not faster than a speeding ballot.

☞ ☜

**FALLACY:**   Some states have many counties, but all states have at least one.

**FACT:**   Delaware has only three counties: Kent, New Castle, and Sussex. California has fifty-eight, including the nation's most populous, Los Angeles County. New York City alone has five counties. The states of Alaska and Louisiana, however, have no counties at all. In place of counties, the equivalent geographical areas in Alaska are called divisions, and in Louisiana they're called parishes.

☞ ☜

**FALLACY:**   Citizens of Washington, D.C., have the same representation in Congress as all other citizens.

**FACT:**   Citizens of Washington, District of Columbia, are citizens of the

United States, pay the same taxes as other U.S. citizens, and are subject to the same federal laws, but were disenfranchised until the Twenty-third Amendment to the Constitution in 1961. Since then they have voted in presidential elections, and since 1970 have elected a delegate to Congress. Their congressional delegate has no vote, however, and as the District of Columbia is not a state, they have no senators. The U.S. House of Representatives voted on statehood for the District in November 1993, defeating the proposal by a vote of 277 to 153.

☞ ☜

**FALLACY:** States with a death penalty have about half the murder rate of states without one.

**FACT:** That ratio is right, but backward. According to figures released by the FBI in 1994, states with a death penalty had about twice the murder rate of states without one.

☞ ☜

**FALLACY:** The signers of the Declaration of Independence signed as representatives of their individual colonies.

**FACT:** The signers of the Declaration of Independence were members of the Continental Congress. They signed in the name of the people of all the colonies, but as representatives of the United States of America. Although adopted by the congress on 4 July 1776, the only names that appeared on the document that day were "JOHN HANCOCK, President" and "Attest. CHARLES THOMPSON, Secretary." The document was signed by fifty members on 2 August, and by six more after that date. The following capitalization is as in the original:

> We, therefore, the Representatives of the UNITED STATES OF AMERICA, in General Congress, Assembled, appealing to the Supreme Judge of the World for the Rectitude of our Intentions, do, in the Name, and by Authority of the good People of these Colonies, solemnly Publish and Declare, That these United Colonies are, and of Right ought to be, Free and Independent States; . . .

☞ ☜

**FALLACY:** The signers of the Declaration of Independence were born in what became the United States.

**FACT:** Most of the signers of the Declaration of Independence were born in what became the United States, but eight of them were not. Button Gwinnett was born in Down Hatherly, England. Francis Lewis was born in Llandaff, Wales. Robert Morris was born in Liverpool, England. James Smith was born in Dublin, Ireland. George Taylor was born in Ireland. Matthew Thornton was born in Ireland. James Wilson was born in Carskerdo, Scotland. John Witherspoon was born in Gifford, Scotland.

☞ ☜

**FALLACY:** All remaining original copies of the Declaration of Independence are preserved in government museums.

**FACT:** Two hundred copies of the Declaration of Independence were issued by the Continental Congress on broadsheets, large sheets of paper printed on only one side. Twenty-four of those copies are known to exist today. Some are safe in government archives and museums, but some are bought and sold for profit like any other commodity. One of the best-preserved copies was offered at auction in 1993 by Visual Equities Inc. and bought by Kaller Historical Documents, a dealer in rare manuscripts.

☞ ☜

**FALLACY:** The military draft was first introduced in the United States for World War I.

**FACT:** When the military draft was first introduced in the United States, people didn't take kindly to it. The New York City draft office at 677 Third Avenue was burned to the ground, and tens of thousands of people took to the streets. Over the course of four days, more than a thousand people died in the New York City antidraft uprising. And that was in July 1863, when New York City had a much smaller population. The draft was for the Civil War. Ironic, considering that one of the major points of contention in that war was involuntary servitude.

☞ ☜

**FALLACY:** Giving false information on a driver's license application is a misdemeanor.

**FACT:** Each state has its own laws on the matter, but some are trickier than others. The state with the most drivers, California, is a case in point. The Department of Motor Vehicles Driver Handbook says: ''Making A

False Statement On A DMV Document Is A MISDEMEANOR OF-
FENSE. Signing A False Statement Under Penalty Of Perjury Is A FEL-
ONY OFFENSE.'' The capitalization is theirs.

☞ ☜

**FALLACY:** Free speech is the only topic covered in the First Amendment to the Constitution.

**FACT:** The politicians of those days were much less wordy than the
present crop. They managed to pack a lot of meaning into a few words,
rather than the other way around. The First Amendment to the Constitution dealt with much more than free speech. Here it is in its entirety:

### AMENDMENT I

Congress shall make no law respecting an establishment of religion, or
prohibiting the free exercise thereof; or abridging the freedom of
speech, or of the press; or the right of the people peaceably to assemble,
and to petition the Government for a redress of grievances.

☞ ☜

**FALLACY:** Mount Vernon was built and named by George Washington.

**FACT:** Mount Vernon was neither built nor named by George Washington. At the age of sixteen, George went to live with his half-brother,
Lawrence, who had built and named Mount Vernon. Lawrence died in
1752, and George received Mount Vernon by inheritance.

☞ ☜

**FALLACY:** George Washington's false teeth were made of wood.

**FACT:** This bit of folk knowledge has been around for a while, but it's
not true. George Washington's false teeth were made of ivory.

☞ ☜

**FALLACY:** George Washington was a military man and held no political office until he was inaugurated as the first president.

**FACT:** George Washington wore many hats over the years. Between
1758 and 1774 he was a member of the Virginia House of Burgesses,
and in 1770 he was a justice of the peace in Fairfax County, Virginia.
He was a delegate to the First Continental Congress in 1774, and a
delegate to the Second Continental Congress in 1775. In 1787 he was

not only a delegate to the Constitutional Convention, but its chairman. All this was prior to his first presidential inauguration on the balcony of New York City's Federal Hall in 1789.

☞ ☜

**FALLACY:** George Washington delivered his Farewell Address when he left the presidency in 1796.

**FACT:** George Washington's September 1796 "Farewell Address to the People of the United States"—parts of which were said to have been written by Alexander Hamilton, Thomas Jefferson, and James Madison— was never delivered. It was published in *Claypole's Daily Advertiser.* Among the thoughts in the Farewell Address were:

• "Guard against the impostures of pretended patriotism."

• "Overgrown military establishments are under any form of government inauspicious to liberty, and are to be regarded as particularly hostile to republican liberty."

• "Some day, taking its pattern from the United States, there will be founded a United States of Europe."

☞ ☜

**FALLACY:** The main address at the dedication of the Gettysburg Cemetery was given by Abraham Lincoln.

**FACT:** The main address at the dedication of the Gettysburg Cemetery on 19 November 1863 was given by an American orator and statesman, but it wasn't Abraham Lincoln. Lincoln gave his famous Gettysburg Address in about two minutes. The principal speaker at the dedication spoke for about two hours. During his career, this man from Massachusetts was a congressman, senator, governor, minister to England, secretary of state, and president of Harvard University. His name was Edward Everett.

☞ ☜

**FALLACY:** The U.S. Constitution says that citizens have the right to own guns.

**FACT:** There's no problem with what the U.S. Constitution says; the heated debates are about what the Constitution means. Rather than get into the interpretations, which lead to endless arguments, here's what Amendment II to the U.S. Constitution says about the matter: "A well regulated Militia, being necessary to the security of a free State, the right of the people to keep and bear Arms, shall not be infringed.'' That's the entire text of Amendment II.

☞ ☜

**FALLACY:** The only five-cent coin the U.S. has issued is the nickel.

**FACT:** The only *recent* five-cent coin the U.S. has issued is the nickel. In 1792, the government issued a ten-cent coin called a disme, an obsolete English word for "tenth"; that same year it issued a five-cent coin called a half disme. From 1794 to 1873 the U.S. government issued both a five-cent half dime and a ten-cent dime. The dime is still with us, but the half dime hasn't been minted since 1873.

☞ ☜

**FALLACY:** U.S. presidents have included a father-son pair, John and John Quincy Adams, but not yet a grandfather-grandson.

**FACT:** It has happened only once. William Henry Harrison, the ninth president, was a son of the Benjamin Harrison who signed the Declaration of Independence, and the grandfather of the Benjamin Harrison who was the twenty-third president.

☞ ☜

**FALLACY:** The Speaker of the U.S. House of Representatives must be a member of the House.

**FACT:** The members in the U.S. House of Representatives can choose anyone at all to be their Speaker, whether or not that person is a representative. Although there are several Constitutional requirements for membership in the House, Article I, Section 2, Part 5 of the U.S. Constitution has only this to say about the Speaker: "The House of Representatives shall choose their Speaker and other officers; and shall have the sole power of impeachment." Improbable though it is, it's possible that a citizen who is not a Representative could be Speaker of the U.S. House of Representatives. The odds of that happening are only slightly less than the odds of your winning a lottery.

☞ ☜

**FALLACY:** President Andrew Johnson's only claim to fame is that he was the only president ever impeached.

**FACT:**  President Andrew Johnson has at least one other claim to fame, although it's not as widely known as his impeachment. He was also the only president ever elected to the U.S. Senate after leaving the presidency.

☞ ☜

**FALLACY:**  The Louisiana Purchase increased the size of the United States by almost half.

**FACT:**  The Louisiana Purchase of 1803, during the presidency of Thomas Jefferson, came as a surprise to almost everyone. Jefferson sent envoys to France in the hope of buying New Orleans and West Florida for $2 million. Napoleon offered to sell the entire area between the Mississippi River and the Rocky Mountains, from British North America to the Gulf of Mexico, for $15 million. The Louisiana Purchase *doubled* the size of the United States.

☞ ☜

**FALLACY:**  Abraham Lincoln was the only president born in a log cabin.

**FACT:**  Six U.S. presidents were born in log cabins. Abraham Lincoln was the fifth. The others were Andrew Jackson, the first U.S. president born in a log cabin; Zachary Taylor; Millard Fillmore; James Buchanan; and James Garfield.

☞ ☜

**FALLACY:**  Congressional Medals of Honor cannot be revoked.

**FACT:**  The U.S. Army awarded 2,625 Medals of Honor in the name of Congress between 25 March 1863 and World War I. A review before the outbreak of World War I resulted in the revocation of 911 of those medals. That was more than double the total number of Medals of Honor awarded during World War II, 432, and nearly ten times the total number awarded during World War I, ninety-six.

☞ ☜

**FALLACY:**  Memorial Day is the U.S. military holiday.

**FACT:**  Memorial Day, also known as Decoration Day, is only one of the U.S. military holidays. Flag Day is usually celebrated as another. Veterans' Day, which used to be Armistice Day, is another. Each branch of the service also has its own, with the Navy stretching it to an entire

Fleet Week. Independence Day is not officially a military holiday, but Fourth of July parades always feature military contingents. And then there's Armed Forces Day.

☞ ☜

**FALLACY:** "In God We Trust" has been the official motto of the United States since the founding of the country.

**FACT:** Secretary of the Treasury Salmon P. Chase put that phrase on some U.S. coins in 1864 as a morale booster during the Civil War, much as Germany once put *Got Mit Uns* (God is With Us) on its army's belt buckles as a morale booster. "In God We Trust" appeared on various coins off and on for almost a century. Then, in 1955, Congress ordered that the phrase appear on not only all U.S. coins, but also on the nation's paper money. In 1956, Congress declared the phrase to be the U.S. national motto.

☞ ☜

**FALLACY:** Grand Canyon National Park is the oldest national park in the United States.

**FACT:** The Grand Canyon of the Colorado—up to one mile deep, eighteen miles wide in some places, and more than two hundred miles long—was initially protected in 1908, and became a national park in 1919. Yosemite is older, becoming a national park in 1890. The oldest national park in the United States, though, is also the oldest national park in the world: Yellowstone. The worldwide national park movement began in March 1872 when Yellowstone National Park was established. Yellowstone wasn't established in a state, but in the Territories of Montana and Wyoming; the 3,500-square-mile park is now in the states of Idaho, Montana, and Wyoming.

☞ ☜

**FALLACY:** President Richard Nixon realized immediately that discovery of the Watergate break-in was serious trouble.

**FACT:** Apparently, Nixon didn't have a clue as to how serious discovery of the 1972 Watergate burglary was. On one of the famous White House tapes, recorded four days after the break-in but not released until 1993, he said: "I don't think you're going to see a great, great uproar in this country about the Republican committee trying to bug the Democratic headquarters.'' Nixon was not noted for his ability to predict the future. On 7 November 1962, after losing the California gubernatorial election, he said to reporters: ''You won't have Nixon to kick around anymore—because, gentlemen, this is my last press conference.'' If he'd been right in 1962, he wouldn't have been wrong in 1972.

☞ ☜

**FALLACY:** The oath that naturalized citizens take is the Pledge of Allegiance.

**FACT:** The full name of the Pledge of Allegiance, which originated in the 8 September 1892 issue of the weekly magazine *Youth's Companion,* is the Pledge of Allegiance to the Flag. It is not to the flag that new citizens are pledging allegiance, but to the nation. The oath that naturalized citizens take is:

> I hereby declare, on oath, that I absolutely and entirely renounce and abjure all allegiance and fidelity to any foreign prince, potentate, state, or sovereignty, to whom or which I have heretofore been a subject or citizen; that I will support and defend the Constitution and laws of the United States of America against all enemies, foreign and domestic; that I will bear true faith and allegiance to the same; that I will bear arms on behalf of the United States when required by the law; that I will perform noncombatant service in the armed forces of the United States when required by the law; that I will perform work of national importance under civilian direction when required by the law; and that I take this obligation freely without any mental reservation or purpose of evasion; so help me God.

☞ ☜

**FALLACY:** Although Ross Perot did well in a couple of small states in the 1992 election, he didn't do well in any large state.

**FACT:** H. Ross Perot got more votes in Maine than George Bush did, and he got more votes in Utah than Bill Clinton did. In California, the largest state in population, Perot received 21 percent of the votes. That was the largest California percentage for any independent or third-party candidate since Theodore Roosevelt ran for the Progressive Party in 1912 against Woodrow Wilson (who won), William Howard Taft, and Eugene

V. Debbs. Roosevelt did better than Perot, though: he won California, even though it was by less than 200 votes.

☞ ☜

**FALLACY:**  Oregon's Portland is its largest city and capital; Maine's Portland is one of its smallest cities and capital.

**FACT:**  Oregon's Portland, located on the Willamette River near its junction with the Columbia River, is the largest city in the state but is not the capital. Oregon's capital is Salem, farther south in the Willamette Valley. Maine's Portland, located on Casco Bay, is not one of the smallest cities in the state; it's the largest. It, too, is not the state capital, although it was from 1820 to 1832. The capital of Maine, whose state song is ingeniously named "State of Maine Song," is Augusta.

☞ ☜

**FALLACY:**  Most presidents in this century have come directly from Congress.

**FACT:**  You'd think so from the number of members of Congress who run in each election, but most presidents in this century have not come directly from Congress. As of 1996, the last member of the Senate to become president was John F. Kennedy, in 1960; the last member of the House of Representatives to become president was James Garfield, in 1880.

☞ ☜

**FALLACY:**  Most of the early U.S. presidents were born in New York or Pennsylvania.

**FACT:**  George Washington, Thomas Jefferson, James Madison, and James Monroe were born in Virginia; John Adams and John Quincy Adams were born in Massachusetts. Andrew Jackson was born in South Carolina. That takes care of the first seven presidents. The first president born in New York was the eighth, Martin Van Buren. The first president born in Pennsylvania was the fifteenth, James Buchanan.

☞ ☜

**FALLACY:**  The Constitution says that the vice president is next in line for the presidency, then the Speaker of the House.

**FACT:**  What the Constitution says on the matter in Article II, Section 1, is:

In Case of the Removal of the President from Office, or of his Death, Resignation, or Inability to discharge the Powers and Duties of the said Office, the Same shall devolve on the Vice President, and the Congress may by Law provide for the Case of Removal, Death, Resignation, or Inability, both of the President and Vice President, declaring what Officer shall then act as President, and such Officer shall act accordingly, until the Disability be removed, or a President shall be elected.

This section was modified by Amendment XX, and again by Amendment XXV, but neither of those Amendments mentions the Speaker of the House of Representatives. The key phrase is: "the Congress may by Law provide." In 1947, Congress passed a law naming the Speaker of the House as next in line after the vice president, followed by the president pro tempore of the Senate, and then the members of the cabinet in the historical order in which the cabinet posts were established. It's because of that law, not because of the Constitution, that the Speaker of the House follows the vice president in the line of succession.

☞ ☜

**FALLACY:** Harry Truman was the first president to invite an African-American citizen to a White House dinner.

**FACT:** The first president to invite an African-American citizen to a White House dinner was Theodore Roosevelt, known for many firsts. The guest at the 16 October 1901 event was Booker T. Washington, founder of Tuskegee Institute. Society was far more racist then than it is now, and several socialites were severely shocked.

☞ ☜

**FALLACY:** The faces on Mount Rushmore are, from left to right, George Washington, Thomas Jefferson, Franklin Roosevelt, and Abraham Lincoln.

**FACT:** The sixty-foot-high faces carved into the northeast side of Mount Rushmore in the Black Hills of western South Dakota are, from left to right as you face the sculptures, those of Presidents George Washington, Thomas Jefferson, Theodore—not Franklin—Roosevelt, and Abraham Lincoln. The project was designed and supervised by Gutzon Borglum and his son. Construction took place between 1927 and 1941. The choice of presidents, of course, was made before construction began in 1927. FDR didn't become president for the first of his four terms until 1933.

☞ ☜

**FALLACY:** The founding fathers were superstitious about the number 13.

**FACT:** The founding fathers were no more superstitious about the number 13 than the founding mothers were. Fear of the number 13, known as *triskaidekaphobia,* certainly didn't seem to afflict the committee appointed by the Continental Congress "to bring in a device for a seal of the United States of America." A design by William Barton, approved by Congress on 20 June 1782, became the Great Seal of the United States. Although there are two sides to the seal, both shown on the back of a $1 bill, only the side with the eagle is used as a seal on documents. There are 13 of many things on the Great Seal of the United States, including 13 stars, 13 arrows, 13 olive leaves, and 13 vertical stripes, on the obverse side; and 13 layers in the pyramid, on the reverse side.

☞ ☜

**FALLACY:** Torpedoes were used during the American Civil War.

**FACT:** "Damn the torpedoes! Full speed ahead!" were Admiral David Glasgow Farragut's famous words during a naval attack on Mobile, Alabama in 1864. He didn't mean the same thing by "torpedoes" that we do today, though. That was the word used at the time for what we now call mines.

☞ ☜

**FALLACY:** The only specific crime mentioned in the Constitution is treason.

**FACT:** Although treason is the only specific crime defined in the Constitution, it is not the only one mentioned. Article I, Section 6, for example, mentions breach of the peace:

> The Senators and Representatives shall receive a Compensation for their Services, to be ascertained by Law, and paid out of the Treasury of the United States. They shall in all Cases, except Treason, Felony and Breach of the Peace, be privileged from Arrest during their Attendance at the Session of their respective Houses, and in going to and returning from the same; and for any Speech or Debate in either House, they shall not be questioned in any other Place.

Article II, Section 4, mentions bribery:

> The President, Vice President, and all civil Officers of the United States, shall be removed from Office on Impeachment for, and Conviction of, Treason, Bribery, or other high Crimes and Misdemeanors.

Campaign contributions were not mentioned.

☞ ☜

**FALLACY:** No former president has become part of a government at war with the United States.

**FACT:** John Tyler was elected vice president in 1840, and became president when William Henry Harrison died on 4 April 1841. He accepted his party's nomination in 1844 but withdrew before the election. In 1861 he was chairman of a conference in Washington called to avert the Civil War. When the conference failed, he supported secession of the southern states. He not only sat in the provisional Confederate Congress, but became a member of the Confederate House of Representatives. He never sat in the Confederate House, however, because he died in Richmond on 18 January 1862, before the House had its first session.

☞ ☜

**FALLACY:** There is no street address for the White House because it doesn't need one.

**FACT:** It is highly probable that the U.S. Postal Service could find the White House without a street address, but it is highly improbable that they'd let even the president of the United States get away without one. The address they gave to the White House is 1600 Pennsylvania Avenue, NW, Washington DC 20500. As of the Clinton administration, you can also reach the White House by Internet e-mail at either president@-whitehouse.gov or vice-president@whitehouse.gov. The World Wide Web address is http://www.whitehouse.gov.

☞ ☜

**FALLACY:** Lincoln won the Lincoln-Douglas debates.

**FACT:** Abraham Lincoln, the challenger, and Stephen A. Douglas, the incumbent, were candidates for the U.S. Senate from Illinois. They held seven debates between 21 August and 15 October, 1858. Douglas was re-elected.

☞ ☜

**FALLACY:** The Post Office introduced Zip codes in the mid-1970s.

**FACT:** The U.S. Post Office, now called the U.S. Postal Service, introduced ZIP codes in the summer of 1963. The name is obviously not an abbreviation of "zippy," which would mean fast; all three letters are capitalized because ZIP is an acronym for Zone Improvement Plan.

☞ ☜

**FALLACY:** John Brown's body is buried at Harper's Ferry, Virginia.

**FACT:** First off, that's Harpers Ferry, West Virginia—no apostrophe and a different state. Second off, John Brown's body is buried at John Brown Farm State Historic Site at Lake Placid, New York. And the truth goes marching on.

☞ ☜

**FALLACY:** According to the Constitution, a president has to be sworn into office with his hand on the Bible.

**FACT:** There is no such requirement in the Constitution. There is no such federal law. Theodore Roosevelt, for one, refused to conform to that tradition. And that's all it is—a tradition. When the people of the United States elect their first Animist or Atheist or Baha'i or Buddhist of Confucian or Hindu or Jain or Jew or Muslim or other such to the presidency, there will be no Constitutional problem.

☞ ☜

**FALLACY:** When National Guard troops shot Kent State students in 1970, several students were wounded but none was killed.

**FACT:** On 4 May 1970, during a demonstration against the Vietnam War on the Kent State University campus, Ohio National Guard troops opened fire on the students. Although no one was ever convicted of any crime, four students were shot to death: Allison Krause, Jeffrey Miller, Sandra Scheuer, and William Schroeder.

☞ ☜

**FALLACY:** The Erie Canal was important because it connected Albany, New York, with Erie, Pennsylvania.

**FACT:** Built between 1817 and 1825, the Erie Canal never left New York state: it connected Albany with Buffalo, providing a navigable waterway between the Hudson River at Albany, and Lake Erie at Buffalo (hence its name). That made it much easier to ship farm products and raw materials from the Midwest to East Coast population centers, and for immigrants on the coast to move inland. On a larger scale, the Erie Canal opened a major shipping route between the Great Lakes and the Atlantic Ocean. The Erie Canal is now part of the New York State Barge Canal.

☞ ☜

**FALLACY:**   Stephen Cleveland, John Coolidge, and Thomas Wilson are not well-known Americans.

**FACT:**   Those three are definitely well-known Americans, although not by those names. Each of the men became famous using his middle name rather than his first name: Stephen Grover Cleveland, John Calvin Coolidge, and Thomas Woodrow Wilson.

☞ ☜

**FALLACY:**   Philadelphia, not Washington, was the first capital of the United States.

**FACT:**   Neither Philadelphia nor Washington was the first capital of the United States. That honor goes to New York City, which was the capital for a brief period in 1789–1790; the first Congress met at Federal Hall on 4 February 1789, and regular sessions began on 6 April. On 6 December 1790, Congress met in the new temporary capital, Philadelphia, which held that status from 1790 to 1800. In 1800 the government moved to the permanent capital, Washington, D.C.

☞ ☜

**FALLACY:**   Franklin and Eleanor Roosevelt were related only by marriage.

**FACT:**   Eleanor's maiden name was Roosevelt; so was Franklin's. Her full name was Anna Eleanor Roosevelt. She was the daughter of Elliott Roosevelt, Theodore Roosevelt's younger brother. Franklin and Theodore had a distant relative in common, Nicholas Roosevelt, making them fifth cousins.

☞ ☜

**FALLACY:**   The Constitution says that all U.S. presidents must be born in the United States.

**FACT:**   Article II, Section 1 of the U.S. Constitution contains this sentence: ''No person except a natural born Citizen, or a Citizen of the United States, at the time of the Adoption of this Constitution, shall be eligible to the Office of President; neither shall any Person be eligible to that Office who shall not have attained to the Age of thirty-five Years, and been fourteen Years a Resident within the United States.'' The United States came into existence with the adoption of the Declaration of Independence on 4 July 1776. Considering that a president must be at least thirty-five years old, the early presidents could not have been born in the United States. The first president born in the United States was the eighth, Martin Van Buren, born 5 December 1782.

☞ ☜

**FALLACY:**   Juneau, Alaska's capital, is connected to the rest of Alaska by a modern road system.

**FACT:**   Situated on the Alaskan Panhandle southeast of most of the state, Juneau was founded as a gold rush camp in 1880, but what made it a major town was its year-round ice-free port on Gastineau Channel. Alaska's capital since 1906, Juneau is not connected to the rest of Alaska by a modern road system, is not connected to the rest of Alaska by any road system, and does not have a single road connecting it with the rest of Alaska. It's not true, as some contend, that Alaska's official state bird is the mosquito; the official state bird is the willow ptarmigan.

☞ ☜

**FALLACY:**   In the 1860 presidential election, Abraham Lincoln received an overwhelming majority of the votes.

**FACT:**   In the 1860 presidential election, Abraham Lincoln did not receive even a simple majority of the votes. He received only 1,866,352 of the 4,676,853 votes cast—slightly less than 40 percent. Lincoln won because the other votes were split among three candidates: 1,375,157 for Stephen A. Douglas, 845,763 for John C. Breckinridge, and 589,581 for John Bell.

☞ ☜

**FALLACY:**   New York has the largest population after California.

**FACT:** New York had the largest population from 1810 until 1970, when it was replaced by California. New York had the second-largest population from 1970 until early 1994. New York now has the third-largest population, after California and Texas—a position it hasn't held since 1800, when it had the third-largest population after Virginia and Pennsylvania.

☞ ☜

**FALLACY:** It costs more than a penny to make a penny.

**FACT:** "A penny for your thoughts" costs less than it used to. When pennies were made of copper, it sometimes cost more than a penny to make a penny, depending on the current price of copper. Now that pennies are copper-coated zinc, it costs about eight-tenths of a penny to make a penny. Give or take a piggy bank, there are roughly 200 billion pennies out there somewhere.

☞ ☜

**FALLACY:** There haven't been any poor presidents, but even the richest of them has accepted his salary.

**FACT:** Two presidents publicly stated that they would not pocket their salary. Herbert Hoover, 1929–1933, gave his presidential paychecks to charity. John F. Kennedy, 1961–1963, simplified the process by not accepting them.

☞ ☜

**FALLACY:** Chief Justice William H. Rehnquist is the richest member of the U.S. Supreme Court.

**FACT:** Members of the U.S. Supreme Court and other high government officials report their wealth only within a very broad range. Although hardly a candidate for welfare, Chief Justice William H. Rehnquist is not the high court's richest member. Several justices, including Sandra Day O'Connor and John Paul Stevens, are millionaires. Figures are inexact, but the richest member of the U.S. Supreme Court is probably either Stephen G. Breyer or Ruth Bader Ginsberg, each of whom has an estimated net worth of more than $6 million.

☞ ☜

**FALLACY:**  The Speaker of the House is as likely as any other representative to lose a reelection bid.

**FACT:**  The Speaker of the House has usually been an incumbent for a long time. For a number of reasons, incumbents have a decided advantage over challengers; generally speaking, the longer they've been in office, the more likely they are to win. The last Speaker of the House to lose a reelection bid was Thomas Foley of Washington, in 1994. The next-to-last was William Pennington of New Jersey, in 1860.

☞ 🕸

**FALLACY:**  Mary Todd, Abraham Lincoln's wife, was born in Illinois.

**FACT:**  Mary Ann Todd Lincoln was born in the South, not in the North. During the Civil War, at least eight of her relatives, four brothers and four brothers-in-law, fought on the side of the Confederacy. Wartime rumors ran from her being a Southern sympathizer to a Southern spy. Rather than simply ignoring the rumors, President Lincoln condemned them at a U.S. Senate hearing.

☞ 🕸

**FALLACY:**  No two ex-presidents of the United States have died in the same year.

**FACT:**  The odds of it happening are small, considering the small group involved. It has happened, though. John Tyler died on 18 January 1862; Martin Van Buren died on 24 July 1862. During the first year of the twentieth century, Benjamin Harrison died on 13 March 1901; William McKinley died on 14 September 1901, eight days after being shot. The most interesting example is that of the three ex-presidents who died on the same day, although not all in the same year. James Monroe, who studied law with Thomas Jefferson, died on 4 July 1831. John Adams, one of the signers of the Declaration of Independence, died on 4 July 1826; Thomas Jefferson, main author of the Declaration of Independence, also died on 4 July 1826—the fiftieth anniversary of the Declaration of Independence.

☞ 🕸

**FALLACY:**  Washington, D.C.'s airport is in Washington, D.C.

**FACT:**  Washington, District of Columbia, is served by three public airports: Baltimore–Washington International Airport, Dulles International

Airport, and National Airport. National is four miles south of downtown Washington, directly across the Potomac River in Virginia. Dulles is twenty-five miles west of Washington, also across the Potomac in Virginia. Baltimore-Washington is twenty-five miles northeast of Washington, in Maryland. The president helicopters back and forth between the White House and Andrews Air Force Base, also in Maryland.

☞ ☜

**FALLACY:** The U.S. flag adds stars for new states, but has always had thirteen stripes for the original thirteen states.

**FACT:** The U.S. flag came into being through this resolution of the Marine Committee of the Second Continental Congress, adopted on 14 June 1777: "Resolved: that the flag of the United States be thirteen stripes, alternate red and white; that the union be thirteen stars, white in a blue field, representing a new constellation." Vermont became a state in 1791 and Kentucky in 1792, and they wanted to be represented on the flag; so in 1795, two stars and two stripes were added. Realizing that the flag could end up with more stripes than a zebra, Congress decided that after 4 July 1818, the flag would revert permanently to thirteen stripes. If Congress hadn't had such a foresight, this fifty-state country would now have a pinstriped flag.